POVERTY
AMIDST
PLENTY

World Political Economy and
Distributive Justice

About the Book and Editor

Edward Weisband's pioneering text is destined to transform the current teaching of world political economy at both the introductory and the advanced level. Outlining the moral principles and ethical concepts fundamental to grasping the human significance of poverty, he clearly reveals what is often hinted at but rarely stated—that the political dimensions of poverty and distributive justice constitute the organizing framework of the study of world political economy.

Against a backdrop of readings, Professor Weisband's insightful, interpretative essays generate an interdisciplinary discussion, a synthesis of theoretical perspectives and value orientations, providing students with a critical comprehension of the complex workings of the world economy.

The essays link basic approaches to world politics and international relations, international law and organization, international sociology, development studies, and moral philosophy to give texture to such basic theories as modes of production, dependency, world systems, unequal exchange, the labor theory of value, free-trade liberalism, neomercantilism, Marxism, and neo-Marxism. Alternative value orientations are also explored, including realist and neo-realist, conservative and liberal, egalitarian and cosmopolitan, radical and materialist.

Poverty Amidst Plenty combines theory and analysis with historical and normative perspectives to offer students a relevant, prescriptive, and most of all, human picture of the far-reaching system that governs much of our lives.

Edward Weisband is a Distinguished Teaching Professor in the Department of Political Science at the State University of New York at Binghamton. Winner of numerous commendations, he was selected as the 1987 New York State Professor of the Year and was a gold medal finalist in the Professor of the Year national competition sponsored by the Council for Advancement and Support of Education. He was awarded the 1975 Christopher Society Literary Award for contribution to ethical discourse in American public life for his coauthored publication, *Resignation in Protest*.

POVERTY
AMIDST
PLENTY

World Political Economy and Distributive Justice

edited by

EDWARD WEISBAND

State University of New York at Binghamton

WESTVIEW PRESS
Boulder, San Francisco, & London

A Note to the Reader: All editor's royalties derived from sales of this book will be contributed to charitable causes or nonprofit institutions in support of the quest for social reform and distributive justice.

All rights reserved. No part of this publication may be reproduced or transmitted in any form or by any means, electronic or mechanical, including photocopy, recording, or any information storage and retrieval system, without permission in writing from the publisher.

Copyright © 1989 by Westview Press, Inc.

Published in 1989 in the United States of America by Westview Press, Inc., 5500 Central Avenue, Boulder, Colorado 80301, and in the United Kingdom by Westview Press, Inc., 13 Brunswick Centre, London WC1N 1AF, England

Library of Congress Cataloging-in-Publication Data
Poverty amidst plenty.
  1. Economic history—1945–   . 2. Distributive
justice. 3. Poor. I. Weisband, Edward, 1939–
HC59.P639 1989   330.9   87-12829
ISBN 0-8133-0523-3
ISBN 0-8133-0524-1 (pbk.)

Printed and bound in the United States of America

⊙ The paper used in this publication meets the requirements of the American National Standard for Permanence of Paper for Printed Library Materials Z39.48-1984.

10   9   8   7   6   5   4   3   2

To Joan,
the victims of poverty,
and the students of P.S. 117

Contents

Acknowledgments   xiii

Statement of Purpose: Toward a Pedagogy   ·   1

Transformations in the World Economy, 1
The Absence of an Appropriate Pedagogy in World
    Political Economy, 2
A Pre-Theoretical Guide to the Study of Political
    Economy: Unity and Diversity, 2
The Dangers of Building-Block Concepts and Linear
    Logic, 3

Introduction   7

Poverty Amidst Plenty: Theoretical and Normative
    Linkages, 7
Blaming the Victim: Circular Analysis in Political
    Economy, 8
The Subfields of World Political Economy, 9
Distributive Justice: An Unwanted Stepchild, 10

PART ONE
THE POLITICAL ECONOMY OF DEVELOPMENT   15

Developmental Economics and Political Economy
    of Development, 15
The "Relative Autonomy" Debate: Do States Make
    a Difference? 18
Policy Strategies, State Realism, and Political Economy, 19

Chapter One
Preliminary Questions   23

READING #1   What Is Justice? *John Arthur and
    William H. Shaw*, 23
READING #2   What Is Political Economy? *Martin
    Staniland*, 28

READING #3   What Is Poverty? *The Independent
Commission on International Development Issues
(The Brandt Commission)*, 30
READING #4   What Is Relative Poverty? *Paul Harrison*, 34
READING #5   What Is the Economics That Really Matters?
Gerald M. Meier, 37
READING #6   Why Do the Poor Stay Poor? Urban Bias
in World Development, *Michael Lipton*, 43

Chapter Two
**Inequality and Income: Measuring the Dimensions
of Injustice**   **51**

READING #7   Who Gets How Much of What? A Simple
Illustration, *Michael P. Todaro*, 51
READING #8   Who Gets What, How Much—and Where?
David M. Smith, 53
READING #9   Drawing the Poverty Line, *Malcolm Gillis,
Dwight H. Perkins, Michael Roemer, and Donald R.
Snodgrass*, 59
READING #10   Ugly Facts and Fancy Models: Poverty in
the Third World, *Keith Griffin and Azizur Rahman Khan*, 63

Chapter Three
**Class, Capital, and Policy Strategies:
Is Justice in Development Possible?**   **69**

READING #11   Politics, Population, and the Pathways
to Poverty, *William W. Murdoch*, 69
READING #12   Inequality in the Third World: An
Assessment of Competing Explanations, *Atul Kohli,
Michael F. Altfeld, Saideh Lotfian, and Russell Mardon*, 72
READING #13   Equity for Whom? *Richard R. Fagen*, 77
READING #14   Class Formation in the Periphery, *James
Petras*, 82
READING #15   Class, Capital, and the Autonomy of
States, *Martin Staniland*, 85
READING #16   Models of Development and Social Change,
Paul Steidlmeier, 89

PART TWO
**THE POLITICAL ECONOMY OF
UNEVEN DEVELOPMENT**   **111**

The Impacts of International Sociology on Political Science
and Economy, 111
How Wide the Realm of Political Economy: National,
International, World, or Transnational? 112

Chapter Four
Core and Periphery: The History and Theory of
Uneven Development   115

READING #17   The Second Image Reversed: Impact of
the International Economy on Domestic Politics, *Peter Gourevitch,* 115
READING #18   Imperialism, Dependency, and World
Capitalism: A Historical Outline, *Anthony Brewer,* 122
READING #19   Marxism and Dependency, *V. Kubálková and A. A. Cruickshank,* 136
READING #20   Dependency Theory and Modern World
Systems: A Liberal Critique, *Robert Gilpin,* 146

Chapter Five
The New Transnationalism: Toward a Political Economy
of Transnational Modes of Production   155

READING #21   The Multinational Corporation and the
Law of Uneven Development, *Stephen Hymer,* 155
READING #22   Dependent Development and the Product
Cycle, *Peter Evans,* 172
READING #23   The Global Factory: Foreign Assembly in
International Trade, *Joseph Grunwald and Kenneth Flamm,* 176
READING #24   The Core-Periphery Structure of Production
and Jobs: The Internationalizing of Production,
Robert W. Cox, 186

PART THREE
THE POLITICAL ECONOMY OF STATES IN
THE LIBERAL INTERNATIONAL ECONOMIC ORDER   197

The Conflicting Pulls of State Sovereignty and
the New Transnationalism, 197
The Nationally Poor as a Segment of the Globally
Poor, 199
The Polar Values in the Liberal International Economic
Order: Political Autonomy and Economic Reciprocity, 201

Chapter Six
States and Distributive Justice: The Search for Grounds   205

READING #25   Justice in the International Society
of States, *Terry Nardin,* 205
READING #26   Three Levels of Justice: National,
International, and Global, *W. H. Smith,* 209

READING #27   Global Egalitarianism: Can We Make
Out a Case? *Charles Beitz,* 215

Chapter Seven
The Liberal International Economic Order
and Distributive Justice   223

READING #28 The Liberal International Economic Order,
Miriam Camps, with Catherine Gwin, 223
READING #29   Protectionism and the Myths of Liberal
Doctrine, *Susan Strange,* 230
READING #30   What the Third World Really Wants,
Stephen D. Krasner, 246
READING #31   The International Monetary Fund,
Conditionality, and Basic Needs, *Richard E. Feinberg,* 250

Conclusion: The Morality of States
and Cosmopolitan Justice   263

The Impacts of International Regimes: Realism
Revisited, 263
Freedom and Justice: Theoretical Questions and
Political Answers, 264
READING #32   The Future of Distributive Justice, *Robert
O. Keohane,* 265

Acknowledgments

Teachers as fortunate as I am to have stood before hundreds of interested and challenging students possess many debts. The State University of New York at Binghamton attracts an outstanding student body, and I have been privileged for many years to have benefited from the extraordinary energies and enthusiasms it has generated. There are so many students for whom I possess such regard. They should be remembered here for their very real contribution to the thoughts presented in this book. But their very number prevents me from acknowledging them in a reasonable amount of space. I merely wish to take the opportunity provided by this publication to express my abiding gratitude to all of them for the exciting, sometimes exhausting, hours we have spent together grappling with the ways of the world in the name of theoretical clarity and moral insight.

In particular, I would like to thank those who have served as my teaching assistants, both graduate and undergraduate. It is my firm and often-repeated conviction that one does not learn until one starts to teach. One of the greatest joys of accomplishment I have known at SUNY-Binghamton stems from my having witnessed the process by which students learn from other students—and they are learning not just facts but also how to think analytically and conceptually.

The SUNY-Binghamton Department of Political Science is a great teaching department, and I thank my colleagues, one and all, for their collegiality. I am especially indebted to Professor Arthur S. Banks, Chairman, for his outstanding stewardship and for his many, many kindnesses to me; to Professor Richard I. Hofferbert, for his insights regarding theories of development; to Professor James P. Young, for his willingness to share his grasp of the political theory literature and, in particular, his understanding of the theories of distributive justice; to Professor Andrew Milnor, for his illumination of the linkages between research on public policy and the study of values; and to Professor H. L. Nieburg for his great political understanding and for his personal wisdom, which he has so generously shared with me, as well as for his valor in teaching me the intricacies of word processing.

I also warmly thank Professor Robert M. Rosh, in the Department of Political Science at Clark University, and Professor Kent Trachte, in the Department of Political Science at Gettysburg College. As former students in whom I take great pride, they helped to inspire my interest in political economy and provided many years of friendship for which I shall always remain grateful.

I thank SUNY-Binghamton President Clifford D. Clark, former Vice-President George H. Stein, and former Acting Vice-President David Gitlitz for their support over the years and for the research semester that allowed me to bring this project to fruition.

Miriam Gilbert, Vice-President and Director of the College Division of Westview Press, nurtured the inception of this book and patiently awaited its long overdue completion with fortitude and understanding. Her talents and energies as an editor in the social sciences are well known to many in the field, and her reputation is more than deserved. I am very grateful to her.

I affectionately extend my appreciation to David V. and Donna M. Snover for allowing the gypsies of Sherwood Forest to remain in seclusion on Nottingham Road during several months of writing.

I am deeply indebted to Everett Walter Chapman for his many kindnesses and for his generous support proffered in connection with this as well as other projects.

Above all, I would like to thank my wife, Joan, who has devotedly lived through each and every hour of this project and whose abiding faith in its validity and importance has helped to sustain us both.

Edward Weisband

POVERTY
AMIDST
PLENTY

**World Political Economy and
Distributive Justice**

Poverty we think it not a disgrace to acknowledge but a real degradation to make no effort to overcome.

—Thucydides

I have ceased, my dear friend, to love my sorrows, since the same God has scorned the rights of the poor.

—Chaim Nachman Bialik

When the West gives the impression of abandoning itself to forms of isolation, and the East in its turn seems to ignore for questionable reasons its duty to cooperate in the task of alleviating human misery, then we are up against not only a betrayal of humanity's legitimate expectations—a betrayal that is a harbinger of unforeseeable consequences—but also a real desertion of a moral obligation.

—Pope John Paul II

For in the end we are all in the same position as Locke's outlaws and thieves: with no innate principles to guide us—nor even, as Locke himself thought, laws of nature discoverable by reason—we have to find principles of equity and ways of making and keeping agreements without which we cannot hold together.

—J. L. Mackie

Statement of Purpose:
Toward a Pedagogy

Transformations in the World Economy

As we veer toward the last decade of the twentieth century, two trends emerge clearly: The world economy is complex and it is rapidly changing. Two economic shocks of the early 1970s punctuated the beginning of a new era. One signified the gradual erosion of U.S. economic supremacy, and the other, the rise of non-Western economic power.

The Nixon administration's decision in 1971 to close the U.S. "gold window" by ending the automatic convertibility of the U.S. dollar into gold and to allow the value of the American dollar to "float" against the value of other currencies, in effect, truncated a main pillar of the postwar international system of monetary management instituted by the 1944 Bretton-Woods agreement. Henceforth, the value of the American dollar would no longer serve as a fixed standard against which all other currencies and all other national economies could be measured. One would be hard-pressed to find greater evidence of economic pluralism or even of economic multipolarity.

In an event of equal historic magnitude, the OPEC oil boycott of 1973 generated unprecedented shifts in financial resources—initially *from* the West through the creation of petrodollars but subsequently *back to* the West, largely by means of what came to be called the Eurodollar market. This expansion of the Eurodollar market, in turn, led to a major acceleration in the volume and speed of financial flows within the world economy, a phenomenon virtually unlimited in its potential impact.

Later developments confirmed the significance of these first harbingers of change in the world economy. Symptomatic of these later developments was the continuing erosion of the paramount U.S. leadership role within the world economy—an erosion characterized by massive trade and budgetary deficits paralleled by increasing degrees of vulnerability to economic forces beyond U.S. control.

The evolution of a more pluralistic world economy seemed as well to be symbolized by the growing prominence of the Pacific rim as the probable economic hub of the world economy during the next century and by the rise of major but as yet largely unrealized economies of the newly industrializing countries, typified by India and Brazil.

Such developments within the world economy have attracted many individuals to the subject. But this burgeoning interest in world political economy among students of international politics, sociology, and economics reflects one other fact of world economic life: widespread poverty.

Chastened in the early 1980s by the horrifying images of famine in Ethiopia and other parts of Africa, students and scholars from several established disciplines have turned in increasing numbers toward the study of political economy for explanation and research. As a result, poverty, exploitation, and socioeconomic disparities of all kinds have emerged as mainstream topics, alongside traditional topics such as domination and conflict. Indeed, standard concepts in political science such as state and power have been "deconstructed" in order to be "reconstructed" for the purpose of explaining how power, in all its modes and guises, relates to poverty and distributive justice.

The Absence of an Appropriate Pedagogy in World Political Economy

Despite these developments and contrary to the wide intellectual appeal of world political economy, the availability of instructional materials for those seeking to develop a basic rather than a specialized perspective has not kept up with demand. Many authors proceed from a particular viewpoint and are unable or unwilling to provide the basis for broad conceptual understanding. The very complexity of the subject also creates obstacles to rudimentary treatment. Thus novice students are left bereft of texts calibrated to their needs and interests.

If a fundamental grasp of the conceptual vocabulary of the various perspectives in world political economy is what a student hopes to attain, such an individual must rely upon multiple resources, many of which have been conceived and written at contrasting levels of difficulty. The consequence is an avalanche of concepts, terms, and theories that topple down upon beginning students. Mastery of world political economy as a subject thus becomes a formidable task—if not, indeed, a forbidding one.

A Pre-Theoretical Guide to the Study of Political Economy: Unity and Diversity

This book is designed to meet the needs of students who wish to survey world political economy in a conceptual manner and in a way that permits them to build theoretically upon what they have learned. Concepts are emphasized throughout the text to encourage students to grapple with their own theoretical and moral preferences and to enable them to define their intellectual identities within this field, which in itself is characterized by contrasting visions and viewpoints.

In order to facilitate such a learning process, this volume includes original as well as reprint materials. Carefully edited readings have been selected to illustrate different, often conflicting, perspectives, all of which nevertheless pertain to the issues associated with poverty amidst plenty. In some cases the titles of the readings have been changed slightly from their originals in order to stress the relationships among them. Original materials by the editor introduce each part and each reading. By emphasizing fundamental concepts, units of analysis, analytical assumptions, theoretical frameworks, and normative approaches, these introductions assist the reader in locating each reading within the broad spectrum created by contending analytical and normative perspectives in world political economy.

This book thus combines the advantages of a systematic text with those of a broad anthology. It is a basic guide to the diverse issues, problems, and approaches within the field of world political economy; but it also seeks to develop the field's substantive unity. It identifies the analytical and normative commitments that inform the study of world political economy as an intellectual enterprise; but it also introduces the subfields in which specialized research occurs. In particular, it stresses the concepts around which the various subfields of world political economy are organized; for example, "markets" are discussed in the context of "free trade liberalism," and "core" and "periphery" are examined in relation to "dependency" and "modes of production" analyses. Thus, this book is designed as a pre-theoretical guide to the study of world political economy.

The Dangers of Building-Block Concepts and Linear Logic

This book introduces world political economy by demonstrating, among other phenomena, how structures of state power and transnational modes of production help sustain inequitable conditions of poverty amidst plenty. The merit of such a pedagogical approach is that it provides comprehensive treatment; but the danger is that this process of learning may inadvertently foster a superficial grasp of theories and concepts.

This very problem has, indeed, impeded the evolution of a systematic pedagogy in world political economy. The field is more variegated than most. It engages not only the main disciplines of the social sciences but also several subdisciplines, including developmental anthropology, agricultural economics, economic geography, urban planning, and world history. Intense debates have been waged over the relative influence of political and economic processes, as illustrated by the arguments contained in this volume between Marxists and realists over the primacy of class and state. Such debates often dissolve into ideological confrontations, which in turn generate oppressive doses of jargon masquerading as genuine theorization. The result is discourse that is rarefied, arcane, and generally inaccessible to the uninitiated.

Consequently, many professors have avoided the shoals of theoretical explanation in favor of calmer but, regretfully, more shallow teaching waters. Students interested in world political economy are presented with introductory texts that describe facts without conceptual explanation or that outline alternative theoretical perspectives so superficially as to ignore the problematic nature of theory. Students sink or swim in analytical waters either too tepid to be intellectually interesting or too choppy to be semantically clear. Teachers and students alike are left without an image of any organizing core to the field and without a sense of the full significance of the central themes within it.

This book, the product of many years of teaching, seeks to remedy this situation. Yet there are serious dangers inherent in the method of presentation employed by this volume. One risk is that concepts and units of analysis will become reified—that is, frozen into universal and unchanging categories robbed of the historical or analytical contexts from which they originally arose. As David Harvey reminds us in his important study *The Limits to Capital*, it is important to reject "linear" reasoning, which assumes that certain "foundations" to knowledge exist and that they can be apprehended by what he calls the "building-block method."[1]

The building-block method presents concepts as axiomatic "givens," thus allowing no room for students' imagination and independent critical interpretation. Conceptual categories become ends in themselves to be labeled and memorized rather than applied as instrumental guides to an under-standing of why things are the way they are. "According to this line of thought," Harvey writes, "it is both possible and desirable to build solid foundations to knowledge by isolating basic components within the social system and subjecting them to detailed investigation. Once the component is understood, we can build upon it as if it were a fixed and immutable foundation for subsequent enquiry."[2]

Harvey calls for "dialectical thinking." By this he means that students must retain the moral courage and imaginative willingness to live with uncertainty and ambiguity. In their use of concepts and units of analysis, they must "grope in the dark" within limited contexts, armed only with certain categories of inquiry. They can aspire only to the possibility of unraveling tiny skeins of reality that yield partial insights into the inner recesses of society.

Thus theoretical and normative concepts must never be thought of as fixed conceptual categories capable of explaining all things for all time. Their usefulness lies in the extent to which they open analytical windows into social phenomena that otherwise elude the nontheoretical eye. One risk built into a volume of this kind is that its conceptual orientation might appear to strip units of analysis from their moorings in the everyday life of social, economic, and political realities. Whenever this occurs, theories begin to appear larger than the occurrences they purport to explain, a problem inherent in much dependency and world-systems analysis.

The reader must remember, therefore, that the abstract concepts and theories identified in this book serve merely as limited devices for under-standing particular and concrete conditions of social existence. Poverty is not an abstraction, but it does need to be theoretically explained. And as we proceed toward that explanation, we must retain a modesty appropriate to the magnitude of the suffering we now survey.

Notes

1. David Harvey, *The Limits to Capital* (Chicago: University of Chicago Press, 1982), p. 2.
2. Ibid.

Introduction

Poverty Amidst Plenty:
Theoretical and Normative Linkages

Poor and rich people live everywhere. The poor live in rich countries as well as in poor ones. The rich live in poor countries as well as in rich ones. Sometimes vast distances in culture and location separate the rich from the poor, as in the contrast between the "modernizing" urban rich and the "traditional" rural poor in many lesser developing nations. In other instances, the poor become concentrated only within short walking distances from the rich, as in the case of the inner city poor in several American metropolitan areas.

That some are rich and others are poor may at first seem no more arresting than that some individuals appear more intelligent or ambitious or attractive than others. Contrasts among peoples and how they live may reflect cultural or value preferences as well as differences in innate capacities or physical stamina. But no one chooses to live in squalor and destitution. Yet one poignant reality in contemporary experience is that, with each passing year, poverty engulfs many more individuals and families around the globe than those who become liberated from it—despite increasing wealth throughout the world economy.

How do we explain this? The aim of the present volume is to enable students to respond clearly and comprehensively to this question and the array of issues it evokes.

But correct answers can be derived only if we first ask correct questions. This is the great secret behind all theory. Theories do not provide correct answers so much as they permit us to inquire precisely and systematically into the complex realities of nature and of human or social experience. The challenge of poverty amidst plenty is to peer behind mere description by asking piercing analytical questions that point toward broad explanation. Thus, our first step is to define not the answers but the questions that nurture the most acute forms of analysis and theoretical explanation.

Questions of theoretical significance must, finally, be posed in terms of a conceptual language or vocabulary, for only by this means can we construct a universe of discourse among persons concerned about the same subjects or issues. The theoretical perspectives we are about to discover represent segments of such a universe of discourse—one which links theoretical or explanatory analysis with normative theory and analysis. The name we give to this enterprise is political economy.

Blaming the Victim:
Circular Analysis in Political Economy

One way to explain poverty is to blame it on the poor. As Pamela Roby notes, for example, "Generally and perhaps not accidentally the *attributes* of the poor—inadequate education, old age, poor health, and so forth— have been incorrectly viewed as the *causes* of poverty."[1] Roby claims that stereotypes of the poor often influence the way in which poverty is perceived by alleging, in effect, that the poor are the sources of their own misery. As a result, the injustice of poverty along with the culpability of political and economic agencies become readily deniable. If the poor cause poverty, they have only themselves to condemn.

This thesis was developed in William Ryan's *Blaming the Victim,*[2] in which the author observes that during the 1960s and early 1970s, in the aftermath of major civil rights legislation, segments of American society routinely exhibited a tendency to blame inequality upon those victimized by it. "The generic process of Blaming the Victim is applied to almost every American problem," Ryan wrote.[3] "The miserable health care of the poor is explained away on the grounds that the victim has poor motivation and lacks health information. The problems of slum housing are traced to the characteristics of tenants who are labeled as 'Southern rural immigrants' not yet 'acculturated' to life in the big city." "The 'multiproblem' poor, it is claimed," he continued, "suffer the psychological effects of impoverishment, the 'culture of poverty,' and the deviant value system of the lower classes; consequently, though unwittingly, they cause their own troubles." "From such a viewpoint," Ryan asserted, "the obvious fact that poverty is primarily an absence of money is easily overlooked or set aside."[4]

Ryan distinguishes "Blaming the Victim" from previous kinds of re- ductionist explanation: "Blaming the Victim is, of course, quite different from old-fashioned conservative ideologies," he noted. "The latter simply dismissed victims as inferior, genetically defective, or morally unfit; the emphasis is on the intrinsic, even hereditary, defect."[5] But the new ideology scrupulously avoided direct references to the poor, criticizing them only indirectly and obliquely. "The new ideology attributes defect and inadequacy to the malignant nature of poverty, injustice, slum life, and racial difficulties," Ryan concluded. "The stigma that marks the victim and accounts for his victimization is an acquired stigma, a stigma of social, rather than genetic, origin. But the stigma, the defect, the fatal difference—though derived in the past from environmental forces—is still located *within* the victim, inside his skin."[6]

Ryan's thesis applies to several interpretations as to why poor countries are poor and why large numbers of people within lesser developing countries remain impoverished despite attempts at development. These explanations manifest similar circular arguments, all of which condense down to the poor are poor because they are poor. Behind such reifications lurks a kind of fatalism about the capacity of these countries to emerge from the dire circumstances they face: the poor are poor and thus do not have the know-how to break out of the cycles of poverty that afflict them; or, the poor are poor and thus do not have the drive or ambition to be able to be anything but poor; or, perhaps most insidious of all, the poor are poor and thus cannot help but bear too many children for their economies to absorb. On occasion, blame is shifted from the poor themselves to ecological forces such as drought or desertification. But these conclusions, too, fall into the category of Blaming the Victim; though regretfully all too real, such environmental problems are easily misappropriated by this kind of illogic to symbolize the very failings of the poor.

The Subfields of World Political Economy

Where, then, do we look for theoretical forms of explanation? And how do we avoid the traps of circular reasoning in which victims are blamed for their own travails by perpetuating self-fulfilling prophecies that confuse the causes of social problems with their effects or symptoms? Within the present context of poverty amidst plenty throughout the world, the answers point to the following subfields of world political economy: the political economy of development; the political economy of uneven or overdevelopment; the political economy of transnational modes of production, or of the new transnationalism; and the political economy of states in the liberal international economic order. This book focuses upon each in order to demonstrate how they together constitute a unified field of theoretical investigation.

One essential element serves to integrate these subfields into an amalgamated body of inquiry and research: the analytical linkage between theories of political economy and normative theories relevant to questions of distributive justice. These subfields establish the following analytical and normative perspectives, all of which are basic to the teaching of political economy and relevant to developments in the world economy:

1. developmentalism;
2. realism;
3. cosmopolitanism;
4. egalitarianism;
5. contractarianism;
6. libertarianism;
7. mercantilism, neomercantilism, and protectionism;
8. classical liberalism and market or neoclassical liberalism;
9. historical capitalism and world-systems;
10. imperialism and neoimperialism;
11. dependency;
12. uneven development;
13. product cycle;

14. modes of production analysis;
15. the new transnationalism.

An imaginative understanding of these perspectives and approaches very much represents the objective of the pedagogy that forms the basis of this book. Together they forge the foundation for a unified study of world political economy—one sensitive to the analytical and normative stature of distributive justice.

Distributive Justice: An Unwanted Stepchild

What is justice? Hardly a more venerable question exists in the annals of political theory. The ancients, enamored of riddles, were as mystified by this puzzle as is the present generation. Indeed, political theory in the Greco-Roman world originated as an attempt to apply justice to the social order. Today the concern for justice is provoked by a pandemic spread of poverty. World poverty is a concrete reality, whereas justice is an abstraction. But both constitute the other side of the same coin: the fundamental issue in the study of world political economy.

World political economy examines the relationship between poverty and justice within, between, and across societies. It allows us to ask how political and economic factors perpetuate injustice and, in turn, how injustice sustains poverty. World political economy as a field of investigation focuses on the questions of how poverty arises, how it is sustained, and under what circumstances expansions in poverty levels reflect injustice.

The subject of world political economy is fraught with moral significance once one accepts the proposition, as we do here, that the plight of vast millions who painfully wither in the face of squalor beyond the bounds of human dignity do so as a consequence of injustices wrought by forces beyond their control. What are the connections between the *empirical* facts of poverty and the *abstract* moral assertions that this poverty is grossly unjust? At what point do differences in how people live add up to conditions of distributive *injustice*? Does injustice occur simply when some people fare well while others hardly subsist? Why or why not, and upon what grounds? Do allegations that injustices exist require evidence that the causes of poverty lie beyond what individuals and groups can do for themselves? If so, what proof can one provide? These are some of the questions that arise when the study of world political economy is guided by a concern for distributive justice.

The research agenda of world political economy thus unfolds as a series of questions:

1. What is poverty?
2. Why are the poor poor, and why do they stay poor?
3. How do we explain rampant increases in poverty?
4. When is poverty unjust?

5. Where are labor, work, and unemployment unjustly distributed, and why?

Without a commitment to analyze the factors that foster injustice, world political economy, as a field of theoretical investigation, is emptied of its thematic content and robbed of its organizing framework—although this is rarely stated and is sometimes even denied.

Distributive justice, the adopted favorite child of certain Third World governments calling for a New International Economic Order (NIEO) in the decade of the 1970s, has returned to its more traditional status as the unwanted stepchild of those interested in world political economy. Students and practitioners of many persuasions tend to envision the concept of distributive justice as an unnecessary obstacle to serious analysis and, even more troubling, as a means of diverting both attention and effort away from the primordial goals of true social and political emancipation in world society.

This tendency has led to a somewhat anomalous situation. Many specialists, for differing reasons, implicitly or explicitly disavow distributive justice as a normative standard or conceptual unit of analysis despite the fact that it undergirds their intellectual commitment to the examination of world political economy.

The reasons are suggestive of the various theoretical predispositions that have shaped the study of world political economy in recent years. They are worth dwelling on for a moment in order to establish how this book applies moral norms—specifically, distributive justice—to the social, economic, and political events associated with poverty amidst plenty.

Distributive justice is avoided, first of all, by Marxist writers who dismiss ethical concepts on the grounds that they obscure the main problematic of social analysis: how capital molds the fundamental categories of class, work, and labor from which social ethics emerge.

Ralph Pettman has outlined this logic as follows: "Justice in this [Marxian] view, then, can never be construed as an independent value since our idea of right is contingent upon the prevailing substructure of material life."[7] How goods or values are distributed within a society is of secondary importance. "The notion of a more 'just' *distribution* is a mere palliative. . . . To tinker only with the *distributive* terms of such a system would be worse than useless, indeed, it would be 'unjust.'"[8] According to this perspective, one cannot isolate distributive processes or outcomes from their sources in the economic structures and social institutions of societies, which, in any event, must be analyzed in their entirety and not merely in terms of distribution. "The fundamental harm comes from the capitalist mode of production as a whole; the mode of distribution derives from the ethos itself, and constitutes only one of its operative components."[9] An emphasis upon distributive justice, in the Marxian view, is therefore counterproductive.

For their part, many non-Marxian students of world political economy also reject distributive justice as an analytical perspective—but for quite different reasons. Realists, those who stress state autonomy and power as being definitive of international society, and who survey the world not from the "bottom-up" vantage point of work, class, and production but from the "top-down" perspective of states and international security, tend to flounder against the bedrock of the state whenever they find themselves distracted by the moral charms of distributive justice.

The morality of states, realists claim, is grounded by the pursuit of self-interest, which may or may not entail promoting the cause of distributive justice at home or abroad. State sovereignty renders irrelevant all claims *across* state boundaries based upon notions of distributive justice. Realist logic is evoked in Part Three to illustrate how even the term *world* economy may be challenged as an accurate means of describing the *international* society of states. The world economy is a manifestation of an international society of states, and the only justice possible in such a society is the justice of, by, for, and most important, *within* states.

Reading #25 by Terry Nardin criticizes even a cosmopolitan logic of egalitarianism that would make it incumbent upon all states to pursue the universal goal of distributive equality. States can never agree to any collective version of the ideal world, Nardin argues; as a result, theoretical and normative emphasis upon process and interaction is more politically effective and more morally relevant than stress upon the attainment of global or cosmopolitan aims. Agreement over procedural order governing how states interact is possible, at least in some degree, whereas collective goals, however worthwhile—such as distributive justice—are not. Therefore, realists come to the same conclusion as Marxists: Distributive justice as an analytical device and as a theoretical perspective confuses rather than clarifies. Whether for reasons of class or states as conceptual categories, both Marxists and realists seem to agree that distributive justice is at best irrelevant and at worst contrary to theoretical insight and social change.

Why bother with it, then? The answer points to the very nature of world political economy as a transdisciplinary research field. Despite misgivings to the contrary, world political economy—shorn of its commitment to the investigation of poverty, its causes, and its injustice—loses its theoretical and moral roots. One might as well return to the more restrictive disciplinary approaches to development traditionally found in anthropology, political science, economics, or sociology.

What transforms world political economy from a field of separate disciplines into a unified perspective is the fact that it consolidates disciplinary approaches around a single focus: the interrelationship of poverty and injustice. An analytical commitment to the primacy of either class or states does not require one to reject distributive justice as the primary focus of research or as a fundamental normative standard. On the contrary, states and class, as units of analysis, acquire special relevance when connected to the dynamics of distributive *injustice*.

To examine world political economy, therefore, is to assess how socioeconomic differences, particularly those involving poverty amidst plenty, arise among peoples. But to an even greater extent, the subject of political economy is concerned with the dynamics of political power and the role of political forces in poverty and distributive outcomes. If the question as to what constitutes the study of world political economy is posed in terms of those elements that are necessary and those that are sufficient, we find that an interest in the linkage between politics and economics is necessary but insufficient until combined with an inquest into the sources of injustice— on the grounds that the ultimate test of the moral mutuality between economics and politics in any society depends upon the extent to which plenty works to alleviate the existence of poverty.

The study of world political economy thus combines the analytical question of how poverty can persist in a world of plenty with the moral or normative question of when and why this is unjust. To disconnect these issues from each other is to destroy the need for the very transdisciplinary approach that makes world political economy the field that it is.

Notes

1. Pamela Roby, ed., *The Poverty Establishment* (Englewood Cliffs, N.J.: Prentice-Hall, 1974), p. 12 (original emphasis).

2. William Ryan, *Blaming the Victim* (New York: Random House/Vintage Books, 1976), pp. 5–6.

3. Ibid.

4. Ibid., p. 7.

5. Ibid.

6. Ibid. (original emphasis).

7. Ralph Pettman, *State and Class: A Sociology of International Affairs* (London: Croom Helm Ltd., 1979), pp. 88–95.

8. Ibid. (original emphasis).

9. Ibid.

PART ONE

THE POLITICAL ECONOMY
OF DEVELOPMENT

Developmental Economics and
Political Economy of Development

The objective of world political economy is to explain poverty amidst plenty in a noncircular manner relevant to the normative concerns of distributive justice. We thus turn to the set of preliminary questions raised in Chapter One: What is distributive justice? What is political economy? What is poverty? But in order to answer these questions, we must first consider the specific analytical enterprise that concentrates upon economic change in poor countries—namely, economic development.

Economic development involves the process of transforming the aggregate economic conditions of societies that sustain some or all of the following characteristics: high levels of unemployment, bare levels of subsistence, slow or distorted forms of growth, low levels of national income or savings and high levels of indebtedness, low levels of domestic investment, high levels of urbanization, and depleted rural or agricultural sectors.

Developmental economics as a subfield of the discipline of economics concentrates on the evolution of developing economies and thus upon the methods of assessing economies stricken by poverty. To accomplish its aims, developmental economics seeks to alter deplorable socioeconomic conditions by

1. fostering efficient use of domestic resources;
2. promoting increases in levels of economic productivity; and
3. accelerating economic growth as measured by rising levels of national income, domestic savings, and internal investment.

Economic development is thus the substantive theoretical and analytical focus of developmental economics. The analytical perspective of this subfield differs from that adopted within the subfield of **political economy of development.** The character and scope of inquiry of the latter are outlined in Part One.

Michael P. Todaro, an economist, suggests possible connections between the two subfields by providing an especially broad definition of development, one that suggests a realm of investigation beyond developmental economics:

> Three equally important aspects of development are: (1) raising people's living levels, i.e., their incomes and *consumption* levels of food, medical services, education, etc., through "relevant" *economic growth processes;* (2) creating conditions conducive to the growth of people's *self-esteem* through the establishment of social, political, and *economic systems* and *institutions* which promote human dignity and respect; and (3) increasing people's *freedom to choose* by enlarging the range of their choice variables, e.g., increasing varieties of consumer goods and services.[1]

Todaro's emphasis on the relationship of political and social institutions to economic growth and, in turn, his stress on the relationship of economic growth to human dignity and welfare are not only suggestive of technical economic issues relevant to developmental economics; they also demonstrate the transdisciplinary concerns of political economy of development. Developmental economics is a subfield of economics focusing on the technical aspects of development; the political economy of development is a subfield of world political economy dedicated to the examination of political economy and, thus, of the social, political, and moral consequences of change brought on as a result of economic development. The political economy of development is a subfield of world political economy in that it is devoted to the analysis of social change within the confines of individual societies rather than across two or more economies as in the case of world political economy.

The subfield of political economy of development therefore evaluates the possibilities of fundamental change designed to permit the poor to benefit from the social gains wrought by economic growth or development. It examines the relationship between politics, power, class, and social structure, on the one hand, and the dynamics of social change in development, on the other. In particular, political economy of development depicts the processes by which transformations in social, economic, and political structures affect the living standards of massive numbers of people within societies located mostly in South and Southeast Asia, Africa, and Central and Latin America.

Political economy of development as a subfield of world political economy thus examines economic growth and/or economic development from the precise perspective of how the poor fare when economic growth or economic development occurs. It asks whether their quality of life, however calculated, becomes better or whether it actually worsens once aggregate or overall economic conditions have improved. These questions represent the major concerns of a political economy of development, and they are illuminated in Chapters One, Two, and Three.

To speak of development is usually to speak of events, institutions, processes, and structures within specific societies. One way to study development from a political economy perspective is to measure and explain poverty domestically *within* more than one society and to compare findings *across* them. This set of procedures enables us to balance our assessment of the conditions of poverty on a country-to-country basis. As a consequence of these analytical orientations, moreover, political economy of development tends to dwell upon the socioeconomic and political dynamics *internal* to particular societies.

This method also permits us to scrutinize on a comparative basis the factors that accelerate poverty, as opposed to those that appear to diminish it. In this way, we can identify patterns of consistency and deviation, which in turn may yield further insights. The specific aim of Chapter Two is to illustrate possible ways of analyzing alterations in poverty and distribution of income during the process of development within poor countries. The purpose of such an exercise within a perspective devoted to political economy is to observe whether and to what extent distributive justice is enhanced by development.

To ask *where* poverty occurs is a question that appears simple enough— simple, that is, until we ponder the sheer variety of living standards around the world. Accordingly, the readings of Chapter Two briefly outline the units of analysis relevant to a systematic examination of poverty, including that of the "poverty line." It is only by locating, or "drawing a line around" the precise incidence of poverty that we are able to examine it. Such an effort represents a preliminary phase in judging how injustice occurs within the world political economy.

Another critical unit of analysis in political economy of development is *income distribution*. Is development conducive to greater or lesser degrees of equality in income distribution? Empirical examination of income distributions, especially those of households within and across lesser developing countries, provides a quantitative measure that enables us to discern how income is disbursed and how "unfair" gaps in income levels appear or disappear as a consequence of economic growth and development. This approach, in turn, permits us to review how inequalities in income distribution reinforce or weaken social divisions relevant to poverty amidst plenty.

The readings in Chapter Two also explore a thesis initially proposed by the well-known economist, Simon Kuznets—namely, that as poor countries develop economically, income distributions within them establish a statistical path traceable in the shape of a "U-shaped curve." Accordingly, gaps in income distribution worsen once development in poor countries commences, but they diminish as development matures. The validity of the Kuznets thesis, and of various hypotheses subsequently put forth to explain it, has led to a lively debate that is partially conveyed by the selected readings.

Political economy of development is thus a subfield seeking to establish generalizations about income distribution, social change, and economic growth based upon observations concerning development within many individual societies. In addition to this, however, measuring income distribution represents an important first step in the process of applying philosophical standards of justice to explanations of poverty. But we must also undertake a prior exercise central to the field of political economy. This involves an investigation of the relationship of power to distributive justice. It is this very orientation that distinguishes a political economy of development from developmental economics. Such an analytical perspective is illustrated in Chapter Three, which assumes awareness of the debate in political economy often referred to as the "relative autonomy of states."

The "Relative Autonomy" Debate:
Do States Make a Difference?

As previously suggested, the field of world political economy looks broadly at the relationship of politics to economics against a background created by normative standards of distributive justice. Since sovereign states are the primary political units within the world political economy, their capacity to pursue effective policies relating to poverty, income distribution, and distributive justice becomes a matter of great theoretical interest and, occasionally, intense debate.

Furthermore, since the specific emphasis within the subfield of political economy of development is domestic processes of change affecting poverty and justice, Chapter Three inquires into the role and status of states, politics, and governmental institutions and policies in pursuing the goals of distributive justice and equity. To raise this issue is to begin to ponder the extent to which sovereign states may be deemed liable for not pursuing justice at home in accordance with transnational standards of distributive justice.

Analysis of the major instrumentalities within the world economy, capable of advancing the causes of distributive justice, centers on a discussion widely referred to as the "relative autonomy of states" debate. Chapter Three, especially the readings contributed by Richard R. Fagen, James Petras, and Martin Staniland, introduces this debate, which is fueled by conflicting views over the capacity of states and the willingness of governments to bring about changes favorable to the poor. More specifically, controversy swirls around the theoretical issue of whether development can operate independent of economic and class forces, given that these forces predominate over the occurrence of change within lesser developing countries and in ways that tend systematically to disadvantage the poor.

This debate, located at the heart of the subfield of political economy of development, consists largely of disagreements that result from an intellectual clash between those who stress the influence of socioeconomic or class networks and structures, on the one hand, and those who emphasize the role of political institutions of governments, on the other, in determining patterns of social change relevant to poverty and distributive justice. In other words, disagreement has arisen over the relationship between "class" forces and government policies within poor countries during development. Many Marxist-oriented scholars consider the state to be less sovereign than has been widely assumed by mainstream observers. Economic forces and class structures, they argue, severely limit the policy options and developmental strategies available to the governments of lesser developing countries, particularly the options and strategies geared toward the poor. Consequently, domestic development within these societies does not—indeed, cannot—occur autonomously.

Why this emphasis upon *relative* autonomy, then, as opposed to no autonomy at all? Responses to this question vary, but Marxian analysis often refers to struggles among segments of the rich and ruling classes that control production and the flows of capital investment. It follows, so the argument goes, that governments must retain some degree of autonomy from ruling classes, even though they are ultimately controlled by them, in order to mediate the conflicts that occasionally break out among the ranks of ruling elites. If governments could not act independently of the class elements that dominate them, they would fail to protect the interests of the ruling classes as a whole—and such protection, from this standpoint, is their very purpose. Governments are not sovereign entities but merely the relatively autonomous creatures of the class forces that dominate them. Therefore, the political decisionmaking process that determines economic development invariably reflects, directly or indirectly, the web of class interests that binds states and restrains governments. For those who accept this argument, politics remains secondary to economics.

If politics and state sovereignty are assumed to be relatively autonomous, moreover, so must be the process of development. Analysts of the relative autonomy persuasion suggest that patterns of domestic development can best be understood as the **articulations,** or reflections, of class forces beyond the control of states or of politics. This assertion contains major implications for any attempt to link concrete instances of poverty to abstract standards of distributive justice. Domestic poverty, according to those who subscribe to this view, represents an articulation, that is, an expression of deeply structured forces in which states and their governments are embedded. One should look not only at the impacts of power and domination but also at those generated by class and exploitation. As a result, sovereign states and the governments that represent them cannot but pursue policies that in the long run reinforce, rather than diminish, the intractabilities of poverty.

The conclusion derived from this logic is clear: Injustice is the natural consequence of states; wherever states are, so will there be injustice. The dismal conclusion to be drawn is that there exists no political mechanism by which to pursue social change and development configured around notions of distributive justice except revolutionary resistance. Accordingly, one should stress not development but **underdevelopment** in the study of political economy. The proper framework regarding the problems of poverty and equity should be not the political economy of development but the political economy of **uneven development**, a topic outlined in Part Two.

Policy Strategies, State Realism, and Political Economy

Within the framework established by the "relative autonomy of states" debates, there exists an alternative perspective to that posited by Marxist authors. Loosely identifiable as **realism**, or the **morality of states** perspective, it rejects both the logic and the conclusions of these propositions. The logic of realism in the context of the relative autonomy debate is as follows:

1. The primary mechanism for collective decisionmaking and for the articulation of development in modern society is the sovereign state and its political institutions.
2. The political instrumentalities of sovereign states remain autonomous of the class interests of ruling elites in order to preserve and protect the self-interests of states as a whole within the international society of states.
3. The autonomy of states is revealed by the capacity of governments to reduce poverty and to create wealth, as, for example, in the recent experience of the People's Republic of China, the mainland communist state, by contrast to that of Taiwan, Republic of China, the entrepreneurial, Western-oriented island society off the coast of mainland China.
4. Governments, whatever their ideological and political character, are free to choose developmental policies that either do or do not promote distributive justice.
5. Therefore, types of governments do make a difference.

According to the positions of realism, it matters greatly whether a government is democratic or, at the very least, humanistically oriented toward improving the living conditions of its population.

Atul Kohli and his colleagues outline one version of realism in Chapter Three. Based upon their empirical assessment of competing explanations of the causes of inequality in lesser developing countries, they claim to show that types of governments and political regimes do make a great difference as to whether economic growth conduces to greater or lesser degrees of distributive justice. They refer to this set of propositions as **state realism**. Their basic assumption is that political regimes can select among development policy strategies and thereby play a determining role in how an economy evolves.

This controversy regarding the autonomy of states and of political processes, however, is not resolved by the readings in Part One, which deal entirely with the domestic settings of poverty. For this debate must also consider how economic forces function *outside* the confines of individual societies. It is, after all, the very argument of those who favor relative autonomy as one explanation of the relationship of politics and economics that global or transnational modes of production and finance operate across state boundaries and that these manifestations of transnational influence and control further reduce state autonomy. Thus the "relative autonomy" debate will resurface later in this volume—implicitly during our discussion of free trade liberalism and explicitly in the context of the political economy of uneven development and the new transnationalism.

For now, the task remains to define poverty, to understand how and why it occurs, and to reason why poverty amidst plenty represents an injustice subject to moral condemnation. Accordingly, chapters of Part One outline the basic concepts and assumptions of the political economy of development. They attempt to do this in a way that not only reveals the issues and debates within the field but that also remains sensitive to the abiding normative orientation that transforms developmental economics into a political economy.

Note

1. Michael P. Todaro, *Economic Development in the Third World*, 2nd ed. (New York: Longman, 1981), p. 524 (original emphases).

CHAPTER ONE

Preliminary Questions

READING #1 What Is Justice?
John Arthur and William H. Shaw

Justice is only one form of morality, while economic or distributive justice is but a single form of justice. A grasp of differing conceptions of morality and justice represents an initial step toward understanding how standards of distributive justice apply within the frameworks of political economy of development. To facilitate this understanding is the aim of the first reading.

John Arthur and William H. Shaw observe that justice operates as a set of "claims." Claims are based on various grounds, such as the principles or precepts denoted by terms like *fairness, merit, need, rights, duty, equality,* and *equity.* Whatever the form of their legitimation, all claims consist of assertions made by certain individuals or groups toward others, or that others regard as beholden upon them for reasons of moral right or beneficial good. Claims thus impose obligations of action, sometimes even sacrifice, on behalf of parties deemed to be unduly harmed or unfairly deprived.

In the case of economic or distributive justice, claims appeal for the redistribution of economic benefits and burdens throughout a society as a whole. The authors of this first reading suggest that claims of distributive justice within a society are valid, but only when social and economic processes demonstrably produce unfair advantages for some and unfair disadvantages for others. In other words, injustice must be manifestly present before claims to distributive justice can be rationally established.

If "demonstrable and unfair disadvantage" within a society becomes the threshold test of injustice, as Arthur and Shaw would have us believe, a formidable barrier is created in cases of claims arising out of the dynamics of international society—claims that result, after all, from the interactions of many states. The mere existence of "foreign poverty" in societies other than our own, the authors suggest, does not in itself validate claims to distributive justice requiring action on our part.

Why not? Their answer is clear. Distributive justice is a normative standard relevant only to how fairly or unfairly distributions of economic benefits occur within *particular* integrated societies. Only within single countries, they argue, could the quality and quantity of economic relations ever be so extensive as to allow a claim to be logically made that the enrichment of a few has been paid for by the unjust impoverishment of others. Thus, Arthur and Shaw conclude, it is the "economic interrelatedness" generated within a society that alone can serve as the basis for claims of distributive justice.

The unanswered question in this reading, however, is as follows: Given the nature and volume of economic relations within the modern world economy, can international society be considered sufficiently interrelated such that standards of distributive justice now apply? In other words, how dense or interdependent do economic relations among different societies have to become before the claims of distributive justice can be advanced by "foreign" citizens or groups across the sovereign jurisdictions of states?

—E. W.

The Concept of Justice

Justice is an old concept with a rich history, a concept which is fundamental to any discussion of how society ought to be organized. Philosophical concern with it goes back at least to ancient Greece. For Plato and some of his contemporaries, justice seems to have been the paramount virtue or, more precisely, the sum of virtue with regard to our relations with others. "Justice" had the ring of "righteousness," and to know an act was just was to know it was right. Although there is still a sense in which to do what is just is to do what is right, philosophers today generally distinguish justice from the whole of morality.

To claim something is "unjust" is a more specific complaint than to say it is "bad" or "immoral." I may be rude to you, behave selfishly, sleep with your spouse, and engage in a variety of other naughty or immoral behavior without—it seems—being unjust to you. On the other hand, an act which is unjust might be morally justified on the whole, as when the necessities of war require denial of legal due process to a traitor. We can make sense of the thought that the act is unjust but, on balance, still should be done. This suggests that in speaking of justice or injustice we are discussing only one sphere of the moral picture. In general, however, an injustice is acceptable only if it can be shown that the consequence of not committing it would be very bad indeed, and to know something is unjust is to have a good reason to think it is wrong overall.

John Arthur and William H. Shaw, *Justice and Economic Distribution*. Copyright © 1978 by Prentice-Hall, Inc. Excerpt, pp. 2–8, adapted by permission of Prentice-Hall, Inc., Englewood Cliffs, New Jersey; endnotes deleted.

If justice is a part of morality, what sorts of facts make an act unjust rather than simply wrong in general? Consider someone who is locked up for criticizing the government; here liberty has been violated and an injustice done. Similarly, if someone else is punished for a crime he did not commit or is singled out from his philosophy class and required to write twice as many papers as the others, then we naturally speak of injustice.

What seems to be going on is that talk of justice or injustice focuses on at least one of several related ideas. First, a claim that one is treated unjustly often suggests that one's moral rights have been violated—in particular, that one has been made to suffer some burden one had a right to avoid or has been denied some benefit one had a right to possess. If we agree to go into business together and you back out without justification, costing me time and money, then you have violated a right of mine and I may well claim that you have treated me unjustly.

Second, the term *injustice* is often used to mean *unfairness*. Justice frequently concerns the treatment of members of groups of people or else looks backwards to the compensating of prior injuries, demanding fairness in our handling of such situations. Exactly what fairness requires is hard to say, and different standards may well be applied to the same case. If Nixon committed high crimes and misdemeanors, he is justly impeached under the Constitution. If Presidents Kennedy and Johnson committed equally heinous acts, then Nixon suffers a comparative injustice since he was singled out. On the other hand, our treatment of Nixon and other white-collar lawbreakers is unjust, although this time for the opposite reason, when compared to the stiffer sentences meted out to "common" criminals for less grave offenses.

Injustice in one sense of unfairness occurs when like cases are not treated in the same fashion. Following Aristotle, many philosophers believe that we are required, as a formal principle of justice, to treat similar cases alike except where there is some relevant difference. This principle emphasizes the role of impartiality and consistency in justice, but it is purely formal because we are not told which differences are relevant and which are not. Satisfying this formal requirement, furthermore, does not guarantee that justice is done; for example, by treating like cases similarly a judge can administer non-arbitrarily a law (like an apartheid regulation in South Africa) which is in fact unjust. (Similarly it may be noted that a fair procedure can lead to unjust results, as when a guilty man is mistakenly acquitted by an honest jury, or vice versa, as when the police unscrupulously trick a person who turns out to be guilty into confessing.)

Related to Aristotle's fairness requirement is a third idea commonly bound up with the concept of justice, namely, that of equality. "All persons are morally equal," it is said, and so justice is frequently held to require that our treatment of them reflect this fact. While Aristotle's formal principle of justice does not say whether we are to assume equality of treatment until some difference between cases is shown or to assume the opposite until some relevant similarities are demonstrated, a claim of injustice based on *equality* is meant to place the burden of proof on those who would endorse unequal treatment.

The demand that equality be respected, though still abstract, does have more content than the two previously mentioned aspects of justice. Even so, to claim simply that all persons are equal is not to establish a relationship between justice and economic distribution. We all believe that *some* differences in the treatment of persons are consistent with equality (punishment, for example), and neither respect for equality nor the requirement of equal treatment implies by itself an egalitarian distribution of economic goods.

Despite equality, then, individual circumstances—in particular, what a person has done—do make a difference. We think it is unfair, for example, when a guilty person goes free or an innocent person hangs, regardless of how others have been treated, because the first fails to get his or her due and the second suffers an undeserved fate. This suggests that justice sometimes involves, as a fourth aspect, something beyond equal or even impartial treatment: justice requires that individuals get what they deserve. But what do people deserve? A substantive theory of justice is needed to answer this as well as to explain when a failure to get what one deserves is a failure of justice. (For example, if I study hard for the exam, while Roger with his photographic memory goofs off all term, it may seem that I deserve to pass more than he. But when Roger breezes through the test and I fail, have I been done an injustice?) Nonetheless, the idea of desert, however it is fleshed out, is frequently tied up with discourse about justice.

Social and Economic Justice

Justice, then, is an important subclass of morality in general, a subclass which generally involves appeals to the overlapping notions of rights, fairness, equality, or desert. Justice is not the only virtue an individual or a social institution can pursue, and many of the most difficult moral dilemmas arise when the requirements of justice conflict with other goods or obligations.

Within the general category of justice, however, further distinctions must be drawn. In particular, many cases of injustice are not instances of *social* injustice. Consider, for example, parents who permit only their favorite daughter to attend college, when it is within their means to send all their children. They behave unfairly, but the injustice in question is not a social injustice. While justice is in a sense a social virtue, since it is a characteristic of our relations with others, the concept of social justice is not used to capture this simple fact. Rather, social justice refers to the *structure* and *policies* of a society, to its political, legal, economic, and social institutions. (Are they fair? Do they violate rights? Do they reflect the equality of citizens?) Thus a constitutional structure which gives undue influence to one group is unjust, as is a policy requiring the registration of Jews. Both cases involve the shared institutions of a society; they are failures of social justice. A corrupt judge who abuses the legal system by throwing an innocent into jail perpetrates a grievous injustice, but such an individual transgression is not a matter of social injustice unless the social system in question tolerates or encourages such corruption.

Justice in general and social justice in particular involve the distribution of benefits and burdens, but distributive justice has come to be synonymous with economic justice, that is, with the distribution of *economic* benefits and burdens. Social justice includes but is not identical to economic justice, although both are concerned in part with how to distribute things that people care about. Political powers and liberties may be distributed unjustly, yet this is not a problem of economic justice as such (unless, perhaps, the political injustice in question results from a particular economic distribution).

Distinguishing the distribution of economic from other social goods goes only part of the way toward defining our subject. Worldwide poverty and starvation, for example, raise serious moral problems involving the distribution of economic goods, yet these problems are not obviously ones of economic *justice* at all. How can this be if, as some philosophers maintain, there is no relevant moral difference between aiding a person in your own town and helping someone overseas?

Some, of course, think that for one person to have more than another is intrinsically unjust, but disparity of wealth itself cannot be the source of the injustice. (Only in a cosmic or poetic sense is it unjust for me to thrive on my Iowa farm while you barely eke out an existence in the Yukon.) If we are to speak of justice at all, there must be some relation between the parties by virtue of which a right is violated or an unfairness done. And furthermore, if we are to speak of hunger overseas as being a matter of social or, more specifically, economic justice for us, the situation must reflect upon the policies or structure of our society as a whole. (Other moral considerations, of course, may oblige us to assist those in need outside our own country, if justice does not.)

However, even if foreign poverty were a matter of economic justice for some wealthy country (perhaps because it enjoys an economically exploitative relation with the countries in question or because its hoarding of resources violates some right of theirs), there would still be the issue of the justice of its own economic institutions as this affects its citizens. The joint enterprises and shared institutions of a society, the economic interrelatedness and mutual dependence of its citizens, and the fact that its members often view themselves as a community of persons who share certain aims and ideals suggest that the question of intrasocietal economic distribution is different from moral problems concerning relations between persons in separate societies. In addition, it may be, as some philosophers think, that resolving the former issue will shed light on the latter, just as, in general, determining the requirements of justice will take us some way toward understanding our overall moral obligation.

READING #2   What Is Political Economy?
Martin Staniland

Principles of distributive justice extend no further than one's conception of the socioeconomic boundaries of any society. Economic borders, however, tend to be demarcated by political ones. How one depicts the economic domain relevant to claims of distributive justice depends upon how one envisions the moral status of political boundaries defined by the sovereignty of states.

The intersection of politics, economics, and distributive justice lies squarely at the heart of world political economy. But, according to the reading that follows, they each must be kept in balance. Staniland warns against "economism" and "politicism," by which he means the exaggerated emphasis upon either economics or politics in developmental approaches to political economy. He concludes by stressing the significance of normative standards and values for the design and implementation of policy strategies to promote distributive justice.

—E. W.

"Political Economy" and Culture

As long as there is a variety of cultures, there is likely to be a variety of theories about important social issues, and there will be no strictly logical or intellectual way of choosing between them. For this reason, there is clearly no such thing as "*the* theory of political economy," and there never will be, in the sense of a single, universally accepted complex of assumptions and methodology. There are various ways of conceptualizing political economy—by which I mean not just any theory bearing the label, but rather a set of theories concerned with depicting relationships between political processes and economic processes. The term *political economy*, used generically, refers to a continuing intellectual enterprise, a particular agenda, a specific object of theoretical ambition.

Because "political economy" is an agenda rather than a method, there will always be a variety of theories of political economy. And because a variety of assumptions and values underlies such variety of theory, it may be possible (indeed, it is very desirable) to criticize each theory; but it will never be possible to decide between them, to end the debate, and to remove the variety by purely logical means.

Martin Staniland, *What Is Political Economy? A Study of Social Theory and Underdevelopment.* Copyright © 1985 by Yale University Press. Excerpt, pp. 198–200, reprinted by permission of Yale University Press; endnotes deleted.

This point is reinforced if we examine the two main deterministic forms of political economy theory identified in this book—"economism" and "politicism." One posits the actual and the explanatory primacy of economic forces; the other, the same primacy of political forces. As [Joseph] Cropsey has pointed out, a careful scrutiny of both formulas shows them to be incomplete and question-begging. Take first the "economistic" approach, adopted by liberal pluralist ("interest group") and Marxist theory. In both, the substance of political life is held to be competition or conflict between predominantly economic interests: "to that extent, the relation between politics and economic life seems to be that political activity grows out of economic activity." But, then, such competition is carried on within a certain structure of laws and institutions that imposes distinct advantages and disadvantages on the various competitors. Politics thus regains its primacy— until we ask what the origins of this structure of laws and institutions are.

The conundrum is not resolved by resort to historical argument about man's ascent from the state of nature. On the one hand, it is argued that economic needs are fundamental, that production and survival are in every way prior to political organization. On the other hand, it is argued that beyond a very rudimentary point of development, economic production and distribution depend on a structure of laws that, most importantly, converts matter into property and regulates its transfer. But here we face not only the question of how this structure came about, but also the further question of how the consequent control of property (or lack of it) affects a person's ability to assert the rights he or she enjoys, including the right (if granted) to take part in making the laws. As Cropsey remarks, the posing of *this* question seems again to make economics the foundation of politics and the determinant of power, and the conundrum remains unsolved: "we seem unable to break out of the endless alternation of the political and economic at what appear to be the foundations, each incontrovertibly determining the other and dependent on the other." Cropsey's point is that the conundrum cannot be "solved" at this level. The two processes are ultimately indistinguishable from each other, and to the extent that they can be distinguished (as separate sets of institutions), they are related in a continual, interactive fashion. Empirically, therefore, one cannot be assigned primacy over the other.

The only primacy possible is a normative one—that is, a return to the subordination of economic processes to morality (and the return of economics to the bosom of normative political theory). In short, we are back with the idea that economics cannot be regarded as morally neutral or self-sufficient any more than politics can. "Values" come first and last. A theory may be—intellectually—a bad theory, even though its creator is "committed" and idealistic. But without some explicit commitment to a value outside of the mere accumulation and circulation of power and wealth it is disingenuous, incomplete, and probably dangerous.

READING #3   What Is Poverty?

*The Independent Commission on International Development
Issues (The Brandt Commission)*

The first fact of life in the world economy is that more than a billion people live in poverty. In the midst of plenty, there are those who suffer dire misery. Squalor, hunger, ignorance, and indignity are the common conditions of the poor, who live everywhere but largely within lesser developing countries. The pain of another is always elusive; any person's suffering remains irreducible to generalization. Unless one is willing to imagine the torment of others as one's very own, however, one cannot understand the moral significance of poverty.

To provoke the conscience of the world and to sound a humanitarian claim on behalf of distributive justice, an independent commission on development was established in 1977 under the chairmanship of former West German Chancellor Willy Brandt. The Brandt Commission released two reports and called for a rejuvenated political commitment to helping the poor in both the northern and the southern regions of the world.

Poverty, the Brandt Commission observed, exists in two types of settings: the more or less prosperous areas in which wealth is poorly distributed, and the mostly poor regions in which little or no wealth is available for distribution. The reports thus characterized poverty as both *relative* and *absolute*. Any political economy of development truly embued with the exigencies of justice, the reports added, must recognize the special plight of women under conditions of poverty who, along with children, suffer the worst hardships. Development with justice is not only morally correct; it is also economically advantageous, since fairness in distribution and in exchange represent crucial vectors of development.

—E. W.

Development never will be, and never can be, defined to universal satisfaction. It refers, broadly speaking, to desirable social and economic progress, and people will always have different views about what is desirable. Certainly development must mean improvement in living conditions, for which economic growth and industrialization are essential. But if there is no attention to the quality of growth and to social change one cannot speak of development.

The Independent Commission on International Development Issues (Brandt Commission Report), *North-South: A Programme for Survival*. Copyright © 1980 by The MIT Press. Excerpt, pp. 48–51 and 59–60, reprinted with permission of The MIT Press, Cambridge, Massachusetts; endnotes deleted.

It is now widely recognized that development involves a profound transformation of the entire economic and social structure. This embraces changes in production and demand as well as improvements in income distribution and employment. It means creating a more diversified economy, whose main sectors become more interdependent for supplying inputs and for expanding markets for output.

The actual patterns of structural transformation will tend to vary from one country to another depending on a number of factors—including resources, geography, and the skills of the population. There are, therefore, no golden rules capable of universal application for economic development. Each country has to exploit the opportunities open to it for strengthening its economy. Structural transformation need not imply autarky. Some countries might find it feasible to pursue inward-looking strategies that rely, at least in the early stages, on using their domestic markets. Others may diversify and expand their exports. Exports can become more fully integrated with the rest of the economy, as the domestic market comes to provide a larger base, or as export industries secure more of their inputs from local sources. Yet others will concentrate initially on distributing income more evenly in order to widen the domestic market for locally produced goods and to lay the foundations for a better balance between the rural and urban sectors. But all countries need an international environment that will be responsive to their development efforts. Herein lies part of the rationale for a new international economic order.

Statistical measurements of growth exclude the crucial elements of social welfare, of individual rights, of values not measurable by money. Development is more than the passage from poor to rich, from a traditional rural economy to a sophisticated urban one. It carries with it not only the idea of economic betterment, but also of greater human dignity, security, justice and equity.

The Nature of Poverty

Few people in the North have any detailed conception of the extent of poverty in the Third World or of the forms that it takes. Many hundreds of millions of people in the poorer countries are preoccupied solely with survival and elementary needs. For them work is frequently not available or, when it is, pay is very low and conditions often barely tolerable. Homes are constructed of impermanent materials and have neither piped water nor sanitation. Electricity is a luxury. Health services are thinly spread and in rural areas only rarely within walking distance. Primary schools, where they exist, may be free and not too far away, but children are needed for work and cannot easily be spared for schooling. Permanent insecurity is the condition of the poor. There are no public systems of social security in the event of unemployment, sickness or death of a wage-earner in the family. Flood, drought or disease affecting people or livestock can destroy livelihoods without hope of compensation. In the North, ordinary men and women face genuine economic problems—uncertainty, inflation, the fear if not the reality of unemployment. But they rarely face anything resembling the total deprivation found in the South. Ordinary people in the South would not find it credible that the societies of the North regard themselves as anything other than wealthy.

The poorest people in the world will remain for some time to come outside the reach of normal trade and communications. The combination of malnutrition, illiteracy, disease, high birth rates, underemployment and low income closes off the avenues of escape; and while other groups are increasingly vocal, the poor and illiterate are usually and conveniently silent. It is a condition of life so limited as to be, in the words of the President of the World Bank, 'below any rational definition of human decency'. No concept of development can be accepted which continues to condemn hundreds of millions of people to starvation and despair.

Eight Hundred Million Destitute

Precisely how many people in the Third World live in such conditions of poverty, no one can say. The International Labour Office estimated the number of destitute at 700 million in the early 1970s. World Bank estimates today put them at 800 million. This suggests that almost 40 per cent of the people in the South are surviving—but only barely surviving—in the kind of poverty we have been describing, with incomes judged insufficient to secure the basic necessities of life.

Mass poverty remains overwhelmingly a rural affliction, and it is rural poverty that seems so harshly intractable. The mass urban poverty of Kinshasa, Mexico City or Cairo is a relatively modern phenomenon. For all its squalor, it is one step up from rural deprivation. To some extent, that is why these cities have grown. But the poor in India, Bangladesh, Pakistan, Indonesia and nearly all of Africa, are still, to the extent of 70 per cent or more of the total population, in the rural villages.

Differing Conditions of Poverty

People are poor in two kinds of circumstances: in countries which have reached relatively high average levels of income, where this income is not well distributed; and in countries which have low levels of income where there is little to distribute. Poverty in the North is entirely of the first kind. There are pockets of poverty, and deficiencies in housing and other services, all the less defensible for existing in the midst of what several commentators have called 'overdevelopment'. In the South, the great majority of the 800 million poor live in the low-income countries of sub-Saharan Africa and South Asia, though many better-off countries have large layers of acute poverty which show that the benefits of growth have not trickled down to the poorest. This does not necessarily mean that these governments are indifferent to their poor or lack the political will to improve their lot. But some of the richer ones, especially in Latin America, could do much more:

the growth performance of Latin America in the 1970s (of about 7 per cent per annum), if sustained, could enable them to solve their problems of extreme poverty. In Latin America as a whole, the absolute poor number about 100 million; in twelve out of twenty-three countries where reliable estimates exist, over one-half of the population has incomes insufficient to buy a basket of goods and services deemed essential for a minimum level of welfare.

The experience of some countries confirms that, where assets are distributed more fairly in the first place, sustained economic growth can provide jobs and better conditions for the poor. The better-off countries have sufficient resources to mitigate extreme forms of poverty; if they can maintain high growth rates, they can eliminate it. But for the elimination of poverty in the world as a whole the outlook is bleak. Recent World Bank projections (which contain fairly optimistic assumptions about economic growth, but do not incorporate any major changes in international or national development efforts) suggest that there will still be 600 million absolute poor in the countries of the South by the year 2000. . . .

Women in Society

Any definition of development is incomplete if it fails to comprehend the contribution of women to development and the consequences of development for the lives of women. Every development policy, plan or project has an impact on women and cannot succeed without the work of women. And development with justice calls urgently for measures that will give women access to better jobs; that will diminish the arduous tasks that hundreds of millions of women face in their domestic and agricultural occupations; and that will distribute more fairly between the sexes opportunities for creative work and economic advancement.

Yet economic development is often still talked about as if it was mainly a subject for men. Plans and projects are designed by men to be implemented by men on the assumption that if men, as the heads of households, benefit from these projects, the women and the children in those households will benefit too. Women's problems still tend to be regarded as separate, rather than as facets of the culture and structure of all societies. Women's progress needs to be treated as a conscious element in every programme directed towards development.

Experience shows that some projects will not succeed at all unless they give positive incentives to women employed in them; some, such as the introduction of new crops, are quite likely to have adverse effects upon women's welfare; some industrial developments which recruit women as a source of cheap labour may harmfully affect both the distribution of work within the household and the quality of family life. Even welfare projects designed specifically for women and children have been found to have negligible impact unless arrangements are built in to make certain that the benefits reach them.

Women participate in development everywhere. But they are not equal participants because very frequently their status prevents them from having equal access to education, training, jobs, land ownership, credit, business opportunities, and even (as mortality statistics show in some countries) to nutritious food and other necessities for survival. The development of production-oriented societies and the use of capital (whether socially or privately owned) have mostly widened the gap between the different evaluations which society accords to men's and women's work. As the majority of inventions and technical improvements have been applied to what have been traditionally regarded as men's jobs, the effect has been to increase men's dominant role. If economic modernization is not balanced by deliberate social and institutional reform, it may work to the comparative detriment of women. As long as women have unequal access to education, technology and other assets affecting their productivity, the 'unequal exchange' which many commentators see as characteristic of North-South relations will in a not wholly dissimilar way obtain between men and women. For this to be overcome women in developing and industrialized countries must achieve equal status, equal opportunity and equal pay for equal work.

READING #4   What Is Relative Poverty?
Paul Harrison

Few have all they want; but some have more, some have less, of what they want than others. People are absolutely poor if they do not enjoy at least a minimal standard of living consonant with human dignity. But how much must a person or a family have before their deprivations add up to what may be considered **relative poverty** rather than absolute poverty? This question is difficult to answer precisely. Personal and subjective factors as well as objective ones must be considered.

Paul Harrison, in the reading that follows, illustrates the distinction between absolute and relative forms of poverty by reference to the **demonstration effects** produced by developmental social change. He describes the processes of impoverishment leading to the worldwide spread of what he calls the "worm of envy." This "worm," which distorts perceptions and often leads to rage, constitutes the psychological bases of relative poverty.

Destitution below the level of biological subsistence constitutes the objective condition of absolute poverty. Absolute poverty does not revolve around relative conceptions of cultural values, although different cultures respond differently to it. Absolute poverty is simply grounded in the raw facts of a brutalized life and early death regardless of culture or perception.

But there exists another and somewhat less immediate form of denial, one that also sentences a person to a lifelong struggle against misery, but usually in more prolonged ways. This form of poverty stems from demonstration effects, perceptions of how one is faring *relative to others,* during the course of social change wrought by development. In lesser developing countries, those individuals able to obtain sufficient amounts of disposable income and who thus enjoy sufficient supplies of food, clothes, shelter, health services, and education, create special problems for those whose purchasing power remains at traditional levels—even if these levels are adequate for survival.

Relative poverty is thus the bitter pill many must swallow in societies where the gap between haves and have nots leaves some clearly ahead and others manifestly behind—not an uncommon event given accelerating income disparities that typically attend early phases of development. Goods and services newly available and thus considered very desirable are often so expensive as to be, in effect, off-limits to the "relatively" poor.

The pervasive irony of much modern economic growth is that the number of people enduring the plights of relative poverty increases as a consequence of it. Large segments of the population find it more, rather than less, difficult to break out from the hold of poverty during the course of the very social changes held to be designed in their favor. Paul Harrison examines this phenomenon, which he calls the "pauperization of the poor," and shows how the process is both circular and self-reinforcing.

—E. W.

The concept of poverty is not easy to define, as it comes in two models: absolute poverty and relative poverty. When we talk of absolute poverty, we are implying a level of income that imposes real physical suffering on people in hunger, disease and the massacre of innocent children.

Hunger is the painful focus of absolute poverty. Disease goes hand in hand with it. Both bring physical discomfort and, worse, prevent children and adults from reaching their full physical and mental potential. Those who cannot afford to eat enough to provide protection against disease and productive labour invariably suffer in other ways: their housing and sanitation will probably be bad enough to contribute to disease, their education inadequate to obtain employment paying enough to feed them. All aspects of absolute poverty work together in denying the victims a fully, or sometimes even minimally, human existence.

Absolute poverty has been increasing, both in total numbers and in the proportion of the population affected. Two-thirds of the absolutely poor live in Asia. Recent surveys from the continent paint an alarming, even

Paul Harrison, *The Third World Tomorrow: A Report from the Battlefront in the War Against Poverty.* Copyright © 1980 by Penguin Books, Inc. Excerpt, pp. 406–408 and 418–426, reprinted with permission of Penguin Books, Inc., and the author; endnotes deleted.

horrifying picture. In many countries the proportion under the poverty line has increased and the real incomes of the poorest groups have declined. . . .

Relative poverty can be almost as destructive as absolute poverty, in the sense that it can preoccupy or even obsess one's thoughts and divert him from the enjoyment of his life. The man who is not suffering physically may suffer mentally when he compares himself with people vastly better off than he, and he can see no good reason for the discrepancy. Relative deprivation depends very much on expectations. An untouchable in India may not feel deprived in comparison to a Brahmin, if the caste system has brainwashed him into believing that the differences are natural and just. But expectations are high in the Third World today and the rhetoric of equality is universal. Elites compare their countries with the West, and feel deprived. Poor men compare themselves with the elites, and feel deprived. Poverty, in the egalitarian mood of the twentieth century, brings with it the worm of envy, as an inevitable reaction to unjust inequalities. Relative poverty, in most of the Third World, often means shame, too: shame that your house has a thatched roof while your neighbour has tin, shame that your children go barefoot to school, shame that your daughter's dowry or wedding feast is so pitiably small.

Relative poverty, in other words, is the mental suffering that derives from inequality. Pronounced inequalities make the burden of poverty that much harder to bear. Indeed in many cases one man's excess wealth may be the direct cause of another man's destitution.

Inequality, like poverty, has been increasing both internationally and in many individual countries.

The distribution of the world's income is more unequal than even the most grotesquely unjust of national distributions. In 1976 the industrialized countries made up only 24 per cent of the world's population, but raked in 78 per cent of the income. The developing countries—76 per cent of the people—got only 22 per cent of the income. The average income in the industrialized countries was $6,110 per person, eleven times that of the developing countries ($542). At the bottom of the heap, the poorest 43 per cent of the world's population got only 3.6 per cent of the world's income, giving them an average income one thirty-eighth of that of the top 24 per cent.

The absolute gap between rich and poor countries is widening. Between 1974 and 1975, for example, the average *increase* in income per capita in the richest countries—$480—exceeded the average *total* income per head in the developing countries, or $416, and was four times greater than the poorest countries' increase. . . .

One can distinguish four modes of impoverishment—geographical, where the main factor is a natural or ecological process; social, where pauperization develops out of the agreed ground-rules of the society; economic, where it results from the forces of the marketplace; and political, where it is imposed by the use of state power. Some of these modes have two or three variants.

In many situations, indeed, they are all at work together, and to cope with one while ignoring the others may lead to oversimplified solutions. . . .

These, to summarize, are the principal mechanisms by which the poor get poor: natural impoverishment, and ecological impoverishment; social impoverishment; the impoverishment of unequal exchange and of unequal competition; and the impoverishment of state repression, state bias and state privilege. Most of these have their international counterparts by which poor nations get poor: social impoverishment corresponds to the growing burden of debt; unequal exchange to the unfair terms of trade; unequal competition to the destructive effect of the most efficient producers on the industries of those countries that are not protected against them. Political impoverishment is thankfully getting weaker, but was widespread when the United States used to intervene to defend reactionary governments and multinational investments, and still occurs in the bias of aid flows, and the overpayment of international bureaucrats and consultants.

Once the poor get poor, they tend to stay that way. . . . The poor man has no capital, human or physical, to improve his lot. He is malnourished and therefore diseased, and so his labour is less productive—but he cannot make it more productive as he lacks money to invest in improving his land or his tools. Therefore he stays poor, and because he is poor, is less able to organize with others of his kind to improve their lot. And, if he finds himself in a situation of competition with the rich, he will probably get even poorer. Nations stay poor, strangely enough, by exactly the same process writ large. And the children of the poor also stay poor, because the environment of poverty is hereditary. Like their parents, the children of the poor are malnourished and unhealthy. Therefore they fail at school (if indeed they ever attend it), lose out in the employment race and remain in poverty.

Poverty is self-perpetuating, and inequality is self-reinforcing. Competition between social groups is like running several Monopoly games at once so that the tokens you have won on one game can be used to enable you to win the other games more easily. As long as you are in a competitive situation, that kind of advantage can go on for ever unless someone comes along and knocks the board over.

READING #5   What Is the Economics That Really Matters?

Gerald M. Meier

One of the striking or salient characteristics of our century is the broad expansion of wealth among those not necessarily wealthy. Upward mobility encapsulates the expectations of large segments of society in affluent countries, especially the so-called middle class, whose talents, energies, and consumption patterns have fueled the world economy since the middle of the last century. For many of the middle class, especially within advanced developed countries, the goal of possessing more than previous generations is integral to the personal expectations that are fostered by national dreams.

The absence of a surging middle class pinpoints a major difference between rich and poor countries. Poor countries are poor and, in the minds of some, remain so because they sustain neither a middle-class sector nor the widespread values associated with middle-class habits in respect to work, spending, and consumption. Thus, creation of a middle class often becomes the aim of development, especially when development policies are shaped by liberal orientations. Indeed, as we shall later see, classically oriented liberals, who extol the social and political worth of a free market system, assume that economic systems favoring middle-class affluence will prove to be more productive, even for the poor, than those that do not.

Not surprisingly, the effect of the middle-class sector on development represents a major issue in development theory. The reciprocal influences of growing affluence for some and relative poverty, or what is sometimes referred to as **marginalization,** present a serious problem in any political economy of development. The important question is this: Is marginalization—that is, expansion of relative poverty—brought about by policies favoring the middle-class sector in lesser developing countries? Alternatively, does the rise of a middle-class sector itself depend upon whether large remaining portions of the population become marginalized? Individuals sink into relative poverty and become marginalized once they are impelled to leave their traditional ways of life and livelihoods to eke out a living from within the ''margins'' of society—for example, from within the slums or shantytowns surrounding many of the large cities in lesser developing countries, or from the margins of often barren rural areas newly depleted of both their produce and their productivity.

Gerald M. Meier, in the reading that follows, unravels the plight of the marginalized and provides many examples to support the proposition that their numbers increase with development. His analysis provides some answers as to why the rise of a middle class coincides with marginalization and the spread of both relative and absolute poverty, by referring to *urban pull, rural push,* and *capital-intensive investment strategies* versus *labor-intensive employment strategies.* The observed direct correlation between a rising middle class and expansions in marginalization in lesser developing countries helps to explain why distributive justice stands at the very point at which political economy of development and policy strategies for development meet.

In the context of distributive justice we are compelled to ask how much relative poverty is necessary for the creation of a viable middle class, or how much marginalization we are willing to permit as the price to be paid for long-range economic growth. Distributive justice thus represents an essential perspective in the evaluation of developmental strategies of growth, since the policies that systematically create marginalized masses of people—however attractive they may have appeared initially—*ought* to be challenged on moral grounds.

—*E. W.*

Absolute Poverty

Average rates of growth in GNP [Gross National Product] for the LDCs [lesser developing countries] and rates of growth in per capita income mask the persistent problems confronted by the most underprivileged groups in the most underprivileged countries. In spite of respectable achievements in rates of growth in GNP, it has been tragic that the low-end poverty groups below a poverty line, based on minimum standards, have not received more of the benefits of this growth. Instead of a "trickling down" of income to the poorest and a reduction in the numbers below a poverty line, there has actually been an increase in the enormous number of people suffering from what the World Bank terms "absolute poverty." Relative poverty in the sense of being at the lower end of a nation's income distribution will exist in any country. But the existence of large numbers in absolute poverty is the agonizing condition of a poor country.

Those in absolute poverty can be identified as approximately the bottom 40 percent of the population, those whose per capita incomes are less than one-third of the national average per capita income. The absolute poor are mainly small subsistence farmers, tenant farmers and sharecroppers, landless workers in agriculture, unemployed and underemployed urban laborers.

Too few of the benefits of economic growth have reached these groups. The failure of these groups to attain a minimum level of income above the poverty line is now of more concern than that of relative poverty, or a "widening gap" between rich and poor countries. With the increase in population, the number of people in absolute poverty has grown and is now in the order of 800 million. For these millions, development has failed. The less developed economies may have done well in terms of GNP growth rates, but hundreds of millions of people in the lowest income groups have not been able to emerge from their poverty.

Malnutrition is especially prevalent among the absolute poor. Fifteen to 20 percent of mankind still suffer from moderate to severe chronic undernutrition. Evidence of serious protein-caloric malnutrition for several hundred million people comes from estimates of food consumption, medical studies, and data on child mortality. Consumption by large sections of the population is still far below what is needed for a minimally satisfactory diet. Undernutrition is most widespread in Africa and South Asia. About 70 percent of all hunger is in nine countries (India, Pakistan, Bangladesh, Indonesia, Philippines, Kampuchea, Zaire, Ethiopia, and Brazil). Moreover, there is evidence that the size of the malnourished population has grown.

From *Emerging from Poverty: The Economics That Really Matters*, pp. 89–96, by Gerald M. Meier. Copyright © 1984 by Oxford University Press, Inc. Reprinted by permission; endnotes deleted.

Studies by the Food and Agriculture Organization and World Bank estimate that the number of malnourished in the world has grown at a rate that exceeds population growth.

Why do people go hungry? Contrary to the common belief that the cause is a failure of food supply relative to the population, malnutrition is largely a reflection of poverty. People simply do not have enough income for food that will provide adequate calories and protein requirements. Undernutrition has persisted even when food supplies meet market demand at acceptable prices. Not deficiencies in food supplies but inadequate entitlements through inadequate incomes are most important in accounting for hunger. A World Bank Report estimates that at the global level, if income were distributed differently, present output of grain alone could supply every man, woman, and child with more than 3,000 calories and 65 grams of protein per day—far more than the highest estimates of requirements. Eliminating malnutrition would require the redirection of only about 2 percent of the world's grain output to the mouths that need it.

To reduce hunger, the employment and income effects of agricultural development are much more important than increasing food output per se. To the tourist, poverty and hunger are more visible in urban areas, but the vast numbers of undernourished people are actually in the countryside. Many of these people have no direct access to land to grow more food or to income to purchase it. Agrarian reforms have not been forthcoming to ameliorate their lot, nor have sufficient productive jobs been created. The lack of income generation and the inequitable income distribution have kept more people in hunger than has a failure to expand food production.

The absolute poor tend to be concentrated in the least developed countries of South Asia and Africa, and mainly in rural sectors. Some 200 million of the absolute poor are in cities, unemployed or underemployed in self-employed pursuits of very low productivity that yield a precarious and meager income. For the 600 million subsistence farmers, tenants, and landless laborers in the rural areas, the weakness of rural development has provided no escape from absolute poverty.

Why have there not been greater benefits from growth for the bottom 40 percent? In part, the failure is related to the other disappointments of failure in agricultural development and the explosive population growth. But there are also other explanations. The pattern of growth, with its emphasis on capital accumulation instead of human-resource development, has failed to raise the productivity of the poor. Those in absolute poverty have not had sufficient access to essential public services such as education and health. Illiteracy, malnutrition, and ill-health keep too many entrapped in absolute poverty. There have not been the necessary opportunities for access to productive assets—land, credit, and education. And employment opportunities have been limited in the face of a growing labor force and rural-urban migration.

Children of Poverty

Absolute poverty takes its greatest toll in denying a future for the children living in poverty. Some 1.6 billion individuals in the world are age 15 or under; most of them—1.3 billion—live in developing countries. These individuals were born with 1 chance in 6 of not living a year. Mortality rates among children age one to four years in low-income countries are frequently 20 to 30 times those in Europe or North America. Even in a country with as good a development record as Brazil, 48 percent of all deaths as late as 1975 occurred among children under five years. . . .

For those who do enter school, 60 percent will not complete more than three years of primary school. The quality of schooling is poor, repeaters occupy 15 to 20 percent of school places, and the school leaver and dropout rates are high. In the low-income countries, less than 10 percent of the secondary school age population is enrolled.

Far removed from the classroom, the poor child is often a working child who endures long days on farms, in mines, in workshops, or in street trades such as cleaning shoes, selling chewing gum, washing cars, or collecting rubbish in the urban centers. The International Labor Organization estimates that 75 million children under 15 years of age are working at a fixed job. Some 17 million Indian children have gone straight from "swaddling clothes into working gear." The child is obviously obliged to accept simple jobs that call for no previous experience or training. These jobs are by their nature low-productivity jobs, and they yield only an irregular and inadequate income. Moreover, children doing this kind of work remain no more qualified for a better job after years of cleaning shoes or selling lottery tickets than they were when they started. But the conditions of child labor have stunted their physical and mental growth—their future has been mortgaged.

Unemployment and Underemployment

Associated with the rising number in absolute poverty is the rising number in unemployment and underemployment. In spite of high rates of investment and growth in national output, the growth process has not provided sufficient employment opportunities. A large labor surplus remains underutilized in many poor countries; the problem of labor absorption is still as acute as three decades ago. . . .

The unusually fast growth in the labor force in many developing countries is only part of the explanation of the disappointing record of labor utilization. Also significant has been the widening gap between the urban and agricultural wage levels. The employment problem in the urban areas has resulted in part from a premature increase in the industrial wage combined with a premature reduction in agricultural employment. It might be thought un-reasonable that urban wages should rise while alternative earnings in agriculture have not, and while the supply of labor coming to the cities is still greater than the demand. But the institutional determination of wages by minimum wage laws, social security legislation, trade union activity, and growth of public-sector employment have created a high-wage sector. Being two or three or more times higher than agricultural earnings, the high urban wage has continued to "pull" the rural to urban migration at the same time as rural employment opportunities have not expanded to reduce the "push." Techniques of production have also been biased toward more capital-intensive production methods, either through the introduction of labor-saving machinery in response to rising wages or through improvement in personnel and production management practices that have trimmed labor requirements. The maintenance of too low a rate of interest and too low a price for foreign exchange have also promoted the use of capital-intensive methods of production. The more intensive use of labor has also been restrained when the government has been attracted to the most modern capital equipment and when foreign enterprises continue to use advanced production techniques more suited to their home countries where labor is scarce.

The urban employment problem is, in turn, a reflection of the rural employment problem—the failure of agriculture to hold and provide sufficient income for all the people whom the urban sector is not yet ready to employ. The urban "pull" was not offset by lessening the "push" through rural development. Many countries failed to follow a labor-using, capital-saving approach to agricultural development. And many failed to realize the employment potential in rural modernization. Without the absorption of more workers in agriculture, and without rising productivity and rising earnings in agriculture, which accounts for 70 to 80 percent of employment, it has not been possible to generate sufficient demand and opportunities for the unemployed and underemployed. The rise of the numbers in absolute poverty and the persistent underutilization of surplus labor are thus related to the neglect of agriculture. The development strategies of the 1950s and 1960s that emphasized rapid capital accumulation and industrialization led to the employment problems of the 1970s and 1980s.

Inequality

Also disappointing has been the persistence of a highly unequal distribution of income in many developing countries, and even an increasing inequality in some countries that have had high rates of growth. Much of the poverty problem is a reflection of low levels of per capita income, but highly unequal distribution patterns are also important. For example, because of the more unequal income distribution in Colombia than South Korea, the proportion of the population below the poverty line is twice as high in Colombia than in South Korea, even though the average incomes of the two countries are close. The development strategies of some countries have succeeded in raising the level of per capita income markedly without having much impact on the poverty problem because of the deterioration in relative income shares. The growth in income has been concentrated in the higher income levels.

A typical distribution of income in a less developed country shows that more than 50 percent of total income is received by the top 10 percent of the population, while the bottom 20 percent receive less than 5 percent. About three-quarters of the total GNP goes to the top 40 percent of the population, while the bottom 40 percent receive only about 10 to 15 percent of the total national income. Even in countries such as Mexico and Brazil, with impressive rates of growth in GNP, the richest 10 percent receive six to eight times the share of income of the poorest 40 percent. The level of employment and remuneration to the owners of capital, land, and labor explain only part of the distribution of income. The low income for the bottom 40 percent is to be explained by underemployment, self-employment in low-productivity activities, and especially the lack of productive assets owned by the lowest income groups—land, physical capital, access to public capital goods, and human capital embodying education and skills.

READING #6   Why Do the Poor Stay Poor?
Urban Bias in World Development
Michael Lipton

In the reading that follows, Michael Lipton's brilliant analysis of marginalization expands upon Meier's analysis of urban "pull" and rural "push" in the previous selection.

Lipton views modern development as a process distorted. Urban bias, built into government policies and strategies for development throughout the developing world, reinforces poverty and marginalization, even during economic growth. Economic growth does not ameliorate the oppressive conditions of the poor. On the contrary, its very mechanisms retard social development. Thus, as the economic picture of any developing society appears to improve *as a whole*, the lives of the poor remain the same or even worsen. This is the story of the modern political economy of development, Lipton asserts, and he asks, But why?

Lipton's examination peers beyond the shroud of ideological sloganizing to scan how urban-oriented policy decisions relating to rural and agricultural sectors often lead to unfortunate consequences for the poor almost everywhere within lesser developing countries. What he sees is the concentrated power of urban-based governments. He also detects the force of urban incentives and values. These, he argues, directly or indirectly, intentionally or unintentionally, erode the viability of rural livelihoods and the vitality of rural life. Accelerating marginalization is the result.

Lipton uses a specific example—food prices—to demonstrate how urban bias in development promotes impoverishment or marginalization. Ironically, government policies that are intended to lower food prices depress rural markets and lead to the malevolent effects of marginalization. Artificially inexpensive food destroys a rural economy. It entices villagers to migrate to large cities where they live in slums and squalor, whereas profits from the sale of food flow not back into farms or villages but into the cities—thereby also accelerating distributive injustice. Lipton's message is clear: A flourishing rural economy is the very key to genuine social development in most lesser developing countries.

—E. W.

The Coexistence of Poverty and Development

The Problem Stated

'In the midst of plethoric plenty, the people perish.' So wrote Carlyle in 1852, addressing himself to the 'condition-of-England question'. Today the distribution of resources is seen in a world perspective. We now notice the coexistence of mass hunger in Bengal and mass obesity in Los Angeles. Many people, even in rich countries, condemn it. For various reasons— political, economic, moral—some people in rich countries have tried to develop policies to alleviate the poverty of poor countries, and in particular to help them to help themselves.

Yet even policies sincerely intended to help poor *countries* often do little for poor *people*. Leave aside insincerity—'aid' to help British or French building companies to supply air-conditioned airports, or trade 'concessions' to one's sugar companies in the West Indies. Even policies apparently aimed directly against individual poverty, and towards self-help, often fail. For instance, when the World Food Programme of the Food and Agriculture Organisation gives food to enable workers to eat while they build a dam, the food can end up enriching speculators, or impoverishing small farmers by replacing their sales; and the dam may well enrich mainly big farmers growing vegetables for middle-class townspeople. More and more people are aware of such things. The new enthusiasm for integrating aid into a country's development plan underlines the growing understanding that a donor is unlikely to succeed in helping poor people, unless he first understands what has kept them in poverty, and then supports an attack upon its root causes ('supports' because that attack has to be mainly the responsibility of the poor countries themselves). But what are the causes?

The key observation is this. In the last thirty years, almost all the hundred-odd LDCs have enjoyed growth and even 'development' at un-precedented rates. Yet—with a few exceptions, such as China, Malaysia and Taiwan—the proportion of their populations below a fixed acceptable min-imum standard of feeding, housing, clothing, and freedom from chronic illness has not fallen much.

Michael Lipton, *Why the Poor Stay Poor: Urban Bias in World Development.* Copyright © 1976 by Michael Lipton. Excerpt, pp. 27–28, 39–40, and 66–69, reprinted with permission of Harvard University Press, Maurice Temple Smith Ltd., and Gower Publishing Co., Ltd.; endnotes deleted.

Marx wrote, 'The philosophers have only interpreted the world, in various ways; the point, however, is to change it.' The economists, turned philosophers of international development, have too often sought to change the world without understanding it. In poor countries, they have helped to persuade governments to tax, borrow and print money to pay for investment and education. In rich countries, they have done a good deal to increase guilt, and something to increase aid. Both aid and domestic savings have produced growth in poor *countries*. Yet the world of poor *people* remains almost the same, partly because its analysts have failed to understand the forces that keep it so.

Let us begin with three facts. First, the poor countries have enjoyed a long period of unprecedented economic growth; the true value of output and income available per person in poor countries has about doubled in the last quarter-century, after many preceding centuries without any long-term upward tendency. Second, this is not 'growth without development'; on any sensible interpretation of development as modernising structural change, the poor countries have enjoyed more development in the last two decades than in the previous two millennia. Third, during this unprecedented growth and development, the condition of the really poor has undergone little improvement, except in important areas of social provision, especially health and education.

What does this add up to? The worst-off one-third of mankind comprises the village underclass of the Third World. This underclass includes landless labourers, peons, sharecroppers, owners of dwarf holdings, and even pseudo-urban (but usually jobless and temporary) migrants. This underclass has become less prone to malaria and illiteracy since 1945. It has thereby become more fit, and better fitted, to enjoy the good things of life. Yet these good things have not become available to it. Meanwhile, on a world scale, the decolonisation, growth and development of poor societies and economies have progressed quickly, smoothly, and—despite the 'cult of violence' and despite isolated horrors like the Brazilian North-East, Vietnam and Algeria—with a degree of peacefulness without historical precedent. Hence we have an astonishing contrast: rapid growth and development, yet hardly any impact on the heartland of mass poverty. Among the steel mills and airports, and despite the independent and sometimes freely elected governments, the rural masses are as hungry and ill-housed as ever. . . .

The most important feature of poor countries today, tending to prolong the period during which growth and 'development' do little for the poorest people, is the imbalance between city and country. Not only is this the main single component of inequality; it weakens the poor, as compared with their situation in Northwest Europe during early modern growth.

By 1811, barely a third of British workers depended on agriculture, and rural interests (though not rural workers as such) were heavily over-represented in Parliament; in most poor countries today, with the rural-urban income gap far greater . . . rural areas are politically *under*-represented, yet still contain over two-thirds of the poor. A relatively impoverished, weak rural sector is an unpromising source of pressures towards equalisation; for how inequalities will be affected by development depends not just on the development but on the inequalities. Many ascriptive inequalities are natural to a fairly immobile, static, nonaccumulating society; where there is not much scope for societal economic advance, society loses little output by rewarding not merit but old age, male sex, or ostentatious piety. Conversely, with growth, the new prospects of social gain can lead to rewards on merit, reducing the old inequalities. Mobility does that too; when men from villages near Bombay leave their farms to seek new urban opportunities, they improve the position of their sisters (who often run the farms they have left) *vis-à-vis* the traditional male gerontocracy. Unfortunately, however, urban-rural inequality, unlike inequality of age or sex, is likely to be strengthened by early development. The bourgeoisie whom capitalism enriches are also burghers—townsmen—and their new power weakens the rural interest. Therefore, if the masses are rural, while power and wealth are heavily concentrated in the cities before the early developmental upsurge, there is little prospect that such an upsurge will soon benefit the masses.

The accelerated growth of the now-rich world took place with 35 to 60 per cent of its people already outside agriculture, and averaging only one and a quarter to twice the income per person of the farming community; but today's poor countries, with only 10 to 35 per cent of their peoples outside agriculture, endow them with an advantage of three to ten times. . . . Those weakened by the concentration of power in the urban centres— the rural people—though relatively more numerous, are also relatively more dispersed, poor and weak in today's South than in yesterday's West. This enormously reduces the prospects of a rapid transition to equalising growth processes. Even in the West, the outlook for mass consumption would have been bleak, had it depended on a shrinking urban-rural gap; for it took a century of growth before that gap began to shrink. In today's South this gap is (1) initially much larger, (2) a much more important component of total inequality, (3) supported by a much more pro-urban balance of ideologies and political forces, (4) not shrinking, (5) not being made significantly less important by townward migration. All these factors militate against the 'automatic' conversion of development into mass welfare along the lines familiar in yesterday's West. . . .

Urban Bias and Class Structures: The Example of Food Prices

A glance at the real class structure of most poor countries casts doubt on the usual analyses of classes defined by their relationship to the means of production—land, capital and labour. One sees rural rentiers—big land-lords—certainly, but also many thousand small farmers, tenants or proprietors. They live in no communal idyll, and are poor and exploited by local monopolists—suppliers of credit, marketing facilities or land. Nor are these peasants egalitarian; they are highly differentiated. But, on the whole, they are consumer-producers for whom the separation of capital and labour, profit and wage, process of production and use of end-product, is meaningless.

Nor is the urban sector inviting to the classical Marxian analysis. One sees a mass of urban jobless, but they are often in reality *fringe villagers*, waiting until penury forces them back to the land and meanwhile living on casual work—or on their rural relatives. They hang around the city slums more in temporary hope than in expectation of work. They are kept half-employed partly by employers' preferences for machines and small workforces: preferences due to subsidised imports and high wages, both maintained in part by unions or other skilled-labour pressures. The wage levels (and less obviously the import subsidies) are paid for by villagers, who could otherwise find urban jobs (or get more imports themselves). They are enforced through naked urban power; they lead to situations where employers prefer heavy capital equipment worked well below capacity to more employment-generating strategies of production. The existing urban labour aristocracy enjoys high wages largely because it is small: it is too costly for the employer to do without their skills, cheap to pay them off, and easy to acquire capital subsidies to keep employment levels low.

Yet if he did go for more labour-intensive methods, he would advance equality. More people would be employed at a slightly lower urban wage. Despite some vulgar *Marxisants*, the basic conflict in the Third World is not between capital and labour, but between capital and countryside, farmer and townsman, villager (including temporarily urban 'fringe villager') and urban industrial employer-cum-proletarian elite, gainers from dear food and gainers from cheap food. While the urban centres of power and government remain able and willing to steer development overwhelmingly towards urban interests, development will remain unequalising.

The systematic action by most governments in poor countries to keep down food prices . . . clarifies the operation of class interests in urban bias. Town and country are polarised, yet the powerful country interests are bought off (by subsidies for inputs, such as tractors and tubewells, that they are almost alone in using). The urban employer wants food to be cheap, so that his workforce will be well fed and productive. The urban employee wants cheap food too; it makes whatever wages he can extract from the boss go further.

Less obviously, the *whole* interest of the rural community is against cheap food. This is clear enough for the farmers who sell food to the towns (largely big farmers, bought off by input subsidies); but even the 'deficit farmer' or net food buyer (who grows too little to feed himself from his land alone) often gains when food is dear, except perhaps in the very short term. Deficit farmers cannot make ends meet on their land alone, and to buy enough food must work for others. Often they work on farms for a fixed share of the crop, which is worth more when food prices are high. Whether they work for crop wages or for cash, it pays the big farmer to hire more labour when food is dearer, and this bids up farm wages as well as rural employment. The rural craftsmen who serve the big farmers' production and consumption needs—carpenters, ropemakers, goldsmiths— receive more offers of work, at higher wages, when their patrons are enriched because food is dearer; and many poor agriculturists eke out their income by traditional craft activities. Moreover, the richer farmers have more cash to lend out when food is dear and their income high, so the interest rate to the poor borrower is reduced as lenders compete. Even the people on the fringe of the countryside, the recently migrant urban unemployed, find their remittances from the village increasing when their farming fathers and brothers benefit from high food prices.

There is a 'deep' reason why an issue such as the price of food polarises city and country into opposing classes, each fairly homogeneous. The reason is that within each rural community (though hardly one is nowadays completely closed) extra income generated tends to circulate. The big farmer, when he gets a good price for his output, can buy a new seed drill from the village carpenter, who goes more often to the barber and the laundryman, who place more orders with the village tailor and blacksmith. When food becomes cheap, this sort of circulation of income is transferred from the village to the city, because it is in the city that the urban worker will spend most of the money he need no longer use to buy food.

We shall see . . . how urban power, urban government in the urban interest, has made farm products artificially cheap and farmers' requirements artificially dear in most poor countries. In Pakistan, in the early 1960s, the total effect of State action and private power balances was to *triple* the number of hours the farm sector had to work to get a typical bundle of urban goods. By severe restrictions on cheap imports of industrial consumer goods, by cheap imported raw materials for factory-owners but not farmers, and by many other means, the ratio of industrial prices to agricultural prices was trebled! This is by no means unusual in poor countries. It shows a degree of exploitation, of unequal dealing, next to which intra-urban conflict between capitalist and proletariat is almost negligible.

There is nothing wicked or conspiratorial about this. It is the natural play of self-interest and power, only obfuscated by moralising from outside—*cosi fan tutti*, moralisers as well. And it is only one of many ways in which the city (where most government is) screws the village (where most people are) in poor countries. In tax incidence, in investment allocation, in the provision of incentive, in education and research: everywhere it is government by the city, from the city, for the city.

In isolated moments of war or revolution, a nation may develop a sense of shared interest between landless agricultural and casual industrial labourer, or between city capitalist and village landlord; even when things are quiet, the urban elite pacifies the big farmer by allocating him most of the few resources that can be spared for agriculture. But usually the contradictions between city capitalist and city proletariat can be resolved by negotiation—are not 'antagonistic'—because they can be settled at the expense of the rural interest.

Poverty persists alongside development largely because poor countries are developed from, by and for people in cities: people who, acting under normal human pressures, deny the fruits of development to the pressureless village poor. Few of these can escape the trap by joining the exploitative city elite, because high urban wages (and subsidised capital imports) deter employers from using extra labour. Many villagers, once migration has failed to secure entry to the urban labour aristocracy, return to an increasingly land-scarce village: a village that is by policy denied the high food prices that would normally be linked to land scarcity, by policy starved of public investment allocations, and hence by policy prevented from sharing in development and thus from curing its own poverty.

This is one reason why . . . we are dealing not with temporary inequality caused by a passing weakness of the impoverished proletariat, but with self-confirming inequality caused by the alliance of the urban employer and proletariat against the rural poor. Population growth, moreover, makes it unlikely that the rural poor will be sucked out, and up, by a labour shortage for a very long time. But what is the structure of power that prevents poor villagers, even in democratic countries, from calling the tune? Why is that power structure not generally recognised for what it is?

CHAPTER TWO

Inequality and Income: Measuring the Dimensions of Injustice

READING #7 Who Gets How Much of What? A Simple Illustration

Michael P. Todaro

The following reading illustrates how inequality in income distribution distorts the developmental process in poor countries. Whenever inequalities in income distribution are characteristic of economic growth, the rich in society tend to dominate economic decisionmaking. The economy thereby becomes skewed toward capital-intensive forms of production; in addition, it encourages luxury consumption patterns that are wasteful of aggregate social resources.

Todaro concludes that some degree of equality in income distribution during development must be created if "self-sustaining economic growth" is truly desired. He thus reaffirms the observations made earlier by Meier and Lipton.

—E. W.

A simple and convenient way to approach the twin problems of poverty and income distribution is to utilize once again the production-possibility framework. To illustrate our point, however, let us divide production in our hypothetical developing economy into two classes of goods. First, there are *necessity* goods such as staple foods, simple clothing, and minimum shelter—

From *Economic Development in the Third World,* Third Edition, by Michael P. Todaro. Copyright © 1977, 1981, and 1985 by Michael P. Todaro. Excerpt, pp. 117–120, excluding tables, reprinted with permission of Longman, Inc., New York; endnotes deleted.

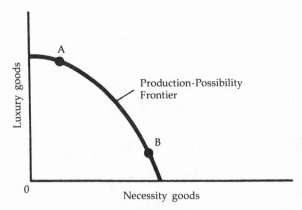

Figure [1]. Choosing what to produce: Luxuries versus necessities

goods essential to basic subsistence. The second class of goods, luxuries, might include expensive cars and houses, sophisticated consumer goods, fashionable clothes, and specialty foods. Assuming for the present that production occurs on the possibility frontier (i.e., that all resources are fully and efficiently employed), the question arises as to what combination of economic necessities and luxuries will actually be chosen by the society in question. Who will do the choosing and how?

Figure [1] illustrates the issue. On the vertical axis we have aggregated all luxury goods and on the horizontal axis are grouped all necessities. The production-possibility curve, therefore, portrays the maximum combinations of both kinds of goods that this economy could produce by making efficient use of all available resources with the prevailing technological know-how. But it does *not* tell us precisely *which* combination among the many possible ones will *actually* be chosen. For example, the same *real* GNP would be represented at points *A* and *B* in Figure [1]. At point *A* many luxury goods and very few necessities are being produced, while at point *B* few luxuries and many necessities are being supplied to the population. One would normally expect the actual production combination in low-income countries to be somewhere in the vicinity of point *B*. But, with the exception of "command" economies where production and distribution decisions are centrally planned, the basic determinant of output combinations in market and mixed economies is the level of effective aggregate demand exerted by all consumers. This is because the position and shape of society's aggregate demand curve for different products is determined primarily by the level and especially the distribution of national income.

Take for example, the simple case of an economy consisting only of two consumers and two goods, luxuries and necessities. We know from both historical and cross-country expenditure studies that individuals or families with low incomes spend very high proportions of their incomes on basic necessities such as food, clothing, and simple shelter. On the other hand, relatively rich people spend a low proportion of their income on these necessities and a relatively high proportion on what we have called luxury goods—luxurious at least in the context of what poor societies can afford. . . .

Two countries with the same levels of GNP and income per capita may have entirely different production and consumption structures (i.e., they may be operating at different points on the same production-possibility curve) depending on whether or not personal incomes are distributed equitably. *For a given low level of GNP and per capita income, the more unequal the distribution of income, the more aggregate demand and production will be influenced by the consumption preferences of the rich.* In spite of the fact that they may constitute only a small proportion of the population, the rich can control a very disproportionately large share of national resources. Their dominant purchasing power can bias production and imports toward manufactured luxury goods even while the masses of people are barely subsisting. This provides a good example of a situation in which the traditional theory of consumer sovereignty, as manifested in market demand curves, represents in fact the sovereignty not of all consumers but of the very few rich ones who dominate the market and determine what goods should be produced. . . .

We see, therefore, that in spite of the relative poverty of the country as a whole, the very unequal distribution of income means that the rich individual can dictate the overall pattern of production since his demand preferences carry more weight in the consumer goods market than those of the poor person. . . .

As a result of highly unequal income distributions, we find a number of low-income Third World countries devoting a sizable proportion of their financial, technical, and administrative resources to the production of sophisticated consumption goods with large import contents (e.g., television sets, stereophonic equipment, electronic components) to cater for the demands of a very small but economically powerful minority located mostly in urban areas. If incomes were more equitably distributed, the pattern of demand would be geared more toward the production of basic foods and other necessities, which would further help to eliminate rural poverty and raise levels of living for broader segments of the population. An additional implication . . . of a demand pattern biased toward expensive consumption goods is that these products normally require relatively sophisticated capital-intensive production techniques compared with the relatively more labor-intensive technology of necessity good production. As a result, fewer jobs are available, profits (including those of resident foreign corporations) are higher, and the distribution of income tends to widen even further.

READING #8   Who Gets What, How Much—and Where?
David M. Smith

Where do the poor live? And how do we compare regions and localities in terms of the incidence of poverty? It is the objective of economic geographers concerned with income distribution in the world economy to answer these questions.

The following selection by David M. Smith illuminates this perspective by defining several important concepts relevant to measuring inequality "cross-sectionally," or across regions and localities. These concepts include gross national income on a per capita basis, the concentration index of world production and population, the Lorenz curve, coefficients of advantage, and the Gini coefficient.

Using these measures, Smith finds that different forms of inequality exist within the world economy—a conclusion he then illustrates with reference to three geographic regions. He thus outlines a geographic or spatial orientation to inequality of income that emphasizes not only who gets what, and how much, but *where* these people live. For a student of world political economy interested in the applications of distributive justice to development, such an approach is important because it maps out the ways in which "spatial concentrations" of poverty and affluence within a developing economy help either to diminish or to worsen inequalities in income distribution.

—E. W.

The geographical perspective may be summarized as a concern with who gets what *where*, and how. The stress on *where* underlines the geographer's preoccupation with spatial or areal inequality—with differences in living standards according to place of residence. These variations may be examined at different geographical scales, to focus on inequality among national populations, regions, neighbourhoods and so on. The geographer thus places primary emphasis on where people live as a contributor to differential life experience. The basic descriptive task is to identify these place-to-place variations, which are often overlooked by economists, sociologists and others who are more interested in inequality among classes, races or other groups in society.

The spatial perspective embraces the process of distribution as well as the facts of spatial inequality. If standards of living vary according to where people live, then geographical space and the organization of life in this space may have a bearing on who gets what. While other social scientists may stress the role of political power, class structure, group conflict or the organization of production and distribution as contributors to inequality, the geographer stresses the way in which the *spatial* structure of the economy and society may work to the advantage of some people in some places and to the disadvantage of others. For example, it might be shown that the

David M. Smith, *Where the Grass Is Greener.* Copyright © 1982 by The Johns Hopkins University Press. Excerpt, pp. 18–19, 25–29, and 89–91, reprinted with permission of The Johns Hopkins University Press; endnotes deleted.

tendency towards spatial concentration of economic activity penalizes people living away from major cities or service centres, or those whose freedom of movement is restricted so that they cannot fully participate in city life.

But before adopting a geographical perspective as a distinctive or separate approach to understanding inequality, a note of caution is needed. No single discipline holds the key to such a complex problem as how the benefits and penalties of life come to be so unevenly distributed. The geographical viewpoint will inevitably stress certain facts and relationships, some of which tend to be neglected by economists, sociologists and political scientists. But there is a risk of over-emphasizing the importance of *spatial* variation in living standards and the role of *spatial* organization in the process of unequal distribution. As we try to show what can be learned from a geographical approach, we will have frequent cause to consider how this relates to the broader structure of society. This inevitably introduces matters conventionally viewed as 'economic', 'political' or 'sociological', as opposed to 'geographical'. The discussion of *spatial* inequality and *spatial* contributions to the process of unequal distribution thus necessarily develops into a broader discussion of political economy. What this . . . seeks to show is that such a broad, multi-disciplinary perspective requires explicit recognition of the role of space in the organization of production, and of spatial elements in distributive processes and outcomes. But on its own, the geographical perspective sheds very limited light on the world, and may obscure more than it reveals. . . .

Measuring Inequality

If we are to say anything precise about inequality, we need methods of measuring the conditions of concern. This requires not only accurate information on what is being distributed—income, health, security or whatever, but also ways of identifying the degree of inequality actually experienced. Putting meaningful numbers to economic and social conditions is a problem common to all approaches to the study of inequality, and indeed to many other aspects of social inquiry. . . . The concern here is with the measurement of inequality itself.

As a simple illustration, we may consider the value of goods and services produced, as distributed among major world regions (Table [1]). The largest shares are accounted for by North America and Western Europe, and the smallest by Oceania (the Pacific countries) and the Middle East. But these figures—the first column in the table—have little meaning in themselves: they must be related to population if they are to tell us anything about comparative standards of living. Calculating GNP on a per capita basis shows North America still first, but second place is taken by Oceania where Australia and New Zealand pull the per capita figure above that for Western Europe. Asia produces more than Latin America and the Middle East, but the size of its population pushes per capita GNP below that of the other regions.

Table [1]. The distribution of world production in relation to population

Major region	GNP (1000 M $US)	Population (millions)	GNP per capita ($US)
North America	1259	231	5450
Western Europe	1057	397	2662
Eastern Europe	748	352	2125
Asia	572	2003	286
Latin America	181	294	616
Africa	78	322	242
Oceania	52	16	3250
Middle East	48	101	475
Total	3995	3716	1075

Source of data: *Business International,* 4 December 1973.

Note: GNP = Gross National Product, i.e. the value of goods and services produced for final consumption or investment including net income from overseas. The figures refer to the year 1972.

The per capita figures in Table [1] offer a rough indication of the degree of inequality among major world regions. The range from $5450 in North America to $242 in Africa gives a ratio of 22.5:1 between the richest and poorest region. In other words, the average African produces only one dollar's worth of goods and services for every $22.5 produced by the average North American. As GNP is identical to national income, this ratio is also representative of differences in consumption possibilities at a given level of prices. Another indication of the magnitude of inequality is provided by deviations of the regional figures from the total world per capita rate of $1075. The average difference between the regional GNP per capita and the world figure is as much as $813. Looking at the individual figures, three regions record more than twice the world average (North America, Oceania and Western Europe), with Eastern Europe almost as high; three regions show half the world figure (Asia, Africa and the Middle East), with Latin America almost as low. Thus there is a clear division between the two worlds of the rich and the poor, on this broad continental scale.

Various descriptive statistics can be used to measure inequality more precisely. How the simplest of these can be calculated is shown in Table [2]. Here the data from Table [1] are first converted into percentage distributions showing each region's proportionate share of world production and population respectively, so that they can be compared directly. If production was equally distributed according to population, then these two columns of percentages would be identical; e.g. North America would account for 6.2 per cent of production instead of the 31.5 per cent shown. The greater the differences between these figures, the greater the degree of inequality. The differences are listed in the third column of the table. Summing them gives us the figure of 102.4; dividing by the number of regions (8) gives the *mean deviation* of 12.8. Taking half the sum of the differences produces a *concentration index* from 0 to 100, where 0 indicates perfect equality (i.e.

Table [2]. The percentage distribution of world production and population, and data for the Lorenz curve

Major region	Percentage distribution GNP	popn	Differences	Coefficient of advantage	Cumulative percentages GNP	popn
North America	31.5	6.2	25.3	5.08	31.5	6.2
Oceania	1.3	0.4	0.9	3.25	32.8	6.6
Western Europe	26.5	10.7	15.8	2.48	59.3	17.3
Eastern Europe	18.7	9.5	9.2	1.97	78.0	26.8
Latin America	4.5	7.9	3.4	0.57	82.5	34.7
Middle East	1.2	2.7	1.5	0.44	83.7	37.4
Asia	14.3	53.9	39 6	0.27	98.0	91.3
Africa	2.0	8.7	6.7	0.23	100.0	100.0
Total	100.0	100.0	102.4			

Source of data: see Table [1].

no differences) and 100 indicates all GNP, or whatever is being distributed, going to one region, i.e. the extreme of inequality. The result of 51.2 shows very considerable inequality on the 0 to 100 scale.

Another way of showing the difference between two distributions is provided by a graphic device known as the *Lorenz curve*. To draw this for the relationship between regional production and population, we have to place the regions in order according to their *coefficient of advantage*. This is simply the ratio between the regional share of the two attributes concerned; i.e. for North America it is $31.5 \div 6.2$, or 5.08. A coefficient greater than 1.0 shows that the region has more of the world's production than its share of population; less than 1.0 indicates the reverse. The regions are in fact listed in order of the coefficient of advantage in Table [2] (see fourth column). Now, the two distributions must be expressed as cumulative percentages; i.e. the first figure is for North America alone, the second is the proportion in North America and Oceania, and so on. These are shown in the last two columns of the table.

To draw the Lorenz curve, we plot the two sets of cumulative percentages against each other. The result is shown in Figure [1]. Reading along the curve from the bottom left, the first dot is 31.5 GNP and 6.2 population (North America), the second is 32.8 and 6.6, and so on until the curve reaches 100 and 100 in the top right. If both sets of percentages had been the same, the 'curve' would have been the diagonal line representing equal shares. The degree of inequality in distribution is shown by how far the Lorenz curve departs from the diagonal. The proportion of the total area below the diagonal that is above the Lorenz curve (shaded in Figure [1] is measured by a device known as the *Gini coefficient*, which is 62 (%) in the present case. The Gini coefficient is the most common general measure of inequality in distribution. . . .

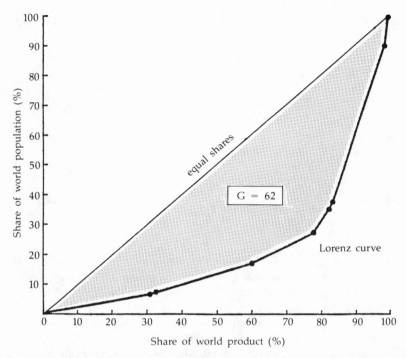

Figure [1]. Lorenz curve showing inequality in the distribution of world production in relation to population, by major regions (source of data: Tables [1] and [2])

Development and Inequality

Human life chances or prospects for happiness vary from country to country. They also vary within nations. . . . But before leaving broad cross-national comparisons, some comments are required on the general question of inequality in distribution. A high degree of internal inequality is characteristic of particular types of societies and particular stages of development.

Cross-national comparisons of inequality are made especially difficult by the kind of measurement problems referred to earlier. . . . The basis on which figures are compiled in different nations often makes them incompatible. However, . . . we find that . . . three world regions are characterized by different types of inequality. . . .

The Central and South American countries generally have a very high degree of inequality in the distribution of land and also marked inequality in income distribution. At the extreme are Peru (G = 93.3 for land, 39.8 for income) and Guatemala (86.0 for land and 48.8 for income). South-East Asian countries have a much more equal distribution of land but considerable variations in income inequality (the range is from G = 43.0 in Thailand to 14.9 in Japan). In Europe, the reverse is the case, with low levels of income inequality but a tendency towards high inequality in land ownership:

for example the UK has the most equal distribution of income (G = 5.0) but a figure as high as G = 72.3 for land. These geographical variations reflect important differences in economic and social structure. Most of the Central and South American countries have a small, wealthy élite of landowners and capitalists, running large ranches or plantations and also gaining most of the wealth generated by industrial activity. South-East Asia has much more intensive agriculture, with smaller holdings of land more evenly distributed among the farming population, but there may still be rich rajahs, princes, merchants and others, along with large inequalities in income as between town and country or skilled and unskilled occupations. In Europe, the concentration of land-ownership is a relic of the pre-industrial era and its feudal aristocracy; economic development and the growing power of organized labour have brought a much more even distribution of income.

READING #9   Drawing the Poverty Line
Malcolm Gillis, Dwight H. Perkins, Michael Roemer, and Donald R. Snodgrass

In attempting to analyze how different groups fare in development, a researcher might trace a so-called **poverty line** around the incidence of poverty. As the poverty line "rises," the number of those who have fallen under it increases. Economic growth in lesser developing countries often forces the poverty line to rise by dislocating traditional patterns of exchange. Traditional barter systems, for example, give way to market exchanges based upon money and prices. Peasants who work their own land, marginalized farmers who toil on the land of others, and rural villagers must now obtain money to survive. New kinds of commodities such as refrigerators, and new kinds of services such as modern transportation, are introduced into a developing economy, but at prices available to relatively few. As a result, the "demonstration effects" of relative poverty are aggravated and the poverty line rises even further.

The authors of the following reading specifically attempt to assess the empirical validity of the Kuznets thesis, which, as suggested earlier, posits a U-shaped or curvilinear relationship between **gross national product (GNP)** and the distribution of income. The Kuznets thesis purports to explain increases of relative poverty and marginalization during development by suggesting that as per capita income rises, inequality in income distribution also rises, until the point at which inequalities taper off.

The following reading focuses upon the extent to which variations in the general U-shaped pattern may be identified and explained. Countries that have achieved intermediate levels of economic growth as measured by GNP and per capita national income do reveal the highest degrees of inequality in income distribution, especially those in which "well-entrenched" elites dominate the developmental process.

Lest one concludes that development and economic growth are contrary to the interests of the poor, the authors remind us that the poor are poor because they tend overwhelmingly to live in poor countries and that helping such countries become less poor continues to be a positive aim. Macroeconomic growth cannot be condemned outright despite the problems that sometimes accompany it, if for no other reason than the fact that economic stasis often spells even greater hardship for the poor living in societies assailed by social or economic paralysis. But the central problem posed by relative poverty and marginalization remains. Increases in GNP may often reduce absolute poverty, but, for reasons suggested in the previous chapter and in the reading to come, aggregate economic growth or expansions in per capita national income, however desirable, often also promotes relative poverty. Key factors, the authors conclude, are the structure of agricultural production and the patterns of domestic employment and labor.

—E. W.

Patterns of Inequality and Poverty

In his 1955 presidential address to the American Economic Association, Simon Kuznets put forward the proposition that the relationship between the level of per-capita GNP and inequality in the distribution of income may take the form of an inverted U. That is, as per-capita income rises, inequality may initially rise, reach a maximum at an intermediate level of income, and then decline as income levels characteristic of an industrial country are reached. Kuznets based this proposition on mere fragments of data available at the time for estimating income distributions in a few rich and poor countries, and on trends in distribution over time in a very few European countries.

Evidence for Kuznets' Inverted U

Kuznets' insight has held up well in later years as much larger bodies of data have been amassed. We now have estimates of income distribution in more than seventy countries, although some of these estimates are of dubious quality. Data published by the World Bank, covering fifty-eight countries for which estimates were made between 1965 and 1982, are summarized. . . . By any of these measures, inequality first rises, then falls, just as Kuznets predicted in 1955. Other studies have obtained similar results. . . .

Reprinted from *Economics of Development*, Second Edition, by Malcolm Gillis, Dwight H. Perkins, Michael Roemer, Donald R. Snodgrass, pp. 84–88, by permission of Malcolm Gillis and W. W. Norton & Company, Inc.; endnotes deleted. Copyright © 1987, 1983 by W. W. Norton & Company, Inc.

But if, as seems likely, there is a tendency toward the inverted-U relationship, two important questions arise. What causes this pattern of changing inequality through the development process? And how predetermined is it? That is, how much latitude is there for differences either in the circumstances of particular countries or in the policies they follow to make a different pattern of inequality consistent with economic growth? . . .

There are many cases in which individual countries depart substantially from the norms. Sri Lanka, South Korea, and Taiwan all have relatively equal income distributions among developing countries. In Latin America, Argentina and Uruguay have inequality measures far below the normally high levels for the region. Several developed capitalist countries have no more inequality than Yugoslavia, a socialist state. Notable deviations on the other side include a number of African and Latin American countries with unusually high inequality (for example, Kenya, Ivory Coast, Zambia, Peru, Brazil, Mexico, and Venezuela), as well as Malaysia and the Philippines in Asia. Among developed countries, France stands out for its high level of inequality. . . .

Analysts have tried to increase the percentage of statistically explained variation in the degree of inequality among countries by adding more independent variables to the equation. One result that emerges clearly from this effort is that socialist countries have much less inequality than nonsocialist countries with comparable GNP per capita. Since socialist countries must, for incentive purposes, maintain wage differentials comparable to those existing in nonsocialist countries, their lower inequality must be attributable mainly to the drastic restrictions they maintain on private ownership of land and capital facilities, assets whose ownership is very unequally distributed in nonsocialist countries.

Among the nonsocialist countries, three factors help to explain inequality in both low-income and high-income countries. Relatively high enrollment rates in primary and secondary schools and a higher GNP growth rate appear to be associated with reduced inequality, given the level of GNP per capita, while a higher growth rate of population goes with greater inequality. Together these factors can raise the total explained variation in a statistical cross-section analysis to about 50 percent. This still leaves a lot of room for country-to-country variation, which has not yet been fit into a general explanatory framework.

Other Explanatory Factors

There have been attempts to identify the types of societies (in social and political as well as economic terms) in which inequality is likely to be high or low. One such study, which measured inequality in terms of the share of income received by the lowest 60 percent of the income distribution, found that relatively equal income distributions are typically found in two kinds of countries: very poor nations dominated by small-scale or communal (jointly farmed) agriculture and well-developed nations in which major efforts have been made to improve human resources. This conclusion is consistent with the Kuznets hypothesis but more suggestive of the factors that may be associated with the inverted-U pattern. The very poor countries may be quite egalitarian, it says, but only if their economies are dominated by small peasant farms and not by large farms or mines. Rich countries can also be egalitarian, but only if their people have been permitted to share in development by upgrading the productivity of the labor resources that they supply to the economy.

By implication, countries with intermediate income levels are likely to have considerable inequality. This same study found the income share of the poorest 60 percent to be smallest of all where well-entrenched foreign or military elites control the most productive economic sectors and receive most of the benefits of development.

There is a school of thought that is pessimistic about prospects that development will better either the absolute or the relative position of the poor. Much of this pessimism stems from study of the South Asian experience. The pessimism does not have strong empirical backing, however, since most studies show that the poor generally do benefit from a rise in GNP, both in terms of absolute income gains and in terms of their share in total income.

Logically speaking, if the income share of the poor rises with growth, their absolute income must rise by definition, since they are getting an increasing share of an increasing total. But what of the situation, apparently common in the early stages of development, in which their share declines?

How Growth Reduces Poverty

The conclusion one reaches will depend on the definition of poverty adopted, but if we define a single worldwide poverty line, it is clear that economic growth is strongly associated with a reduction in poverty. . . . We can ask ourselves how much of the intercountry variation in the absolute mean income of the poor (defined here as the lowest 40 percent of the distribution) can be explained statistically using per-capita GNP as the sole explanatory variable. The answer turns out to be a high 94 percent. In other words, while there are many reasons why people may be poor in an absolute sense, the most important one is that they live in poor countries. Other studies have reached similar conclusions.

Another indication of the close association between poverty and low national income per capita is the locational pattern of world poverty. Calculations made by the World Bank in 1975 show that over half the world's poor (defined as per-capita income below $75) lived in the low-income countries of South Asia. Overall, 79 percent of the poor lived in countries with per-capita GNP of less than $265 in 1975 prices. There are of course absolutely poor people in other regions, such as Latin America and the Middle East, but their numbers are much smaller. Most of these poor people live in rural areas.

Is there any need to qualify the strongly indicated conclusions that poverty is associated with low national per-capita income and tends to be eradicated as per-capita income rises? Only, perhaps, in two respects. First, we have been analyzing absolute poverty using a global poverty line. Relative poverty is far more persistent. There are not many people living on $75 a year in the United States, but there are many who must live on incomes far below a reasonable U.S. standard. Second, some time-series studies for particular countries have shown stagnation or even decline in the incomes of the poor and increases in the number of poor people or both. Many of these findings have been challenged, but they do at least serve to warn us not to assume complacently that economic growth will necessarily eliminate poverty either automatically or rapidly.

READING #10   Ugly Facts and Fancy Models: Poverty in the Third World
Keith Griffin and Azizur Rahman Khan

To what extent do development and growth in lesser developing countries reduce poverty, eliminate inequality, and advance the cause of distributive justice? Keith Griffin and Azizur Rahman Khan present several negative conclusions regarding the fate and future of distributive justice in a world characterized by contemporary forms of developmental growth. Their findings, based upon empirical investigation, suggest that the majority of lesser developing countries, with some major exceptions, face declining income for the already low-income poor, especially the rural poor, and significant increases in the incidence of absolute poverty. These are the "ugly facts" to which their title refers.

Why, they ask, do the poor become poorer, even as the societies in which they live become richer? Their response introduces the concepts of **structure** and **inequity**, which are discussed further in subsequent chapters.

Positions of advantage constitute the structures of inequitable social relations. According to Griffin and Khan, these *structural* positions of advantage in power, status, class, or capital reinforce the very inequities that development policies are designed to eliminate by promoting inequalities in the distribution of disposable income.

The authors proceed by illustrating the connections between political economy of development as a subfield of political economy and the normative issue of distributive justice. A "grow now, redistribute later" strategy, Griffin and Khan conclude, is off the mark. Lesser developing countries must first "get the structure right."

—*E. W.*

Development of the type experienced by the majority of Third World countries in the last quarter century has meant, for very large numbers of people, increased impoverishment. This is the conclusion which has emerged from a series of empirical studies of trends in levels of living in the rural areas of Asia. In most of the countries we have studied, the incomes of the very poor have been falling absolutely or the proportion of the rural population living below a designated "poverty line" has been increasing, or both. Similar things almost certainly have been happening elsewhere, in Africa and parts of Latin America, for the mechanisms which generate poverty in Asia are present in greater or lesser degree in much of the rest of the underdeveloped world. Certainly there is no evidence that growth as such has succeeded in reducing the incidence of poverty. . . .

Indeed, the evidence from the case studies points to an even stronger conclusion. In almost every case a significant proportion of low-income households experienced an absolute decline in their real income, particularly since the early 1960s. . . .

The other major empirical finding concerns the trend in real wages of agricultural laborers. In most of the countries for which measurements could be obtained either real wages remained constant or there was a significant downward trend. . . .

At the same time, it has been shown in our study that the proportion of agricultural laborers below the poverty line increased precisely during the period when real wages are claimed to have risen. If one is to believe both pieces of evidence, then there must have been a change in the occupational distribution of the wage-earners included in the average wage index. In fact, the composition of agricultural laborers does seem to have changed significantly as a result of the widespread adoption of capital-intensive farming techniques, especially by the labor-hiring, large farmers. The importance of skilled labor and of operators of mechanical equipment has increased considerably. The rise in demand for workers of this type, given the initial shortage of skills, undoubtedly led to a relatively rapid increase in their wages. On the other hand, the balance between the supply and demand for more traditional types of labor became increasingly un-favorable over time, and consequently their wages failed to rise.

All the countries included in our sample are characterized by a highly unequal distribution of landownership. Statistical information usually relates to the distribution of farm size, i.e., to the area farmed and not the area owned. It is generally known that the ownership distribution is less equal than the distribution of farm size. Of the seven countries studied, the degree of inequality is perhaps the least in Bangladesh, but even there the bottom 20 percent of the holdings account for only 3 percent of the land while the top 10 percent account for over 35 percent. The Gini concentration ratio is

Reprinted with permission from *World Development*, vol. 6, no. 3, pp. 295–301, Keith Griffin and Azizur Rahman Khan, "Ugly Facts and Fancy Models: Poverty in the Third World." Copyright © 1978 by Pergamon Press, Ltd.

0.5. In the other six countries the distribution is less equal. For example, the Gini concentration ratios of the distribution of landholding for Pakistan, India, and the Philippines have been estimated to be around 0.6.

None of these countries made any significant progress toward redistribution of land during the periods considered. For those countries for which information is available no significant trend toward reducing inequality can be found. Pakistan, the Philippines, and Sri Lanka initiated some land reform measures in the early 1970s. Although our studies were not able to take their effects fully into account, it is reasonably clear by now that the redistributive consequences of these measures are likely to be marginal. . . .

Latent within these inefficiencies and inequities are possibilities for higher output, faster growth, and greater equality. This potential for rural development, however, has lain dormant. Instead of growing prosperity for those most in need there has been impoverishment. The crucial question is why.

The answer to why poverty has increased has more to do with the structure of the economy than its rate of growth. One structural feature common to all the countries studied is a high degree of inequality. Data from the six countries on which information is available suggest that in the economy as a whole the richest 20 percent of households typically receive about half the income, whereas the poorest 40 percent receive between 12 percent and 18 percent of total income. The bottom 20 percent fare even worse, of course, receiving about 7 percent of the income in the least inegalitarian country (Bangladesh) and merely 3.8 percent in one of the most inegalitarian countries (Philippines).

The degree of income inequality in rural areas is somewhat less than in the urban areas and, hence, less unequal than the average for the economy. Nonetheless, the degree of inequality is considerable. According to the available data, rural India is the least inegalitarian while rural Malaysia and the Philippines are the most. Little emphasis should be placed on these differences, however, as the data are not very precise and in the case of India in particular it is widely believed that the data understate the extent of inequality.

The counterpart to the compression of the income of the poor is the concentration of the economic surplus in a very few hands. The disposal of this surplus, in turn, largely determines the pace and composition of economic growth. The preferences of the upper income groups as between present consumption and savings will affect the rate of accumulation. The pattern of demand, itself strongly influenced by the distribution of income, will determine in large part the sectors into which investment flows. And the set of relative factor prices which confront those who invest the surplus will have an effect on the methods of production that are used, the amount of employment that is generated, the productivity of that employment, and the distribution of income.

The structure of factor markets is such that the unequal distribution of income arising from an unequal distribution of productive assets is reinforced by the operations of the price mechanism. Those who have access to the organized capital market are able to obtain finance capital for investment on very favorable terms. Indeed, when nominal rates of interest are adjusted for inflation, the real rate of interest paid by large investors is often negative. This introduces a strong bias in favor of investment in the more capital-intensive sectors and in the more capital-intensive methods of production. As a result, the demand for labor is lower than it otherwise would have been. Paradoxically, the relatively high productivity of labor associated with the more mechanized processes may lead to higher wages for those who secure employment in the sector, thereby further reducing the demand for labor.

This pattern of investment is accentuated in countries where a system of protection is combined with a foreign exchange rate that is overvalued and import permits for foreign equipment consequently must be allocated through a rationing device of some sort. The contrived cheapening of imported goods relative to domestic labor introduces an additional bias in favor of (foreign) capital-intensity, and tends to raise the share of profits in national income while reducing the demand for labor.

The capital markets operate in such a way that a small minority of the labor force is equipped with excessively capital-intensive techniques, given the relative availabilities of investable resources and labor. At the same time, the majority of the labor force (in urban as well as in rural areas) is forced to work with techniques which are insufficiently capital-intensive. As a result, the productivity and incomes of the majority are exceptionally low compared to those employed in the so-called modern, capital-intensive sector. . . .

The initially high degree of inequality of income and wealth, the concentration of the economic surplus in a few enterprises and households, and the fragmented allocative mechanisms constitute a socioeconomic context in which powerful dynamic forces tend to perpetuate and even accentuate low standards of living of a significant proportion of the rural population. . . .

In consequence, the tendency toward diminishing returns and falling output per worker has not always been compensated by rising investment. As population densities and the man-land ratio have increased, the level and share of rents have risen while the wage share, wage rates, and the number of days employed per person have tended to decline. That is, at the going terms of agricultural remuneration, the demand for labor has increased less rapidly than the supply and hence the standard of living of those who depend on work as a source of income has fallen. This has affected some plantation workers, unskilled landless agricultural laborers, pure tenants, and some small landowners who have to supplement their income by engaging in paid labor.

Thus it is that in a world that is far from being perfectly competitive, a rise in national income per head and in food production per head is quite compatible not only with greater relative inequality, but with greater hunger and falling incomes for the poorest members of society. The study of Asian economic development indicates that the initial distribution of wealth and income has a decisive influence over the pattern of growth and hence over the rate of amelioration or deterioration in the standard of living of the lowest income groups. Furthermore, given the initial conditions, it is difficult to change the distribution of income by manipulating standard policy instruments—tax, subsidy, and expenditure levels, exchange rates and trade controls, monetary variables, etc. It follows from this that a "grow now, redistribute later" strategy is not a valid option in most countries; it is necessary first to "get the structure right."

CHAPTER THREE

Class, Capital, and Policy Strategies: Is Justice in Development Possible?

READING #11   Politics, Population, and the Pathways to Poverty

William W. Murdoch

Children born into poverty suffer terrifying forms of deprivation. Yet impoverished parents still bear large families. William W. Murdoch provides a compelling interpretation of this phenomenon.

It is sometimes alleged that poor parents are poor because they have so many children. Murdoch, however, reverses this "causational pathway" by suggesting that if poor parents were not poor, they would not have as many children. Population explosion in lesser developing countries does not cause poverty; rather, it is poverty that causes populations to explode. Eliminate the poverty of poor families and the motivation for large families disappears.

Poor families seek often tragically high numbers of children, Murdoch suggests, as a strategy for subsistence. High rates of infant mortality, the labor and income potential of each child, and the security benefits accruing to parents in old age for each child who survives into adulthood—all of these factors nurture a cycle of high population growth that, in aggregate terms, is disastrous for a developing economy.

Murdoch argues that equity in income distribution and other forms of welfare has a salutary effect upon population growth by making it less beneficial for poverty-stricken parents to have many children. Policies promoting equality and equity are thus a crucial means of population control.

Murdoch's analysis parallels that of Lipton, by indicating that "circular causal pathways" induced by structures of political power and class maintain

high birth rates among the poor. The implications are clear: Only
transformations in the structures of power and economic decisionmaking can
resolve the dilemmas posed by structural forms of disadvantage and
poverty. Murdoch's conclusion thus coincides with that of Griffin and Khan:
Distributive justice advanced by structural equity is essential to social
development.

—E. W.

I have sought to establish that rapid population growth and inadequate
food supply are but the symptoms of poverty and that poverty itself is
maintained by two basic and related causes. These are the internal political-
economic structure of the LDCs and their strongly dependent and unequal
relationship with the rich nations. I will first summarize the analysis that
has led to these conclusions, then discuss what can be done to improve
matters—in particular, what the rich nations ought to do.

Our point of departure was the massive increase in population in the
LDCs, which is caused by persistent high birth rates in the face of greatly
reduced death rates. The evidence is strong that these high birth rates result
from poverty. . . . Large families make economic good sense for very poor
people. This motivation for large families disappears as the family's level
of economic welfare rises during development, and this is reflected in smaller
families at higher levels of economic well-being. No single factor will explain
all variation in family size, of course, and cultural features such as religion,
the status of women, and family structure are likely to affect the timing of
the demographic transition, i.e., the level of economic welfare at which
average family size begins to decline. The rate of decline may also be
increased by access to modern family planning techniques. However, the
fundamental factors are economic.

Above the very lowest levels of national income, average family size
falls sooner and faster when economic well-being is more evenly spread
across the population. . . . Birth rates can be reduced, even at low income
levels, if the nation or state uses its income to provide increased economic
welfare and security to the entire population, as exemplified by China, Sri
Lanka, and Kerala. Conversely, if the benefits of growth are very unevenly
distributed, as in Mexico and Brazil, the national birth rate remains high
even when national income is quite high and increasing rapidly. Thus,
egalitarian patterns of development lead to more rapid population control.
In particular, since the countryside is the great population dynamo, equality
within rural society, and between rural and urban societies, is critical for
reduced birth rates.

William W. Murdoch, *The Poverty of Nations.* Copyright © 1980 by The Johns Hopkins University
Press. Excerpt, pp. 307–309, reprinted with permission of The Johns Hopkins University Press;
endnotes deleted.

The maintenance of high birth rates, then, even in nations where *aggregate* income has increased at respectable rates, is caused by the persistent poverty of the majority, and particularly by rural poverty. I have called this *structural* poverty because it is the result of the economic, social, and political structure of society: the poor stay poor because they do not have access to productive resources.

A similar analysis applies to inadequate food supplies. The poor are malnourished either because they cannot afford to buy enough food or, where they are farmers, because they cannot afford the investment needed to grow more. . . . Since agricultural production is the major source of rural income, low agricultural productivity also causes rural poverty. The effects are widespread; low farm incomes mean low demand for nonfarm goods and therefore low employment for the off-farm rural population.

Two related sets of circumstances maintain the structural poverty of the rural population. Within rural society gross inequities exist in the distribution of land, water, credit, and technical innovations. The poor are thus prevented from making use of the available productive resources. In addition, the rural economy is suppressed because almost all LDCs have concentrated on developing urban industry at the expense of agriculture. A critical feature of this strategy has been the need for cheap labor, both in urban industry and in the production of exports that buy imported industrial goods. This cheap labor would be impossible without cheap food, but cheap food has required the suppression of agricultural incomes. Thus the rural population is exploited so that urban industry can be sustained. . . .

An important consequence of the suppression of agriculture is that this sector is then unable to contribute to overall economic development. Development requires a dynamic agriculture that can supply the needs of the nonfarm population and provide savings for investment. It also requires the integration of agriculture and *appropriate* industry through the meshing of supply and demand from both sectors. This integration is not possible within the distorted "dual economy" of the LDCs. The reason is that farm incomes are highly concentrated in a very small fraction of the farm population, and the demand generated by this group is for goods that are quite inappropriate to the needs and resources of the developing countries. As a result, there is no stimulus to small-scale industry that could provide goods to the farm population at large and could, in the process, make use of abundant local resources and employ many people. . . . This failure of agriculture is crucial: the LDCs cannot expect to develop without attacking the poverty of the rural majority, but the structural biases in most LDC economies maintain this poverty by distributing the costs of failure to the countryside and the benefits of progress to the cities. We thus have a "circular causal pathway" that is self-perpetuating and extremely difficult to break.

The fundamental cause of these problems is the unequal distribution of economic and political power in the LDCs. A small, mainly urban, elite controls the economy and ensures that it produces goods largely for a privileged minority. These goods are typically luxury items in the LDC context. They are inappropriate to LDC needs and are produced by large-scale, capital- and import-intensive industry that is generally inappropriate to LDC resources. This industrial strategy thus accentuates those biases within the LDCs that maintain poverty and underdevelopment. It squanders scarce capital, suppresses employment, increases income inequality, strengthens the position of the elite, and diverts resources from rural society and from the urban poor. . . .

Because development does not grow out of the internal dynamics of the dual economy, and because they have chosen the goal of creating "modern" industry quickly, the LDCs are dependent upon the industrialized nations for modern industrial goods and technology. These require foreign exchange, and so the LDCs depend upon the rich nations for markets for their exports, commercial loans, aid, and direct investment by foreign firms. . . . This pattern of dependence has its origins in colonial history and in the history of economic domination by the West. . . . It has been maintained in recent decades by the nature and aims of the LDCs' ruling elites, and by the unequal relationship between the rich and poor countries, particularly by the West's control over capital and modern technology.

Two important conclusions flow from these analyses. First, to reduce poverty and create sustained development, it is not enough to redistribute income and benefits. *Instead, there must be a redistribution of the productive resources (wealth) that produce income and benefits.* Second, basic changes within the LDCs require equally basic changes in their relationships with the rich nations. The exercise of economic and political power by the rich nations, which is made possible by the dependence of the LDCs, reinforces inequality *within* the poor nations and hence accentuates there the maldistribution of economic and political power—which in turn strengthens the dependent relationship. Thus the two sets of structural relationships—internal and external—must be seen as interlocked; *they have a joint historical origin and they are mutually reinforcing.*

Finally, the economic policies that interfere with real development in the LDCs are the natural result of the distribution of political power there. That political power in turn rests upon the uneven distribution of wealth. That is, the problems we have discussed have a political basis and require political solutions.

READING #12   Inequality in the Third World:
An Assessment of Competing Explanations
Atul Kohli, Michael F. Altfeld, Saideh Lotfian, and Russell Mardon

---

Atul Kohli and his colleagues combine two important strands of research in the following reading. One concerns variations in income distribution; the other deals with the relative impacts of political institutions or economic forces upon distributive justice. In particular, the authors seek to explain why some countries reveal greater, and others lesser, tendencies toward inequalities in the distribution of income during the course of development. They also examine the sources of these variations by empirically testing alternate or competing forms of explanation, including the **developmental, dependency,** and **statist** perspectives.

The developmental perspective, as tested by this research team, essentially focuses upon the Kuznets thesis. The primary hypothesis of the dependency perspective selected by the authors for examination states that international flows of finance and technology generated by multinational corporations represent the major source of marginalization. And the statist perspective stresses the importance of regime or type of government as the key determinant in processes of economic decisionmaking for development.

As this reading attempts to assess the impact of government policies upon economic and social processes in development, it is relevant to the "relative autonomy of states" debate. At the root of this controversy, as we saw, are contrasting views of the standing of politics and the capacity of governments to pursue policies in a manner more or less autonomous of the dictates of class and capital.

This controversy will hardly be settled here. But the following reading is suggestive of the theoretical components of a central question in political economy: Is distributive justice or equity in development possible? The authors conclude that it is. Governments or regime types do make a difference; the actions of democratic regimes are different from those of authoritarian ones in respect to income distributions and distributive justice.

—E. W.

Why are social inequalities greater in some Third World countries than in others? Why are inequalities growing in some of these countries while they are narrowing in others? Most answers to these questions stem from one of three competing theoretical perspectives: developmental, neo-Marxist, or statist. For many students of development, inequalities within countries are best understood as a function of the overall level of economic development. . . . By contrast, neo-Marxist scholars of the dependency school often hold that Third World inequalities result from the penetration of these economies by the forces of world capitalism. . . . Finally, other scholars emphasize the political and policy determinants of inequality, especially the nature and role of the state in molding patterns of social change. . . . The purpose of

Atul Kohli, Michael F. Altfeld, Saideh Lotfian, and Russell Mardon, "Inequality in the Third World: An Assessment of Competing Explanations," *Comparative Political Studies*, vol. 17, no. 3, October 1984. Copyright © 1984 by *Comparative Political Studies*. Excerpt, pp. 283–284, 290, 296–297, 301, 303, 308, and 313, reprinted by permission of Sage Publications, Inc.; endnotes deleted.

this article is to attempt to assess these three competing explanations of inequality.

The Developmental Perspective

An enduring line of thought in the income distribution literature is the one that posits a curvilinear relationship (the inverted U) between inequalities and the level of economic development. Proposed initially by economist Simon Kuznets, . . . the argument suggests that, as economies develop, inequalities first grow and then later diminish. The mechanisms underlying this trend are factors such as the nature of intersectoral shifts (from agriculture to industry) and the changing nature of the labor force (from unskilled to skilled) that industrial development necessarily entails.

The intersectoral shift is often held to explain the increasing inequalities in early industrialization. Development entails the relatively rapid growth of the high-income industrial sector in relation to the low-income agricultural sector. The substitution of skilled for unskilled labor (assuming wages reflect productivity) is then suggested as the mechanism that propels more mature industrial societies toward greater equality. . . .

Much statistical evidence has been gathered over the years to support the hypothesized curvilinear relationship between inequality and development. . . . The thrust of these findings is that countries at an intermediate stage of development indeed show greater income inequalities than do those at earlier or later stages. The existence of the inverted U in such cross-sectional analyses is then cited as indirect evidence for the existence of this type of relationship. . . .

We propose that the process of economic development creates a mild tendency toward increasing income inequalities within the contemporary capitalist Third World. These tendencies can, however, be either accentuated or alleviated by other factors at work within these nations. These factors include variables such as the initial pattern of inequality when industrialization began, the degree of foreign participation in the developing economy, and state policies toward population growth, social welfare, and inequality. . . .

The Dependency Perspective

The idea that the growth of capitalism simultaneously generates improvements in productivity and increases the relative poverty of the lower classes is as old as Marx. Modern-day sympathizers with Marx have pursued this line of thought in various modifications. Contemporary dependency scholars, not unlike Marx, often conclude that the spread of capitalism to the Third World facilitates economic growth and industrialization, but does so at the expense of creating serious distributional distortions. Both the developmental and distortive effects are captured in the concept of "dependent development." . . . While there are many distortions associated with "dependent development," a central one is that the benefits of such development are monopolized by a small elite. Development that is dependent on the forces of world capitalism, especially in the form of the multinational corporation (MNC), is thus associated with sharp income inequalities within the Third World.

Empirically oriented literature has, in recent years, generated support for the proposition that dependency is associated with income inequalities . . . has even concluded that "the relationship between dependence and inequality [is] one of the most robust, quantitative, aggregate findings available." While dependence is conceived to be a many-dimensioned phenomenon, including trade, aid, capital, technological, and perhaps even political and cultural dependence, the aspect that receives most attention is capital and technological dependence associated with MNC participation in Third World economies.

Why should MNC participation be associated with inegalitarian development? Several direct and indirect linkages are often cited. The most important of the direct links is the use, by MNCs, of capital-intensive technology. This is assumed to create a high rate of return for the company, but few jobs. . . . Of the indirect links, the suggested ones include the political and social conditions within which MNCs prefer to operate and that they help perpetuate. These include favorable tax and exchange rate policies, anti-inflationary governmental policies, political stability, minimal labor unrest, and a demand structure favoring income concentration. This last condition aids MNCs in that their products are not generally mass-consumption goods. . . .

Dependency scholars thus expect the participation of foreign investment in development to increase income inequalities within the Third World. Like the developmental perspective reviewed in the last section, dependency scholars would not be surprised by the fact that some of the richer Third World countries have greater income inequalities. The explanation offered for this phenomenon by the dependency scholars, however, would be radically different from that given by the developmentalists. The dependency theorists would argue that greater income inequalities reflect not only or primarily the level of development of a nation, but rather the extent to which that development involves the participation of MNCs. Such participation, they would further argue, is the cause both of the increased level of development and the increased inequalities. We will test the accuracy of this perception below. If the dependency theorists are correct, we should expect that, in our cross-sectional sample, countries showing greater MNC participation would also show greater inequalities. . . .

While the dependency perspective receives some support . . . whether a nation's inequalities increased or decreased appears to bear no systematic relationship to the level of MNC penetration of its economy. . . .

Concentration of foreign investment within a Third World economy probably generates some long-term structural tendency toward sharper income inequalities. Over the short run, however, MNC involvement is not directly or primarily responsible for changes in a nation's pattern of inequalities.

It is important to reiterate here that most debates over Third World inequalities, whether they concern the "Brazilian miracle" or the "wonder" that is Taiwan, are based on short-term evidence. Our findings suggest that long-term hypotheses such as those of the developmental or dependency schools simply do not explain short-term fluctuations in inequality. In order to reconcile the long- and short-term views, it is probably most fruitful to think of long-term trends as being either exacerbated or mitigated at any given time by a number of factors, especially state actions and policies.

The Statist Perspective

While development and dependency have been the major perspectives for understanding Third World economies, a minority but consistent theme has emphasized the significance of regime type. Many development economists, for example, point to the impact of regime policies on redistributive and welfare outcomes. . . . Samuel Huntington, . . . a political scientist, has argued that political order is a necessary prerequisite of social and economic development. Empirical studies have also sought to delineate the impact of democracy, socialist parties and governments, levels of government expenditure, and political stability on economic development in general and income distribution in particular. . . .

A focus on regime type can, of course, proceed from within the assumptions of both development and dependency frameworks. Recent attempts to systematize a statist perspective, however, suggest that the view that the state shapes society tends to rest on assumptions shared by neither liberal nor Marxist scholarship. . . . Rather, the statist standpoint appears to rest on two distinct assumptions. First, it assumes that state forms and actions are not simply derivative of the social structure whether conceived in terms of level of development, class structure, or level of foreign economic penetration. Second, this perspective assumes that state authorities periodically utilize the degree of autonomous authority they possess to mold processes of social change. . . .

This line of thought has important implications for understanding patterns of Third World development. While many of these remain to be spelled out in the literature, . . . from the standpoint of our interest in income distribution it is not difficult to move logically from the statist assumptions to more specific hypotheses linking political variation to income distribution. Third World income distribution patterns, one could argue, following this line of thought, reflect not only levels of development and foreign dependence, but also the actions undertaken by state authorities. As one would expect authorities governing democratic regimes to behave differently than those in authoritarian situations, the obvious hypothesis to examine is one linking the democratic-authoritarian continuum to income distribution. . . .

As societies industrialize and the structure of the economy changes, there is a mild tendency toward increasing income inequalities. Similarly, greater dependence on foreign investment also generates a partially independent tendency toward sharper income inequalities. Both of these long-term propensities are, however, mediated by the nature of the state and its policies, especially over the short run. Thus the manner in which authority in a state is structured and the specific choices the authorities make regarding development strategy seem to have a considerable impact on patterns of inequality. Harsh authoritarian regimes pursuing "exclusionary" models of development tend to produce more unequal distributions of income within their nations. Conversely, a more open regime (whether nominally "authoritarian" or not) tends to allow for the mitigation of the long-term propensity of developing nations toward increasing inequalities. . . .

So many debates on Third World inequalities are carried out between "liberals" and "Marxists" or, specifically, between the proponents of the inverted U curve and those of dependency theory. We have found both of these positions to have some merit for explaining long-term trends, but not for the explanation of the processes of short-term change. As most development experiments are currently of no more than two or three decades, we suggest that a focus on regime types and development strategies is the most useful one for analyzing income inequalities in the contemporary Third World. This is consistent with Adelman and Robinson's . . . judgment that development strategy is the crucial variable determining the course of income distribution. It is also consistent with the statist assumption that state authorities do in fact make choices of far-reaching importance for the societies they govern.

READING #13   Equity for Whom?
Richard R. Fagen

The quest for distributive justice and equity in the world economy has been transformed into a dramatic political struggle by the emergent and highly articulate governments of the developing world. The term **Third World** is used to connote these political aspects of development; in addition, it implies that lesser developing countries represent a discrete political force with singular interests that sometimes veer in directions contrary to the will and aims of the **First World** of advanced developed states and/or the **Second World** of Soviet-bloc command economies.

Richard R. Fagen, in the following reading, counters the "statist" proposition put forward by Atul Kohli and his associates in the previous reading by challenging the assumption that states or political decisionmaking in Third World countries can function autonomously of economic or class structures. Fagen thus implicitly favors those who argue on the side of the relative autonomy of states and governments. He also points out that economic structures of advantage lever the basic mechanisms of exchange, such as markets in developing countries, in ways that are consistently disadvantageous to the poor. His comments in this regard echo the analysis by Todaro provided in the previous chapter.

Fagen concludes that "equity-as-distribution" is not possible because Third World states and governments are caught "in the very web of exploitative class and market relationships" from which they cannot free themselves. Thus developing countries are incapable of arresting inequitable development, for they are subject to the pressures of international capital and class.

These forces, which originate from outside as well as from within states, reveal the crucial role played by agencies that control the transnational flows of investment capital, the circulation of technology, and the organization of production in the world economy. The inference to be drawn from Fagen's analysis is that development within single countries gives expression—or "articulates"—these external influences.

—E. W.

Let us begin by examining the bases for the hypothesized underlying pessimism regarding the feasibility of implementing the democratic rule. One basis for this pessimism is a widely shared understanding that those who control income (or wealth) in Southern societies also to a great extent control or exercise political, social, and cultural power as well. Even persons who reject much of Marxist analysis grudgingly concede that the power resources at the disposal of those who sit at the top of the income-wealth hierarchies in Southern societies are immensely superior to the resources at the disposal of those at middle and lower levels. No matter how those resources are conceptualized (political access, control of the media and the consciousness industry, know-how, allies abroad), the intimate relationship between wealth and power is everywhere manifest. This is not to argue that the top income earners (or the wealthy) necessarily sit in the seats of government or mechanically dictate public policy. Rather it is to stress that the multiple resources which they can assemble, if necessary, in defense of proportionality of distribution (or even regressivity of distribution) are impressive indeed. When the "ordinary" operations of the economy and the polity are not assuring distributional outcomes most favorable to them, they have the capacity to lever the situation back to "normal." In short, we are arguing that class (whether understood in Marxist or more conventional stratification terms) is intimately related to power, and that power, in turn, is used in the service of proportional distribution—or worse. The proposition is hardly new, but it is essential to all that follows.

The second basis for the hypothesized pessimism concerning the future of the democratic norm has to do with the market as an instrument of

Richard R. Fagen, *Rich and Poor Nations in the World Economy*. Copyright © 1985 by the Council on Foreign Affairs. Excerpt, pp. 189–195, reprinted with permission of the Council on Foreign Affairs; endnotes deleted.

distribution. Whatever other virtues neoclassical analysis assigns to the market, a tendency toward democratic distribution is not one of them. As persuasively argued by even the most liberal neoclassicists, the function of the market is efficiency in the allocation of resources (and rewards), not distributive justice. In fact, it is quite vigorously argued at certain points in neoclassical theory that increments of new income *should* accrue disproportionately to certain sectors of the population (entrepreneurs and/or big consumers) so that savings, investment, demand, and ultimately growth will be maximized. At best, market mechanisms will not shift income shares in a democratic direction except as the structure of production itself changes. Within the existing structure, individuals can of course improve their incomes by moving to a higher niche. But this individual mobility, however widespread, does not contain within itself a dynamic seriously challenging the proportional shares going to various sectors of the society. Thus, in speaking of Southern societies, hardly anyone suggests that "the free play of market forces" will bring in its wake movement toward more equitable distribution however defined.

But if class power and the market both militate against equity in distribution, what—in the words of a famous theorist—is to be done? Everywhere the answer, *grosso modo*, is similar: the *state* must ensure that benefits, opportunities, and wealth are pushed against the grain of social structure and market. From the mildest reformers to the most militant revolutionaries, persons who think about these problems are in agreement that the root of the solution—however that solution is conceptualized— must be sought in a revamped political/administrative process that in some fashion empowers those groups that the existing distribution of wealth and the operation of the market currently leave disadvantaged.

This widespread agreement on the centrality of the state and political processes to the problem of equity-as-distribution, however, obscures more than it reveals. For revolutionary socialists, the political scenario envisaged includes *within it* coherent solutions to the problems of class and the market. However imperfect the practice may be, the theory is quite clear in stating that a direct assault on class privilege, intended to strip the wealthy of the bases of their status quo–maintaining (and exploitative) power, is to be combined with the substitution (be it more gradual or more accelerated) of central planning for the operation of market forces in production and distribution. For reformers of all stripes, however, the political scenario must necessarily respect to some degree the existing class forces and forms of production and distribution. The equity-oriented reformer thus faces the historically difficult (impossible?) task of discovering those secondary contradictions and possibilities within existing class and economic structures which will allow the state to spearhead a movement of distribution that runs *against* the basic logic of class and market. . . .

Central to this question is the concept of the "autonomy" of the state and its relationship to class and political power.

Everyday understandings of the concept of autonomy emphasize that it refers to "freedom from exterior constraints." Whereas the concept of power emphasizes capacity to accomplish chosen goals in the face of obstacles, autonomy typically refers to the more limited condition of not being controlled by others. The distinction is important, for what reformist elites purport to seek (among other outcomes) is to escape the control of those class forces that would block public policies conducive to more equitable distribution. The essential question . . . is the extent to which this is possible.

That reformist elites—and others—are busy strengthening and empowering the state apparatus to intercede and direct the process of economic development in the South is everywhere evident. The bureaucracy expands; expertise is developed; critical planning, fiscal, and administrative responsibilities are assumed; and domestic programs proliferate. Everywhere in the South we are witnessing what has aptly been called the "age of state-centric development." But does the sum of this activity (expanding state power) necessarily signal increased long-run state autonomy from those class forces that are in some sense "antidistributional"?

The answer to this key question depends on the kind of economic development that is taking place. To the extent that the model is essentially growth-oriented, energized by private capital (with or without associated state financing), and dependent to any significant degree on foreign investment, the prospects are very dim.* To weave multinational corporations into the development scenario, for example, is to significantly strengthen certain sectors of the domestic class structure while disempowering others. New class alliances with key sectors of the state bureaucracy are formed at home, reflecting the exigencies of attracting and facilitating investment capital. New sociopolitical forces are linked to those sectors of production and distribution that are most fully internationalized (or "modern" in the less pejorative term) and on which aggregate growth depends. The highly tuned and high-technology segments of the domestic economy become ever more susceptible to pressures generated externally but articulated internally by privileged classes and class fractions. The state itself through the techno-bureaucracy increasingly assumes responsibilities for ensuring the continuation of the political, economic, and social conditions undergirding this web of external-internal relationships. The old, conservative, openly antiequity class sectors recede in political importance as this kind of development takes place. But there is no reason to believe that the class forces that are strengthened, in alliance with the state, are any more favorable to equity measures than were the groups they are replacing. Can it be said under this kind of

---

*Codes of conduct and joint ownership notwithstanding, the antiequity implications of the foreign investment scenario are profound. The scenario affects (negatively as far as improved distribution is concerned in the vast majority of cases) the types of technology that will be used, the kinds of commodities that will be produced, the patterns of consumption that will be encouraged, the way in which labor will be rewarded and allocated (and displaced), and the regions or sectors of the nation that will benefit. Many of the same arguments could also be made for development based on domestic private investment as well, although the critique has more bite when applied to the multinational firms.

development that the state is any "freer" from the influence of the privileged than before?

It is this scenario, combining a partially open political process, economic growth, and an *expressed* commitment to improved distribution, that tests the autonomy of the state and thus the limits of equity-enhancing reform. In the worst of cases, the contradictions are excruciating. Is the Mexican state—a long-term articulator of the rhetoric of social justice, a state massively involved in the developmental process, a state that "oversees" an economy profoundly penetrated and multinationalized, with a modernizing industrial sector, export-oriented agriculture, currency no longer tied to the dollar, inflationary pressures and balance-of-payments problems—any more autonomous from domestic, antidistributional class forces today than 40 years ago? Could even the most progressive Mexican regime imaginable consistently decide in favor of impoverished *ejidarios* when the interests of Mexican and international agribusiness are at stake? The answers are obvious for the Mexican case (and well supported by the experiences of the not especially radical Echeverría government), but they would not be much less controversial for any regime, no matter how "progressive" its expressed commitments, as long as these kinds of developmental rules and class alliances guided the processes of accumulation and distribution.

If the autonomy of the Southern state from class interests is seen as quite limited and if—in the typical case—these class interests are understood as closely linked to the modern international system of production and distribution, then the behavior of Southern elites—even those with reformist pretensions—who bargain hard for fairer shares internationally while doing little to increase equity at home becomes quite understandable. There is nothing mysterious or even particularly hypocritical about their behavior. These hard-bargaining elites are themselves deeply enmeshed in the very web of exploitative class and market relationships that are at the heart of the distributional problem in the first place. Fairer shares internationally strengthen them, equity at home tends to weaken them—or at least to trigger opposition. Large increments of additional income (imaginable in any case only through oil and perhaps a few other key minerals) may allow them to buy time through a policy of populist handouts—with enough left over in certain cases to buy expensive weapons and even some international goodwill through developmental aid. But a concerted attack on the root causes of the domestic inequity problem undercuts their own essential bases of authority and support.

This is the real dynamic behind the now oft-predicted *embourgeoisement* of much of the South, particularly those regimes that now or in the foreseeable future may be receiving significant new increments of income as new international bargains are struck. What is feared in some circles—and ardently hoped for in others—is that the richer regimes will "go their own way" with their newly won gains, that the Southern bargaining consensus will fragment, and that eventually the international equity issue will recede in importance. The prediction has the ring of historical probability about it, but not simply because nationalisms will reassert themselves when the initial gains from Southern solidarity have been harvested and new patterns of international inequality have been established. More central is the fact that the majority of elites speaking in the name of the South *have from the outset* been the spokesmen for, and in some cases even the direct agents of, national and international class interests quite satisfied with the existing world economic system if not with their share of the pie. Under these conditions, we will witness the *embourgeoisiement* of the bourgeoisie—hardly a surprising turn of events.

In sum, the international bargaining process now under way, to the extent that it results in fairer shares for the South, serves to strengthen Southern elites who in the main have little autonomy from antiequity class forces at home. Although some among them may genuinely wish to assault class privilege and maldistribution, they are relentlessly pulled back toward policies that favor the few rather than the many. Windfall increments to income may in some cases serve to alleviate certain impediments to more equitable distribution, but sustained progress in the direction of implementing policies leading toward what was previously called the democratic distributional rule is structurally out of the question. Only profound changes in the developmental strategies currently in use (and most probably the elites currently in power) will significantly alter this situation. Whether alterations this profound can be other than socialist *and* revolutionary remains to be demonstrated historically.

READING #14   Class Formation in the Periphery
James Petras

James Petras, in the brief reading that follows, defines the meaning of class in terms of networks and structures. He suggests that these two concepts represent the basic elements of distributive injustice and inequity in development.

What is class? How is it related to the structures of advantage and networks of ruling elites that predominate over the processes of government decisionmaking in Third World countries? If such structures and networks promote inequity, how do they sustain themselves? Petras's questions outline an entire research agenda and raise two key issues in the relative autonomy debate that we confronted earlier:

1. To what extent is the internal development of lesser developing or "peripheral" countries an expression of external or "exogenous" forces?
2. To what extent is the autonomy of states and politics limited by class?

Petras argues that lesser developing countries and Third World politics are embedded in a mode of production dominated by networks of ruling classes. These internal class elites, moreover, are "locked into" transnational class structures. The political systems of peripheral countries and the policymaking processes within them are thus *epiphenomenal*—that is, caused by deeper conflicts among ruling classes operating domestically but based transnationally. If a given government is to be able to pursue equity within its own borders, therefore, it must repel class formations both within and outside itself.

The relevance of the "relative autonomy of states" debate to the quest for transnational standards of distributive justice should now be clear: If governments of lesser developing countries are nested within transnationally based class structures, as both Fagen and Petras suggest, standards of distributive justice arguably apply to economic relations within the world economy as a whole and not merely within specific individual societies.

—*E. W.*

The fundamental problem to consider in discussing the political formulas for transformation is not only of simply transferring one set of institutional end products to another, nor is it merely a problem of locating the historical experience of one set of countries in a time sequence or world setting, but rather of dealing with the very special problem of the inequality of power on a world scale and of the tendency for those "inequalities" to manifest themselves with peripheral polities. More specifically, the issue of transition from one social system to another through electoral processes and within a class society assumes that the events and forces within a country are in "free and equal" competition—independently of the existence of exogenous classes and institutions—an assumption that hardly captures a major facet of political-economic life in the late twentieth century. . . .

Power is to be understood first through an analysis in the following sequence:

A. Modes of production, social relations of production, and the resultant process of accumulation and expansion define the parameters within which "policy" is formulated and discussed.

B. The "foundation" of society is the crucial moment in which control over the mode of production is defined; the class structure which emerges—class-formation—is implicit in any discussion of "foundations."

James Petras, *Critical Perspectives on Imperialism and Social Class in the Third World.* Copyright © 1978 by James Petras. Excerpt, pp. 64 and 68–71, reprinted by permission of the Monthly Review Foundation; endnotes deleted.

C. The new capitalist social formation possesses certain imperatives (dynamic) to which state activity is directed: facilitating the accumulation of capital while safeguarding the "foundations."
D. Policy decisions reflect the efforts by different social interests within the class structure to shape specific allocations of state resources to improve their relative position.
E. Policy studies within a decision-making framework focus on the relative influence of different social interests in the allocation of marginal increments at a certain moment in a social system. The problem of state power cannot be tested by examining derivative phenomena historically and structurally removed from the foundations and organizing principles of a society.

A common mode of production unites the owners of capital in essentials: maintenance of the foundations, state promotion of the dynamic (accumulation) and support for the class structure (especially at the upper ends and among "support groups"). Within those boundaries, individual owners and factions embodying a variety of political, social, and economic orientations can be found competing for influence within the state power. It makes little sense to discuss the plurality of competing groups without first understanding the unitary basis of their involvement.

In peripheral societies, power is cumulative: status, wealth, contacts, access, and communication networks add up to and generate "power." Furthermore, interests overlap: media, industry, and bureaucrats converge to defend and propagate policies and values tending in the same direction.

The organization of power does not begin with the formation of a party, faction, or interest group, but rather those forms embody pre-existing and more fundamental units of power (classes), which organize and control the factors and relations of production (codified perhaps in a constitution), which are directed by a bureaucratic-military apparatus (government) that embodies the foundations and propels its expansion.

The peculiarity of political action in the periphery is that the ruling class does not usually seek out mediating structures but is directly represented in the state, and in some cases the state-classes are combined features of society (the members of the highest state bodies are the ruling class). The rather weak position of parties, interest groups, and the like is not a product of the "underdeveloped nature" of society. The lack of influence of this institutional configuration is an expression of a more fundamental weakness of the ruling classes, the lack of "legitimacy" of the ideology or values of the dominant class within which parties and narrow-focus interest groups can grow. It is specifically in the West, where ruling class ideas circulate generally within the society and where the capitalist mode of production and class divisions are taken for granted, that narrowly focused parties and interest groups have the legitimacy to bargain and compete. Power in peripheral society, then, is located in the structures of production, and policy is largely derivative: the interest groups that emerge and compete for power (short of revolutionary classes, parties, or movements) are expressions of the consolidation and institutionalization of the ongoing structure of power. The terms under which ruling class power is exercised are subject to the class struggle. Therefore, the power of the capitalist is rarely absolute, except in cases of totalitarian dictatorships, under which the class antagonism becomes latent, and rulership appears total. The dominance of a mode of production defines the prerogatives of the ruling class and the role of the state. However, the state, while subject to the laws of development of that mode of production, is also subject to the level of the class struggle. Economic development is, in the first instance, informed by the class struggle; hence, in the capitalist periphery the central problems for imperial and national capital (and its academic apologists) are "stability" or control and subordination of the labor force where possible, segmentation and nonpolitical bargaining activity where necessary. Modes of production and their laws of motion are, in the final analysis, class relations and are thus determined by the capacity of each class to impose its terms of control over production, including the disposition of the surplus. Nevertheless, distribution appears largely as market relations—the behavior of the capitalists apparently being ruled by the demand and supply of market forces.

The crucial difference between the above discussion as it applies to the overall social and political configurations within the periphery and to the imperial countries is the existence of liaison groups, which link the class structures of both peripheral and metropolitan societies. The process of capital accumulation "from the outside" led to the growth of internal classes, which grew in proportion to their capacity to extend and develop their external linkages. The peripheral bourgeoisie expanded, not with the growth of an internal market, but with the expansion of the external market. The periphery is composed of interlocking classes, which integrate and organize production and structure political activity toward facilitating the free flow of capital and goods between areas. The peripheral nation contains classes of double nationality: state rule is shared with economic "subjects" with external political allegiances. An "open" political system is then necessary to facilitate the interlock of classes and the free flow of capital. The "liaison groups" within the periphery (landowners, industrialists, military, etc.) provide the "access" points for economic entry and political influence. This pattern of class formation provides for a skewed political pattern in which great concentrations of capital on a worldwide scale enter into competition with locally anchored class forces—a problem that seriously cripples the notion of political competition.

READING #15   Class, Capital, and the Autonomy of States
Martin Staniland

The transnational class forces to which the previous reading refers are widely understood to be related to the dynamics of capitalism, the motor force behind much world development. World capitalism as a mode of production poses a dilemma for many of the lesser developing countries. Few modes of production have offered the hopes of such expansive development. And yet, in the perceptions of some, world capitalism contains the elements of both exploitation and domination. In the reading to come, Martin Staniland describes the "logics" behind these concerns. The now familiar issues of the autonomy of states and the internal/external linkages between politics and class reappear in Staniland's analysis.

Staniland identifies an *externalist*, or capital, logic and an *internalist*, or class, logic and demonstrates the implications of each for the relative autonomy debate and the political economy of development. Are peripheral societies exploited by world capitalism, as depicted by "externalists"? Alternatively, are they dominated by structures of power as portrayed by "internalists"? One's stance on these questions often helps define one's position in relation to development and the issue of the relative autonomy of states.

—E. W.

Marxism and Third World Politics

Given the perspective just outlined, what is the nature of the class struggle in underdeveloped countries, and what is the class character of the state?

The first injunction of Marxist analysts in treating these questions is that the only meaningful framework is an international one. They reject the premise of most "bourgeois" writing on "modernization" and "nation-building" that domestic processes can be understood using a national framework. Thus the first editorial statement of the radical *Review of African Political Economy* called for an approach that "sees the dynamic of African societies as a complex result of internal and external forces which distort and limit the development of the forces of production under capitalism." In practice two ambiguities mark this position. One is an ambiguity about the desirability of capitalism. As Colin Leys has remarked, much dependency theory is infused with an implicit hankering for "true" capitalist development. But the same ambivalence is present in much Marxist writing, and quite naturally so, given the uncertainty in Marx's successors about the possibility of achieving socialism without capitalism to expand production and create a proletariat.

The other ambiguity concerns the national and international credentials of theory itself. Specifically, it concerns the acceptance of Marxism by intellectual nationalists in the Third World. "Bourgeois" theory is denounced as "cultural imperialism," because it presumes a global process is under

---

Martin Staniland, *What Is Political Economy? A Study of Social Theory and Underdevelopment.* Copyright © 1985 by Yale University Press. Excerpt, pp. 164–169, reprinted by permission of Yale University Press; endnotes deleted.

way that will generalize the experiences and structures of the Western industrialized countries to the underdeveloped world. It equates modernity and development with acquisition of the institutions and values of the liberal capitalist world. Critics argue that such theory offends the integrity and independence of ex-colonial countries by excluding the possibility of development on lines different from those of liberal capitalism. The obvious question is why Marxism, which also originated in the West (albeit as a dialectical adversary of capitalism), which also assumes the preeminence of international processes and the dominance of international forces, and which is even more peremptory in its treatment of nationalism, should be so warmly embraced by so many intellectual nationalists in the Third World, not to mention radicals in the first world.

To explain this interesting paradox would involve some burrowing into the cultural dilemmas of Third World intellectuals. The point of noting it is simply to identify a tension apparent in actual discussions of Third World politics. The tension is one between the external and internal dimensions, which . . . is characteristic of much international political economy, but which takes on a particular idiom in Marxist analysis. Here the tension expresses itself (to use [John] Lonsdale's useful distinction) as one between capital logic and class logic. "Capital logic" means that "the main determinant of action by the capitalist state are the systematic requirements of capitalism in general." "Class logic" means that "the state's, and capitalists', freedom to choose more productive techniques and so on is crimped by the existing class relations of power and production." One way of understanding Marxist debates about Third World politics is to conceive them as pulled, broadly, between these competing logics. To oversimplify, one camp sees the logic of international capitalism as the main dynamic in the development of Third World countries. It thus adopts a clearly externalist view and sees domestic politics as instrumental to the needs and purposes of international capitalism. This view satisfies both the internationalism of Marxism and the intellectuals' yearning for a universal theory of cause and effect. The other camp is uneasy about the mechanical character of such argument and its implied depreciation of the significance of domestic politics. It therefore wants a framework that recognizes the realities of external influence but accords more prominence to internal class struggle. It seeks, if not in so many words, to inject a note of voluntarism, to assert that while Third World peoples may not make their history as they choose, they do nevertheless make it. Such an assertion satisfies the nationalism of Third World intellectuals and also restores a sense of political efficacy to arguments about Third World politics.

In order to make this abstract distinction intelligible, I shall now examine the specific arguments between Marxists about the nature of politics and the state in Africa, an area with which I am relatively familiar and one in which an active, if occasionally theological, debate has occurred in the two decades since independence.

Marxism and the African State

Two quite divergent themes compete in Marxist analysis of African politics. One, arising from the capital logic view, represents the class structure of African societies as shaped by international capitalism. In this perspective, the dominant class in African countries is not a true bourgeoisie, nor is it a true ruling class (the latter is, in fact, the bourgeoisie of the European and North American core). The dominant class in the African state is a *comprador* group, an auxiliary bourgeoisie, in terms of Marx's original formulation, "a kind of sub-committee of the metropolitan committee for managing the affair of the bourgeoisie." The subordination of the African state to capitalism follows ineluctably and is often described in the language of structural Marxism. Thus Michaela Von Freyhold writes of Tanzania:

> The colonial and post-colonial state are both the agents of parts of the bourgeoisie, but the ways in which they *fulfill their function and the tasks they have to perform* are rather different and require a substantial transformation of the state in the process of decolonization . . . [the postcolonial state] is faced with the task of disorganizing the direct producers who have begun to assert their class interests . . . the actual dynamics of economic and social development . . . are determined by the metropolitan bourgeoisie irrespective of the form in which it intervenes.

Writers taking the externalist, capital logic view tend to be uninterested in detailed examination of domestic political life in African societies. Just as earlier, liberal writers of the nation-building school concentrated on elites, so many Marxists concentrate on the character of dominant classes, since they are seen as crucial agents for the penetration and stabilization of capitalism. Because, in this view, domestic politics is essentially a product of larger forces, it holds little interest for the theorist.

The other theme, often associated with the class logic view (and more agreeable to radicals with nationalist sympathies), stresses the systemic autonomy of African states. Writers drawn to this perspective often argue that the major characteristic of the postcolonial elite is its possession of political power. They accept that this elite is not a true bourgeoisie and they may also agree that it is neocolonial in character. However, they assert that the lack of a true bourgeoisie does not imply the existence of such a bourgeoisie elsewhere but a very different basis for class formation in Africa. *Power, not control of the means of production is the basis of class formation and class conflict*: the dominant class is therefore to be seen as a "political class," a "bureaucratic" or "managerial" or "organizational" bourgeoisie. Class logic is thus preserved, but by inverting the classical Marxist conception of the relationship between economics and politics. Power determines access to wealth, rather than wealth determining access to power.

Such observations are often accompanied by the notion that class formation occurs downward. The state provides the organizational foundation any class needs to move from being a "class-in-itself" (a group with identifiable common interests, problems, and values) to a "class-for-itself" (a group that has recognized such community and has started to create collective organizations). Therefore, class formation has proceeded more rapidly within the elite than among the peasants and workers, who are dispersed and lack such an organization ready to hand. The state, then, can be regarded as "a preformed class organization in waiting": "There was thus [at independence] no need for those at the upper levels of society to constitute an organization to represent their class interests—they had the State." The externalist (capital logic) perspective and the internalist (class logic) perspective are not altogether mutually exclusive. They do, nonetheless, constitute distinct ways of dealing with two sets of questions to which a Marxist approach to international political economy gives rise. One set concerns the relationship between international capitalism and the Third World state: is the latter merely a tool of the former, or does it enjoy relative autonomy? The other set concerns the relationship between the state and domestic interests: is this relationship shaped by the exigencies of international capitalism, or is it subject to dynamics that are local in origin, perhaps involving forces other than those generated by capitalism? Are the external imperatives of economic power congruent with the internal imperatives of getting and holding onto power, or may these two sometimes conflict?

READING #16   Models of Development and Social Change
Paul Steidlmeier

What developmental programs should states select, assuming that governments are able to implement policy strategies for autonomous development? How do policy strategies differ, and which among them most effectively incorporate the norms of distributive justice? Paul Steidlmeier, in this final reading of Part One, surveys the entire range of policy strategies available to lesser developing countries in contemporary society; he also assesses their value-assumptions and developmental impacts.

He begins by encapsulating the plight of poverty-stricken countries in terms of the dilemmas created by the world food complex. He then proceeds to describe six development policy strategies: growth, revolutionary, redistribution with growth, basic needs, self-reliance and popular participation, and integrated rural development strategies.

The distinctions among these strategies relate to the questions raised earlier regarding class, capital, the nature of economic growth and social development, and the autonomy of states. For Steidlmeier, authentic social development ultimately depends upon what people do for themselves and the extent to which political and economic structures allow the creative energies of citizens to function freely. Where economic growth impedes distributive justice, however, Steidlmeier recommends leaning hard in favor of equity—even at the price of slower growth. For this reason, he manifestly prefers policy strategies that emphasize self-reliance and integrated rural development.

But the central question in regard to world political economy and distributive justice persists: Can a theoretical explanation of poverty amidst plenty be derived from within an analytical perspective that concentrates almost exclusively upon the policies of individual governments? By extension, we must ask whether a broader explanatory perspective is required and, if so, what might this be? Part One has focused on the domestic side of poverty, class, and economic decisionmaking in ways relevant to a political economy of development. Now this perspective appears inadequate by itself. Regardless of whether one accepts the class and capital logics described earlier by Staniland, it becomes evident that we must evaluate development processes from within a transnational frame of reference.

Why? Part Two explores possible reasons. The criteria for the claims of justice established by Arthur and Shaw in Reading #1 will be reintroduced, but now in the context of international and transnational claims. Claims of distributive justice must be grounded in prior socioeconomic activities that have demonstrably led to unfair results. Indeed, if the claims of distributive justice are to be applicable on a transnational basis and thus relevant to the world economy in whole or in part, we must demonstrate both that the interactions among states and the degree of transnational linkage among their socioeconomic structures are sufficiently complex in quality and appropriately dense in volume as to be representative of an integrated social order, and that these transnational economic relations demonstrably promote conditions of distributive injustice on a global scale. This represents the challenge of Part Two.

For the purposes of the following reading, we shall assume that the political economy of development represents a valid perspective—but one only partially valid given that its analytical focus does not readily permit analysis of the transnational factors that may be relevant to social change within lesser developing countries. Accordingly, we shall turn in Part Two to a framework of analysis that views the world economy not as a collectivity of individual societies but as a transnational order in which the claims and standards of distributive justice may be applied globally and thus across sovereign political boundaries.

—E. W.

The Development Framework: Agents, Ends, and Means

What are the problems development policy must resolve, and who are the agents to solve them? How are they to do it? Development policy must

Paul Steidlmeier, *The Paradox of Poverty: A Reappraisal of Economic Development Policy.* Copyright © 1987 by Ballinger Publishing Company. Excerpt, pp. 200–221, reprinted with permission of Ballinger Publishing Company; endnotes deleted.

be devoted to attacking a wide number of targets simultaneously in an integrated way that anticipates the interaction between specific problems and areas. In Table [1], I present a summary outline of the main dilemmas encountered in the poverty and development equation in terms of the economic dynamics of production, consumption, and marketing in the context of the sociocultural background. The problems listed are referred to in a global aggregate sense. Needless to say, the reality of poverty differs greatly from place to place; accordingly, these factors will assume varying degrees of importance from region to region. Nonetheless, good development policy must simultaneously address some such array of problems.

What sort of policy is called for to adequately address these issues? . . . The question is how ideas about development can be translated into effective programs of social change. It is not possible here to present a plan for a local area, a region, a nation, or the world. But it is possible to analyze the framework that such plans imply. Development aims to bring about social change. The agents are those individuals and groups I delineated in my discussion of social power. They include individuals acting in their various social roles, but most of all the agents of development are groups of people acting in a collective way. There are four possible points of focus for their actions.

The first strategy is a *person-to-person* approach, which attempts to persuade individuals to change their analytical frameworks, priorities, and values. It concentrates on influencing those in key roles. This strategy endeavors to recast individual behavior within social systems.

The second focus of action is social *prophecy*, which attempts to challenge and refashion the pervading models of analysis, cultural value systems, dominant social paradigms and ideologies, and prevalent social interpretations of reality. It does this through a variety of means ranging from discourse on values to innovative programs and forms of social conflict.

The third strategy is *politics*, which is here defined as the art of organizational participation so as to effect the common good. This strategy aims to transform the social system, not only in its individual roles, but also in its general rules, the formal legal system, its ideologies, its patterns of stratification, and its social control mechanisms. Politics in this sense is work on behalf of the common good. It represents a struggle over legitimate social authority and should not be narrowly identified with "government."

The final point of focus is *economic activity*, which involves the use of the market or exchange system to influence behavior. As such it may include strikes, boycotts, shareholder responsibility initiatives, cooperatives, the formation of free economic associations, and the use of economic incentives.

None of the above focal points of strategies is of itself superior, and the proper strategy mix depends upon the situation being addressed. The first two involve strategies that are primarily modes of persuasion. The third and fourth use civil authority systems and economic exchange systems, respectively, to change social behavior. Both are involved with groups and institutions as social agents more than they are with individuals.

Table [1]. Some Leading Dilemmas in the World Food Complex

A. *Production of Food*

1. Allocation of production factors and economic opportunity in a way that does not benefit the poor.
2. Welfare distorting power/profit interests, whether local elites, international business, or former colonial masters.
3. Obstacles to accumulating factors of production both nationally and for the small farmer (especially credit).
4. Agricultural dualism, both national and international, market orientations are pitted against basic needs.
5. Patterns of mechanization that displace labor and cause unemployment.
6. Resource exhaustion and destruction of the ecosystem.
7. High resource consumption levels, especially with energy-intensive agricultural technology.
8. Poor nutritional quality of product (from chemicals, etc.).
9. Inappropriate technology and lack of adequate research and development in soils, new seed uses, pests, climate control, and so forth.
10. Lack of extension services and management training.
11. Unavailability of new technology (to the poor) and general lack of complementary infrastructure.

B. *Consumption of Food*

12. Adequate nutrition is too much correlated with high income.
13. Good quality food is too high priced.
14. Consumption patterns of the affluent world drain away food resources (notably for feed).
15. In processing, consumer value may be sacrificed to profit.
16. The consumer, as price taker, has all costs passed on.
17. Inadequate international reserves in times of crisis.
18. Ignorance regarding nutrition.
19. Population growth (demand) outstrips production supply.

C. *Distribution of Food Products*

20. Poor people who are hungry do not have enough income to enter the market.
21. Food aid in terms of rationing, price controls or an income supplement is necessary.
22. Food has become an instrument of power for personal and national interests.
23. Waste because of poor storage, processing, pests, etc.
24. Patterns of industrialization and urbanization often do not mesh with supply patterns.
25. Lack of market information, transport, and other related services.

D. *Attitudes and Value of Orientations*

26. The grounding of moral values; especially the split between communitarian and individualist orientations.
27. Narrow nationalism and conflicts with international food policy goals.
28. The self-interest of business and government managerial elites.
29. Ignorance of the cultural base of hunger (e.g., the role of religion or philosophy, whether positive or negative).
30. False images of nutrition and hunger in symbolic media.

What do agents of change seek? What is the ultimate purpose of development? These questions focus on the human values of development policy. I approach the ends of development in terms of (1) social participation, (2) growth, and (3) distribution. The pivotal element to underline in any social system is the right of all people to have access to and participate in the structures and offices of that system and of society. To be legitimate any civil society must guarantee participation. Such participation connotes (1) a level of individual liberty compatible with a like liberty for others as well as (2) equality of opportunity. Participation, based upon liberty and equality of opportunity, is the prerequisite of justice in civil society and governs the possibility of attaining a common good that truly represents the public interest rather than the despotic will of small elites. While participation guarantees the "subject character" of development patterns, it is not sufficient. Provision must be made for both growth (to meet demand stemming from both quantitative increments to population as well as affluence) and equitable distribution.

The first task of such a participative society in developing countries is to establish the nature and goals of these other aspects of development. This task is to be carried out through processes of dialogue characterized by fairness, due legal process, and cultural appropriateness. . . . This in itself is a formidable problem, for many developing countries allow very little participation.

I have said that development should be based on culture if it is to be successful. . . . At the same time, it must be recognized that cultural forms can function negatively as well as positively with respect to social participation. A caste system, for example, is openly discriminatory. In such instances, economic development is pushed back to a more fundamental stage: building participatory institutions. Participation can be considered as both a goal as well as a mechanism of development.

Questions of growth and distribution arise within the context of participation. These are areas of very concrete decisionmaking. To the point, the body politic (which is the subject of development) must come to terms with four further questions:

- What rate and composition of growth is desired and how is it to be achieved?
- What would amount to a fair pattern of distribution of offices, goods, and services in society?
- What is the duty of each member of society or group to render service to the public and contribute to the common good?
- What types of incentives for conformity as well as sanctions for nonconformity would be just?

These four questions as well as the two prerequisites for social participation noted above correspond to the main issues of social ethics of development. . . . It goes without saying that any development policy implies such normative questions. When it gets down to the concrete, then, I advocate a certain qualitative orientation in development policy based on the following priorities: the liberty of the oppressed over the freedom of the more powerful, the social opportunity of the marginalized over their exclusion by certain elites, the needs of the poor over the mere wants of the wealthy, the duty to contribute to the common good according to ability rather than be apathetic or merely seek narrow self-interest, and the reinforcement of patterns of social justice through social incentives and sanctions rather than surrendering the determination of due process to mere group egoism or vindictiveness. Each of these goals is a value statement in the sense that it indicates priorities regarding what should happen. I am well aware that others may disagree. Nonetheless, the positions that any society takes with respect to any of these questions will directly determine the overall orientation of development as well as the policy instruments and strategies involved. My point is that these issues must be explicitly addressed. These notions then go together to provide a social ethical component to the assessment of economic efficiency, which provides the foundation of what I call a social market economy.

Such social efficiency includes more than economics. It is normative in a broad sense, and it is very difficult either to summarize or measure. It raises the question of the *quality* of markets and other economic institutions (including bureaucratic planning). The history of development itself attests that there is a need for more explicit attention to social justice in determining the orientation of the economy. In some versions of economics, such as under multiple assumptions of perfect competition, it is assumed that adequate levels of justice and human welfare follow as a corollary from technical and price efficiency. Yet in the day-to-day functioning of economic systems, dysfunctions occur that lead not only to economic inefficiency but social inefficiency as well. There is a social opportunity cost and inefficiency associated with unemployment as there is with the stifling of innovations through overcentralized bureaucracy.

The society-wide delineation of social efficiency, however, is difficult to specify in detail. Social efficiency implies some sort of public choice of priorities. That is, it implies a position of concrete goals regarding the above questions as well as an evaluation of how satisfactorily these social goals are being met. As such, the analysis of social efficiency entails a wide social assessment of benefits and costs. To take a microeconomic example, in agriculture social efficiency includes both the strict economic efficiency of farming operations as well as their effects on ecology and the environment, on farm safety, on levels of wages and employment, and on the nutritional quality of the product. It includes narrow economic efficiency but is more extensive. It can only be concretely assessed if society has reached some performance expectations regarding such broader issues.

Macro applications of the social efficiency notion come to the fore in terms of farm legislation, which provides income support to farmers, supplies food to needy persons, and monitors the areas of employment, ecology and the environment, farm safety, insurance, and product quality. Social efficiency is at least partially based upon ethical analysis and public priorities. It frequently calls for political action in addition to market dynamics, particularly in areas of structural change. Some institutional aspects that are frequently discussed: land tenure policy, extension services and cooperatives, and supportive infrastructure. There is a vast amount of literature on each of these topics. Many of the issues are functional rather than ideological. It is clear that without an economic infrastructure for irrigation, rural electrification, transport and feeder roads, and marketing and storage facilities, local agricultural production and markets will be severely hampered. This in turn will have an impact upon consumer welfare and the broader performance of other sectors of the economy. The point is that more restricted technical economic considerations, such as farm size and land use patterns, must be evaluated within their social setting with a view to adapting them both to higher productivity as well as other social goals.

Theoretically, there are many possible solutions to development problems. The role of management in both public and private spheres and on both micro and macro levels is absolutely pivotal. Both public and private management serves to integrate various social agents, foster the social articulation of goals or ends, and judge the suitability of means and ends as well as outcomes.

What are the means to the end? Even within the same set of social goals and priorities, a number of types of social organizations remain theoretically possible. There is no demonstrably unique path to socially just patterns of economic development. To take the example of agricultural organization, which is so important in overcoming poverty and hunger, the world today confronts a wide variety of agricultural subsystems. The immediate challenge for development is not simply to imagine a theoretical alternative but to figure out how one can go from the status quo to something that, in fact, would be better.

Assuming that the responsible agents in a country reach some consensus regarding general development orientation, what are the means to the end in terms of the economic questions that a country faces? Any economic system confronts three basic questions: What to produce? How to do it? And for whom? These questions provide a concrete framework for development in both its normative and technical components.

What to produce? It has been pointed out in the case of agriculture that myriad production possibilities exist. One must decide to produce final consumer or intermediate goods. If producing food, one must decide whether to produce grain or beef, export crops, or both. Countless farmers make these decisions in terms of their comparative advantage in production and markets. A society guides these decisions in terms of its social goals, in general, and on the basis of human consumption needs and the social environment of markets, in particular. Market demand is a shorthand way of indicating the personal consumption needs and preferences of people when they are effectively able to enter the market. Need and market demand, however, are not necessarily equivalent. One of the functions of public policy is to resolve such disparities.

How to produce? With this question a society touches, first of all, the general principles of organization of the economy; for example, is it to be socialist, market, or "mixed"? Secondly, individual farmers must decide on the composition of inputs and the level of technology employed in producing a certain set of commodities, determining whether the system will be more capital intensive or labor intensive. The social and individual decisions interact reciprocally.

Finally, for whom? Does one produce primarily for oneself or for a cash market? If for a cash market, does one produce luxury goods (for those who are better off) or goods to satisfy basic consumer needs or both? In this question, there is an implicit discussion of the principles of distribution in the political economy: Who is to receive what benefits and why? Again, social choice (in terms of budgets and fiscal policy, for example) reciprocally interacts with individual decisions.

It should be clear that there are many agents of development, ranging from individuals to groups in government, market, and other social circles. It is their task, first of all, to forge a social consensus on the purposes of development and to articulate at least a working definition of social economic efficiency for public policy purposes. There is no demonstrably unique end or goal nor a demonstrably unique set of means to the end. The choice of a particular strategy among alternatives represents a political economic process based upon assessment of probable outcomes of different scenarios and their acceptability. I now turn to examine such scenarios as embodied in development theory.

Development Theory in a Social Change Framework

Most economic models of development have assumed a simplified theory of social change without examining its foundations. Such implicit models of change are often so heavily circumscribed by unrealistic assumptions and conditions that they rarely work out in practice according to the line of development indicated in the theory. It is very difficult indeed to achieve a realistic and integrated perspective on rural development and to identify effective mechanisms of change. . . .

Sociologists and political scientists have never succeeded in developing an adequate theory of social change. Neither "laws of the market" nor socialist "laws of history" are in fact laws. . . . Some recurrent elements in the process of social change have been identified. But there are no universal laws of social change nor is there some kind of blueprint by which economics can abide. Indeed, patterns of change seem to be specific to particular historical and sociocultural milieux. To discover what types of development policies may work in a certain region, it is advisable to master the history and culture of that place in order to understand how things evolve and are accomplished in that specific context. Historical and institutional analysis is the key to discovering the inherent dynamics of change in a particular milieu and that can provide the best hints regarding the most fruitful paths to follow in development policy.

In the literature on economic development one encounters many diverse and even conflicting theories. Most of the theories that have stood the test of time in the literature possess an internal logic; otherwise, they would have been dismissed long ago. The basis of diversity and even conflicting opinion is located more in the presuppositions of the various theories. In this light, I examine a number of theories against the backdrop of their implicit presuppositions regarding social change. I consider in turn theories of (1) growth plus trickle-down, (2) revolution, (3) redistribution with growth, (4) basic needs, (5) self-reliance and popular participation and, finally, (6) integrated rural development in a social market economy. These distinctions are not airtight and some overlapping is evident. Yet it is instructive to consider them as general typologies, which serve to provide development policy with a fundamental orientation in terms of agents, ends, and means. For each model, I discuss the goal of development, criteria of performance, principal instruments, key mechanisms, principal agents and institutions, dominant values and cultural vision, and principal problems (Table [2]).

Growth Models

The dominant Western theory of economic development is a theory of growth. The framework of analysis is narrowly economic and focuses on input/output. The main goals of development are growth in gross national product and growth in GNP per capita. The primary question is how is it possible to stimulate the growth of a country's GNP. The answer is found in the accumulation of the factors of production and their allocation in an economically efficient manner.

In this theory, economic efficiency provides the criteria of performance of development policy. It is defined in a two-fold manner. . . . The first component is technical efficiency. This refers to maximizing output from a given set of inputs. The second component of economic efficiency is variously called price efficiency or allocative efficiency. This refers to minimizing costs or maximizing profits from a given fixed output. Cost minimization and profit maximization are related but not equivalent goals.

Economic efficiency is predicated primarily on the allocation of the factors of production. In practice, efficient farm management is very complex. A farmer faces a number of questions that have to be decided in an atmosphere of risk and uncertainty: What to produce? How? When? Where? And for whom? Those decisions are made first of all on the basis of available resources: the goods of nature (land, water, and climate), labor, capital, management, and technology. They are also made in light of market information and sociopolitical constraints or opportunities.

What is the principal instrument of growth? Growth theorists have traditionally recognized that the many decisions between types of product to produce, what input set to use, and how to optimize the factor/product

Table [2]. Development Typologies and Social Change

Development Typologies	Categories of Comparison		
	Primary Goal of Development	Criteria of Performance	Principal Instruments
Growth	• growth of GNP and GNP per capita	• market-rational growth • economic efficiency	• capital markets and investment • law to assure fairness in markets
Revolutionary	• growth in areas of social priority • radical redistribution of productive resources • egalitarian social relations	• plan-rational growth • economic efficiency	• planned investment • authority of party
Redistribution With Growth	• growth of GNP • incomes policy	• economic efficiency • basic income level for all • improved market quality	• markets/investment guided by income policy • budget/public policy
Basic Needs	• satisfaction of basic needs • growth and improvement of the quality of life	• needs met • growth in needs-meeting capacity	• planning of supply and demand • government authority over markets • limited markets within planned goals
Self-Reliance and Popular Participation	• participatory social relations • meet people—identified needs and goals in growth	• popular self-determination in development • needs met • growth in meeting people's goals	• decentralized: emphasis on grassroots organization • new educational pedagogy • communal economic decisionmaking for investments, etc.
Integrated Rural Development in a Social Market Economy	• sociocultural defined quality of life • growth guided by social choices	• culturally appropriate self-determination • needs met in guided market • integration of resource, population and technology policy with culture and historical institutions	• decentralized grassroots organizations • markets guided by communal decisions, public policy • monetary and fiscal policy are the main tool to guide markets

Table [2], continued

	Categories of Comparison		
Key Mechanisms	Principal Agents	Dominant Values and Cultural Vision	Main Problems
• technical innovation • inculcation of modern mentality • social mobility • individual liberty of action	• entrepreneur • market agents	• liberty/political rights • individual self-interest • utilitarian social goals • meritocracy • due process and opportunity	• exploitive concentration of power • market failure • Western cultural bias
• conflict • thorough social organization • revolutionary consciousness	• vanguard party • proletariat • government bureaucracy	• communal life in an egalitarian society • social duty linked to ability • primacy of need in distribution • collective liberty of disenfranchised	• lack of popular participation • planning inefficiency • poor implementation
• technical innovation • reforms of public policy • appropriate technology	• market agents • public policy, institutions and participants	• individual liberty with utilitarian social goals • long-term mutual self-interest • basic equity and due process	• growth/distribution tradeoffs • inadequacy of income alone to meet needs
• diffusion of values of human dignity • public institutions • appropriate technology	• vanguard elites • poor people • government bureaucracy	• human dignity expressed in political and economic rights • solidarity • distribution in communal life based on needs	• government bureaucracy • "top-down" approach • implementation problems
• diffusion of communal values • popular participation • self-reliance • appropriate technology	• decentralized, self-reliant • grassroots agents • cooperation with outside agents and central government	• communal self-determination and participation • people as subjects • self-reliance • solidarity • equity	• integration of local with central governments and outside change agents • institutional innovation and transformation
• cumulative inter-action of social system • value diffusion • public choice guides economy	• grassroots and traditional cultural leaders lead • central government and outside agents cooperate • primarily market	• priority of human development and cultural pluralism • balance between individual rights and communal self-determination • participation, equity, solidarity in social rights and duties • "wholeness in life"	• overcoming negative aspects of culture • institutional innovation and transformation • integration among various participants

relations all present management difficulties. But they have concentrated on the inputs that are most difficult to accumulate, the lack of which presents the greatest obstacle to development.

The primary focus falls upon capital accumulation and investment. Capital is accumulated domestically—primarily through savings. The possibility of accumulating savings is, of course, tied to technically efficient and price efficient management, on the one hand, and withholding some income from consumption uses, on the other. Countries that go along on a subsistence level are caught in the poverty trap because they always consume all that they produce. Furthermore, when their population is growing, their production-consumption cycle may fall into a vicious circle of increasing poverty. There are two primary ways to accumulate savings: to increase output efficiency leading to higher profits and to decrease consumption, either through population policy or by abstaining from higher levels of consumption.

Capital accumulation catalyzes growth. The key mechanism is technical innovation that leads to the scientific transformation of the economy. Natural resources can be improved through irrigation and reclamation projects, the quality of labor can be raised through education, health, and nutrition programs, needed mechanical and biochemical technological inputs can be acquired, and by [means of] extension training programs the quality of management can be made more efficient. Improved factor accumulation, both in quantity and in quality, will generally lead to overall production increases and higher factor productivity. This process can be represented by an upward and expanding circle where growth produces more savings, which leads to further investment and more growth.

In such an expanding scenario, there is increasing demand for the factors of production. In the context of labor it is assumed (on the basis of the adoption of a certain technology set) that more and more jobs will be created. Entrepreneurial investments produce growth, which benefits workers in terms of increased jobs. They and their families will have more money to spend. Thus, effective demand in the marketplace will increase and entrepreneurs will respond with further increased investment. This theory does not really anticipate limits to growth: the process can theoretically continue in an ever-expanding way.

Growth theory presents a model of change primarily based on private economic agents acting rationally in free competitive markets. Government has a secondary role in maintaining the quality of markets through the legal system and monetary and fiscal policy.

Generally this theory either ignores broader normative discussions or assumes a satisfactory outcome (trickle-down). Nonetheless, there is an implicit normative vision. . . . The emphasis falls upon individual liberty with general equality of opportunity guaranteed by due legal process. Distribution is articulated primarily in terms of meritocracy. Social duty is argued in utilitarian terms and is tightly linked to incentives and sanctions.

Within its presuppositions, the growth theory model is logically complete in charting the course of development and makes considerable sense regarding growth itself. Its weakest point is distribution. Why has trickle-down not worked? Those who support the model defend its inherent logic and cite the interference of governments, the political distortion of factor prices, overvalued exchange rates, and the poor success rate of birth control programs as the causes of failure. With the startling decrease in mortality rates (made possible by modern science and technology) population growth has soared, for birth rates have not come down to a satisfactory level. On the demand side, the trickle-down theory presupposes a demographic transition, if savings are to be made possible rather than being merely consumed by escalating population.

On the supply side, the trickle-down theory has been criticized for its theory of change based upon the entrepreneur. This theory has firm roots in the capitalist world, especially in neoclassical theory. It does not anticipate that the profits and surplus deriving from growth are more and more accumulated in the hands of the entrepreneurial class and that the real bulk of the fruits of growth are not passed on. Skilled managers and workers often benefit, but in the context of a large pool of surplus labor, wages in poor countries have tended to hover around subsistence. The anticipated general increase in consumer welfare in poor countries has frequently not materialized and demand has faltered. Developing countries found themselves in a vicious circle of another sort, which was caused by the concentration of economic power. This is particularly true of the economic scene today, where new investment may utilize a capital-intensive technology and thus entail the creation of very few jobs.

As an historical model, trickle-down has seemed to work in Europe and North America. But it did not do so without critical legislative changes throughout the past century. The socio-cultural institutional framework of the West, however, cannot be presupposed in most parts of the developing world today. In the theory of social change, which underlies the growth model of economic development, the positive functions of wider social factors (such as law, public investment, and social infrastructure) is assumed, rather than explicitly analyzed. This has proven to be improper, both on the production as well as the consumption side of the equation.

Revolutionary Models

The second theory of development that has proven to be of enduring historical importance is the Marxist revolutionary theory. The goal of development is not only growth but a radical redistribution of resources. Marx's analysis of poverty and underdevelopment focuses upon alienation in light of two considerations: production forces and production relations. The former refers to the economic input/output framework discussed above. The latter refers to the structural institutional framework and social relations between various classes. According to Marx, these relations are primarily based upon the control of production resources and the concomitant division of labor. Marx agreed that investment and more efficient management of resources would indeed produce economic growth and greater wealth. What he denied is that these benefits would trickle down to the workers and the poor.

The criteria of performance for Marx were not only aggregate growth but the elimination of poverty and achieving of equality in distribution. He saw the entrepreneurial class as denying the poor the surplus economic value that was produced by means of their labor. He also saw the population and poverty problems as derivative from the dominant social structures. Social structures, not overpopulation, produced scarcity and poverty.

The principal instrument of development for Marx was structural and institutional change: The social system of production relations is indicted for systematically producing underdevelopment, poverty, and misery. The way to development was to overthrow those structures. Marx did not deny that production forces themselves need to be continually transformed on the basis of science and technology. Nor was he against growth; he viewed capitalism as a necessary phase in historical change. His point was that economic development will not reach the poor without political change.

The Marxist model of social change basically centers on class conflict, and its dynamic progress is based on the vanguard party and the proletariat. The members of the party have the task of awakening and leading the oppressed classes in the seizure of power by revolutionary class struggle. After the struggle, there is a period of administration envisioned where the masses become reeducated and the enemies of the people are rooted out once and for all. The principal institutions are political planning and management of supply and demand processes.

The Marxist model presupposes rational and selfless human motivation by the liberated classes. The proletariat is described in terms reminiscent of Rousseau's noble savage. Socialist thought invariably highlights communal solidarity and equality of distribution. Social duty is articulated in terms of ability: one's abilities to contribute constitute a duty. Within this vision of human communal solidarity, individual liberty, due process, social opportunity, incentives, and sanctions emerge. There is a clear subordination of the individual and family to the "will of the people" as manifested in more collective forms of organization and enshrined in party directives and economic plans.

There are a number of problems with Marxist thought. He assumed both that all social evil was located in the oppressive capitalist class and its agents in religious, philosophical, and cultural spheres. Furthermore, he assumed that solidarity existed among all the oppressed people and between these people and the party. One of the main policy problems for radicals has been that the poor and dispossessed, whose cause they champion, are often unwilling clients. They are passive, distrustful, and fearful for themselves and their families. Marx blamed the passivity of the workers on the fact that they were mesmerized by the ideological superstructure and the opium-like hold that religion and other cultural forms had over them. The poor had first to develop a revolutionary consciousness.

Vanguard parties can [do] and have done some good. In accepting Marxist theory, however, one must presuppose (in addition to the above considerations) that the party is in general enlightened, benevolent, honest, and efficient. Furthermore, one must presuppose that its program invites and encourages the participation of the workers and the oppressed. That is quite a bit to presuppose. Wherever Marxist theory has been implemented, the final stage of the revolution—the transformation from the dictatorship of the proletariat (exercised through the tutelage of the party), to democratic and scientific socialism—has never occurred. Marxists continually blame class enemies for this failure. One must ask whether there might not be a fundamental flaw in the theory, especially regarding social change and "laws of history."

I believe that flaw is found in the theory of power and the assumptions regarding social change, which is based on an oversimplified theory of conflict, the seizing of formal power as a solution, and the existence of effective solidarity among the poor. As important as seizing formal power may be, there is a lot more to social change.

Finally, the Marxist notion of planning is based upon an extremely rationalist view of the human person unencumbered by poor data or logistical problems. This is a fundamental miscalculation of both the agents of change (party members and proletariat) as well as of mechanisms and institutions (party rule and planning). More important, the historical economic results of planning models have been generally weak, particularly in agriculture. Historical facts do not completely bear out the theory, especially in growth and productivity. Distribution has been more successful.

Redistribution with Growth

The lack of success of development policies based on either growth or revolutionary models in the post-war era has led to further questioning of both in the sixties and seventies. One model that emerged—primarily in the circles of World Bank emphasis on poverty and income research—was characterized by the goal of redistribution with growth. . . . This theory first emphasized the fact that mere growth models were not adequate to stem the increase in the numbers of the absolute poor in the world. Secondly, growth models ran into other economic problems, for the production growth that was taking place in developing countries was not matched by access to international markets or internal market development. Developing countries increasingly competed among themselves for the limited first-world markets for their raw materials, agricultural products, and light industrial products. The almost exclusive production growth emphasis failed to generate domestic markets for goods and services. Income did not trickle down to the poor, and thus, they could not constitute a market.

The criteria of performance in redistribution with growth theory are not only efficient growth but providing sufficient income to all persons so that they can participate in a market system.

The principal instruments of policy are capital accumulation and development explicitly geared to an income policy. Redistribution with growth is not a precise formula. In an economic sense it emphasizes the simultaneous development of production capacity, improving patterns of income distribution, and hence, the generation of domestic markets.

Insofar as social change goes, the redistribution with growth theory heavily relies upon the diffusion of technology as the main mechanism of change on both the production and consumption sides of the equation. But the technology adopted must be appropriate in terms of generating jobs and channelling adequate income into people's hands. Furthermore, in growth models the demand in the marketplace that did eventually materialize was very often for imported goods rather than domestic products. Domestic products were often of inferior quality and design. In addition, many of the goods and services produced domestically did not correspond to domestic demand. This point amounted to using public policy as a mechanism for restructuring the domestic product mix.

The agent of social change is not merely the entrepreneur acting in markets. The government enters in as a key element of change in basically guiding the investment policy, as well as instituting an explicit income policy. Nonetheless, the key economic institutions remain very much market institutions.

The value set in redistribution with growth models is similar to that in growth models. Primary emphasis falls upon individual liberty, equality of opportunity, and due legal process. But there is more emphasis on mutual self-interest (argued in utilitarian terms) than on mere individual self-interest. Also, while distribution is viewed primarily in utilitarian terms, there is . . . a notion of human dignity in terms of a basic quality of life that should be met. The main shift is in means: public economic policy is called for because the market has not and will not function adequately by itself. Ironically enough, Taiwan and South Korea, which are cited as redistribution with growth successes, are neoConfucian in spirit and authoritarian in practice. They are paternalistic and provide a strange contrast with the value set implied in the Western theory of redistribution with growth.

Redistribution with growth policies have been implemented with some success in Taiwan and South Korea. Growth rates remained high, domestic markets developed, and absolute poverty decreased. It is not clear, however, whether their success can be imitated. Both received something from their status as former Japanese colonies, both followed aggressive export policies, both had very strong and efficient governments (even if dictatorial) and both had Confucian and Buddhist cultural traditions. It has remained difficult to sort out which factors accounted more for the development success and how they related to each other.

What are some of the problems with this theory? It is argued by some that redistribution of income necessarily means less growth. For there would be less money for investment. Furthermore, whatever surpluses might accrue would be so dispersed throughout the country that they could not be marshalled for investment purposes. There has been, therefore, a considerable discussion in development circles over the trade-offs between growth and income redistribution. That there may be trade-offs is not denied, but it is questionable whether these trade-offs are one to one. Income in the hands of consumers can be transferred back to entrepreneurs in two ways: by means of market purchases and by means of savings. While talk of trade-offs tends to focus single-mindedly on production, in many ways it is more important that market structures have not developed and that savings institutions have not been in place to channel savings towards investors.

Basic Needs

As its name states, the goal of the basic needs theory is to ensure that all can, in fact, meet their basic human needs of food, clothing, shelter, health, and education. Redistribution with growth theory attracted wide attention in the seventies. At the same time, it was observed that in countries with different cultural traditions than East Asia basic needs have remained unsatisfied despite growth and even some income redistribution. In the redistribution with growth theory it is assumed that all basic needs can be satisfied in the marketplace: All that is needed is sufficient income to become a market participant. The basic needs critique claims that incomes policy is a necessary but not a sufficient condition to achieve satisfactory levels of social welfare. . . . One problem is that the incomes of the poor generally remain too limited. Another is that producers have not been keying their investments on basic needs, but, instead, have been concentrating on other domestic and export areas, which have promised a more favorable financial return.

The criteria of a basic needs strategy are not all that clear. Often enough in the literature, "basic needs development" represents . . . a general orientation rather than a precise set of goals. Criteria of basic needs activities must be established. Richard Szal . . . has attempted to do just that. He identifies eight criteria: (1) to increase the income of the (socially determined) target group, (2) to contribute to a direct impact upon core needs of health, education, housing, water, and nutrition, (3) to increase the production of other (socially determined) goods and services, (4) to increase decentralization and self-reliance, (5) to use simple equipment, (6) to use low skill technology, (7) to use local material, and (8) to use small-scale labor intensive capital construction. These criteria are not exclusive, but they do provide a relevant series of questions for policy analysis.

The basic human needs and redistribution with growth approaches share many similarities. They both imply a "capacities approach" to absolute poverty and both recognize that the growth with trickle-down model is inherently flawed. Yet basic needs approaches go further in several respects. . . .

What kinds of activities form part of a basic needs strategy? There is in theory almost an infinite variety of instruments. In addition to an agricultural development program to increase production they concentrate on investment in rural works (especially storage, transport, access to roads, and water supply), health and nutrition services, programs of adult literacy and extension, provision of housing and related services, and promotion of the informal sector.

The principal mechanisms of a basic needs strategy are, firstly, public articulation of what are basic needs. Secondly, public policy processes provide the integrative mechanism for all economic decisions.

The agents of change are the people themselves. There is a role for private entrepreneurs. More important, major intervention of the state is envisioned, not merely in income distribution but in production, in what is called "supply management." Development budget priorities are not geared merely to increasing GNP but also to providing public services necessary to meet human needs and build up infrastructure. It is primarily the government that does this. That there may be "trade-offs" with GNP growth rates is accepted. Basic needs approaches do not share the same commitment to growth as that enshrined in neoclassical theory; nor do they share the basic market orientation that redistribution with growth implies. To the extent that a market operates in basic human needs approaches, it is very much a politically guided market economy.

The value set places emphasis upon human dignity and the empowerment of people. This is conceived of, first, in terms of a fair distribution of wealth and economic assets (e.g., land and credit). Secondly, basic community structures of political participation are stressed. Thirdly, the composition of what is produced (i.e., of growth) is clearly weighted against nonessential goods and services, which satisfy wants rather than needs.

Basic needs theory emphasizes equality in distribution as well as the duty of all in society to contribute to meeting the needs of all. A basic needs strategy calls for establishing a minimum quality of life. The meeting of fundamental and identifiable needs is the priority of government budgetary and fiscal policies. As such, it calls for increased direct investment in the provision of core needs: health services, education, clothing, housing, and nutrition (including supplies of clean water). This suggests a significant change in the output of goods and services.

Problems with basic needs are seen in areas of growth and bureaucratic administration. As this idea is relatively new, policies are only beginning to be formulated to make such a strategy operational. What would be the effects of a basic needs approach upon overall economic growth? There has been little time to empirically observe any countries that are trying to implement such a strategy. So far much of the discussion remains quite theoretical, but it is important, nonetheless, in raising questions of priorities for development. As to bureaucratic problems, one significant criticism is that the basic needs approach has emerged from government bureaucrats and academicians who tend to view bureaucracy benignly. Also, the theory tends to favor a view of social change that operates from the top down. It is more a program of doing things for people . . . than [one of] people developing themselves. This reaction has fostered a popular participation variant.

Self-Reliance and Popular Participation

The primary goal of popular participation models is that people truly [become] subjects of their own development. Popular grass roots participation is necessary if development is to be humanistic and if development programs are to succeed. For only then can basic needs be identified, resources mobilized, and measures drawn up (all by the people themselves) to improve the distribution of goods and services. In such a strategy, there is a clear reaction against the authoritarian type regimes found in Taiwan and South Korea, which allegedly squelch the satisfaction of some nonmaterial basic needs. Participation models stress that it is crucial to satisfy the people's desire to participate and to be the active architects of their own destiny. The ordinary people must be responsibly involved in the design, implementation, and evaluation of projects and policies.

The criteria of performance stress popular self-determination through full participation. The basic needs approach is refashioned in terms of national and local self-reliance and the establishment of social structures and institutions that elicit and guarantee popular participation. In this context more specific criteria are discussed that include economic growth, income distribution, and material welfare as well as larger concerns of human development. Basic needs are expressed in terms of both a material and nonmaterial component. The latter recognizes human dignity in terms of self-reliance and participation.

It is not easy to identify the principal instruments of such an approach. The discussion of popular participation models is quite diverse. The general formula emphasizes self-help, local resources, initiative, and leadership; it stresses the effective impact of traditional ways and of rural village organization and insists on "development from below." . . . One of the clearest expositions of an (ideal) participatory development project has been provided by Guy Gran. . . . He lists eight characteristics:

1. A significant percentage of the specified group must participate in and control as many elements of project initiation, design, operation, and evaluation as is possible.
2. The project design must include clearly defined and operational participatory mechanisms to guide administrative, productive, and distributive elements of the project.
3. The institutional linkages of the project with the larger economic and political system must be functional for those at the bottom; the aid inflow and the productive gains must be protected. Thus the hostile development environment and prevailing confidence mechanisms must be explicitly dealt with in project design.
4. Technological and organizational aspects must be culturally feasible. If women are the farmers, it is counterproductive to train only male agricultural extension agents.

5. The project design must reach some reasonable standard of ecological soundness that reflects an empirically defensible analytical framework by the participants.
6. The project must show the potential for self-reliance; resources should serve a catalytic function, not a welfare function encouraging further dependency.
7. Comparable potential for self-sustainment must be evident; conventional aid activities often die when funding stops.
8. The project design must include enhancement of self-directed learning. Intellectual dependency, as much as political and economic dependency, saps creativity and productivity.

In addition to instruments of change seen in basic needs theory, popular participation theory gives considerable attention to pedagogy and to the conscientization of the poor. This pedagogy focuses upon human values, but it also focuses upon conflict as a mechanism of change as in revolutionary theory (although not necessarily violently). The instruments of change are similar to those in basic needs theory, but the spirit of self-reliance places particular emphasis upon local resources. Development is not to be imported from a foreign government or even from the national government but must be based upon and initiated with local resource endowments.

From the above, the key mechanisms of popular participation emerge. It is a program to empower people. This involves creating active citizens by overcoming the underdevelopment state of mind, emphasizing humanist economics in terms of the self-actualization of persons and peoples. On a more practical level, this program calls for small group organization and decisionmaking. This model also features the local selection and training of development catalysts and effective participation in project design.

The agents of change are clearly the local people. Specific roles and responsibilities emerge from processes of dialogue. Institutions tend to be decentralized and fluid. The task for the local people developing themselves is to identify their goals and to figure out what the next possible step for them is on the basis of their own resources. This point does not deny the need for national infrastructure or even for some outside inputs. It aims to overcome simply being passive recipients by becoming active subjects of development. It is also wary of the benefits of tutelage by vanguard parties.

Most of the popular participation models are articulated in close connection with basic needs theory and the leading role it assigns to governments. It should be recognized, however, that there is also a strong private enterprise/market strain of popular participation theory, which is analytically closer to growth and redistribution with growth models. . . . The eventual outcome will be what people decide.

The value set in popular participation typologies emphasizes communal solidarity and more equal patterns of distribution of both resources and economic products. Individual rights and duties are placed within the context of communal solidarity; theoretically, at least, they remain intact through the normative criteria of participation (corresponding to equal opportunity).

The main problem with popular participation is its actual orchestration. The primary agent of change is seen as the poor themselves, and the problem of the "pedagogy of the oppressed" is not easily overcome. In the literature, one also finds an enlightened elite of intellectuals, religious figures, and community leaders who argue the case of the poor both in front of the entrepreneurial class and government bureaucracies as well as to the poor themselves. The identification of the agents of change bears similarity to the revolutionary theory, for it depends on people-based initiatives (as well as upon a vanguard elite).

Finally, the precise role of entrepreneurs and markets as well as the role of government remain unclear. The tendency to decentralize, however, would seem to favor markets and make government more of a facilitator that provides infrastructure and information and maintains public order in a way that effectively protects basic communities of the poor from the predatory instincts of the local elites.

PART TWO

THE POLITICAL ECONOMY OF UNEVEN DEVELOPMENT

The Impacts of International Sociology on Political Science and Economy

World political economy has been characterized in many different ways. Realists emphasize the linkages between national economic policies and state security, and regard the structure and dynamics of balance of power and state sovereignty to be the ultimate determinants of economic order. Economists of liberal persuasion, oriented toward economic growth and the role of markets in the creation of wealth, concentrate upon questions dealing with trade and exchange, supply and demand, scarcity and consumption. Marxist-oriented analysts focus upon the relationship of capital to labor in the world economy and consider capital and class, core and periphery, structure and modes of production, to be among the basic units of analysis.

Realist, liberal, and Marxist observers also hold to different versions of the impacts of power in the world economy. Whereas realists underscore the problematics of domination by some national economies over others, liberals think in terms of imperfect market structures in which international competition becomes restrained, and Marxist commentators concern themselves with national and transnational exploitation through class relations within and across societies.

In recent years, moreover, the study of world political economy has become deeply influenced by the theoretical frameworks of international sociology. The sociological perspective envisions world political economy in terms of national and transnational socioeconomic forces. These include class, capital, and modes of production, among other conceptual categories—all of which refer to elements operating beneath the state or beyond politics.

Top-down perspectives on power, the standard fare of realists, who stress the "high politics" of state behavior, have been either supplanted or extended to include *bottom-up* approaches. These examine the dynamics by which states and international politics become embedded in socioeconomic relations. The depiction of world society as an international society of states, so much the province of international politics, now involves methods of theoretical analysis sensitive to the interplay between transnational modes of production and the politics among nations.

The sociological perspective in world political economy encourages analysis of poverty amidst plenty. Such analysis surveys the dynamics by which "deeply structured" processes reduce the autonomy of political agents, particularly governments and the administrative apparatus of states. It then seeks to reveal the manner in which such hidden but omnipresent forces produce and reproduce impoverishment and marginalization. The controversy regarding the autonomy of states, outlined in Part One, not surprisingly occurs mostly within the disciplinary confines of international sociology and its approach to world political economy.

How Wide the Realm of Political Economy: National, International, World, or Transnational?

Uneven development is the conceptual focus of this perspective, which examines the world economy in terms of the polarities known as **core** and **periphery.** A range of theories and analytical frameworks, including imperialism, dependency, and modern world systems, attempt to explain the relationship between the have's and the have not's by postulating that a so-called core and periphery exist within the world economy, and that the core, by its very nature, exploits or underdevelops the periphery. Chapter Four outlines these approaches. Together they help to establish the political economy of uneven or underdevelopment.

Chapter Four thus identifies competing theories of world political economy, including both a description and a critique of dependency and modern world systems. But the aim of the chapter is not to attach labels to theories as ends in themselves. Rather, it is to assess the most powerful and precise manner of explaining poverty amidst plenty, but now in a global or transnational as well as an international context.

Students of uneven development start from a common scrimmage line: Economic exploitation in one country can be explained only in terms of the uneven development in many countries. They argue, therefore, that attempts to examine the causes of poverty amidst plenty by referring to individual societies, as in the case of the political economy of development, are doomed to theoretical failure. Poverty and plenty within single states are caused by transnational as well as international phenomena, and it is to these, so the argument goes, that we must turn our attention. An examination of the political economy of uneven development thus seems a necessary theoretical measure to accompany our earlier review of the political economy of development, if our aim is to develop an understanding of the relevance of international normative theory in general and of international distributive justice in particular to the study of world political economy.

The political economy of uneven development starts with the following cluster of historical givens:

1. the rise of industrial capitalism within the now mature societies of North America, Europe, Australasia, and Japan;
2. the drive toward imperialist colonization of the three major under-developed regions roughly coinciding with Africa, Asia, and Latin America, Central America, and the Caribbean; and
3. maintenance of an underdeveloped Third World periphery conceived not exclusively in geographic, socioeconomic, or political terms but as a combination of all three.

The emergence of transnational business enterprises and global assembly lines represents, from this perspective, a significant recent feature of the modern world economy. Current analysis within the political economy of uneven development often suggests that transnational business enterprises are fostering dramatic changes in work, labor relations, and patterns of employment in a manner that reveals the possible emergence of a world division of labor along lines that defy neoclassical liberal economic analysis. Such changes are often referred to collectively as the **new transnationalism.** Many observers, both liberal and Marxist, assume that they will continue to carry increasing influence over patterns of *national* economic growth, *international* trade, *world* circulation of finance and technology, and *trans-national* modes of production. Chapter Five accordingly focuses on the following basic elements of the new transnationalism: the changing nature of transnational business enterprises; the socioeconomic and political impacts of the product cycle and circulation of technology; the structure of the global assembly line in terms of transnational modes of production; and the role of transnational modes of production in altering the structures and dynamics of core and periphery as reflected by labor, work, and employment.

The readings in Chapter Five are closely interrelated. They derive conceptually from one another and extend each others' analyses. Together they suggest that the world economy is currently experiencing nothing less than a major revolution. The name of this revolution is the new transna-tionalism.

One transformation directly related to the new transnationalism is the emergence of newly industrializing countries, such as South Korea, Taiwan, Singapore, India, Brazil, Mexico. Such instances of economic power among formerly lesser developing countries are often cited as cases of economic success. Yet the analyses provided in Chapters Four and Five leave one in doubt, or at least less than sanguine, about the capacity of this newly achieved economic power to advance the cause of distributive justice by relieving poverty amidst plenty.

In an attempt to address this concern, these chapters pose the following normative questions in relation to political economy of uneven development:

1. To what extent is the emergence of newly industrialized countries a result of transnational modes of production organized by trans-national business enterprises operating in world markets across na-tional economies?

2. To what extent do transnational modes of production work to improve the conditions of poor people living, on the one hand, in newly industrialized countries and, on the other, within societies that remain impoverished in aggregate terms?
3. To what extent do transnational modes of production allow and/or require application of cosmopolitan norms of distributive justice?
4. To what extent should such cosmopolitan norms be deemed applicable to sovereign states?

The answers to these questions revolve around the possibilities of a new normative order appropriate to a world economy steered both by the new transnationalism and by an emergent world division of labor.

CHAPTER FOUR

Core and Periphery: The History and Theory of Uneven Development

---

READING #17   The Second Image Reversed: Impact of the International Economy on Domestic Politics
Peter Gourevitch

Many regard states as the primary political agent in the world economy capable of contributing to an alleviation of poverty amidst plenty. As a result, analysis of development often concentrates upon the roles played by the states in influencing international economic policies. Typical of this focus is Reading #12, by Atul Kohli and his colleagues. The authors concluded, on the basis of their findings, that states and governments did indeed possess a major influence in determining equalities of income distribution.

In the reading that follows, however, Peter Gourevitch turns this logic upside-down. As his title suggests, he "reverses the image"—specifically, by inquiring if the international economy as a whole is a force in determining the kinds of governments that arise within states. On this basis, he examines the processes by which international economic influences skew or distort economic development within individual countries.

The theories reviewed by Gourevitch thus implicitly examine the question of the autonomy of the state, which was introduced in Part One. Unlike the previous discussion, however, these theories emphasize international, transnational, and global economic factors. The specific theories introduced by Gourevitch include late industrialization and centralized state control; and dependency, core-periphery, and imperialism.

The application of labels to specific perspectives is less important than the theoretical challenge presented by all of them: To what extent does state autonomy exist in a world economy in which world economic forces operate so powerfully? The way in which one answers this question reflects one's approach to the analytical dilemmas created by poverty amidst plenty and thus the normative issues relevant to international distributive justice.

—E. W.

Two aspects of the international system have powerful effects upon the character of domestic regimes: the distribution of power among states, or the international state system; and the distribution of economic activity and wealth, or the international economy. Put more simply, political development is shaped by war and trade. . . .

The International Economy

Recent events and the international relations literature have made us acutely aware of the impact of world market forces upon domestic politics. Citing the oil embargo after the Arab-Israeli war of 1973 makes other examples unnecessary. These effects though are not something new. The Great Depression alone did not bring Hitler to power: German history, institutions, parties, political culture, classes and key individuals did that, but it is impossible to imagine that without the millions thrown out of work by the contraction of the United States economy following the Crash of 1929 these other forces could have brought the result about.

The economic cycle referred to as the Great Depression of 1873–96 also had dramatic effects on political life around the world. Immense increases in agricultural and industrial production caused the prices of both sorts of goods to plummet. In Britain, the flood of foreign grain drove many persons off the land, undermined the landed aristocracy, and hastened democratization of political life (the secret ballot, universal suffrage, elected local government, disestablishment of the Church). In France and Germany, the drop in prices threatened landed and industrial interests. In both countries, these groups managed to protect themselves by erecting high tariff barriers. In France, this served to strengthen the Republic. In Germany, it stabilized Bismarck's newly-fashioned ramshackle empire. In both countries, preindustrial groups were thereby able to prolong their positions with ultimately disastrous consequences for constitutional government: fascism in Germany, the French collapse in the thirties and Vichy afterwards. Italy, Russia and Southeastern Europe could no longer provide even subsistence to much of their populations and sent a tidal wave of migrants around the world. In America, the late nineteenth century depression spawned Populism, a most powerful challenge to the two-party system and to the hegemony of industrial interests. It was ultimately defeated in part because the immigrants hurled ashore by the

Peter Gourevitch, "The Second Image Reversed: The International Sources of Domestic Politics," *International Organization*, vol. 32, no. 4, Autumn 1978. Copyright © 1978 by *International Organization*. Excerpt, pp. 884–891, reprinted by permission of The MIT Press; endnotes deleted.

crisis in Europe sided with their Republican employers against the Populist and Democratic farmers.

In all these countries, what we now call transnational actors were certainly present (at least in some sense of that term): British investors, German steel manufacturers, French engineers, American missionaries.

That international market forces affect politics and have done so for a long time seems incontrovertible. Can we find general arguments which posit systematic relationships between such forces and certain configurations of regime type and coalition pattern?

One of the most well-known of these is Alexander Gerschenkron's famous essay "Economic Backwardness in Historical Perspective." Gerschenkron's argument goes, briefly, as follows: the economic and political requirements of countries which industrialize early, when they have few competitors and simple, low-capital technology, are different from the requirements of those which industrialize when competition already exists and industry has become highly complex, massive, and expensive. The more advanced the world economy, the greater the entry costs. Paying those costs requires greater collective mobilization, which in turn requires greater central coordination. Societies which, prior to industrialization, developed strong central institutions will find these institutions useful if they attempt to catch up with "early" industrializers.

The first industrializer, Britain, enjoyed a congruence between the liberal character of its society and the relatively simple nature of economic development in the first stage of the industrial revolution in the eighteenth century. The society had weak or nonexistent guilds which were unable to prevent the introduction of new practices. It had an abundant labor supply to be pulled off the land into factories and a commercially oriented aristocracy and middle class, both with sharp eyes for new ways for finding profits. Its navy was able to corral world markets. Its state was strong enough to support that navy and to maintain order at home, without curtailing adventuresomeness and profit seeking even when, as with enclosures, these threatened social stability. Industry was at the textile stage, in its first incarnation: innovation was small-scale, relatively individualistic, and dependent on artisans; capital requirements and organizational requirements were low and easily mobilized by market forces.

In the eighteenth century, German society could not imitate this model. Political fragmentation limited demand-pull. Strong guilds inhibited innovation. The regime in the land across what became Germany varied considerably, but in most parts, the peasants, while lacking the freedoms of their English counterparts, could nevertheless not be driven off it. The middle class was of a traditional composition: lawyers, civil servants, teachers, traders, all little inclined toward industrial innovation. The aristocracy varied considerably. In the east the gentry were profit-oriented, but sought to make their money from the land and related activities such as brewing, and were quite disinclined to invest in new activities which might threaten the hegemony of farming. While the German state did not exist, local ones did.

These had very strong traditions of state activity, especially state-directed economic activity.

Over a century later, some of these liabilities became advantages. When the industrial revolution moved from textiles to iron and steel to chemicals, from putting-out small spinning jennys and handlooms to gigantic factories, blast furnaces, mines and so on, capital requirements skyrocketed. Organization and coordination became critical components of productivity. The corporate character of German society, at first a hindrance, now became a help. Once a certain level of technology was reached, it was no longer necessary to become like England in order to copy her. Banks and the state organized very rapid industrialization in a highly centralized way without parallel in Britain. This sort of centralized state corporatism was strongly rewarded by international markets. Germany surged ahead of Britain by the turn of the century.

While Gerschenkron's article deals only with the late nineteenth century, it is possible to extend the argument quite widely. Barrington Moore does so in suggesting that bourgeois democracy, fascism, and communism are successive modes of modernization, rather than options available to any given country at a particular moment. Moore ties the consequences of "lateness" more explicitly to fascism. The very configuration which made it possible for Germany and Japan, and to a lesser extent Italy, to catch up to Britain so rapidly (the survival of classes, institutions, and values from a preindustrial, anticonstitutionalist era) also made those countries more vulnerable to fascism. Moore then extrapolates to the peasant-based revolutions of Russia and China: by the time they were drawn into the world system of states and competition, things had proceeded even farther: even the German-Japanese model was no longer appropriate. The landlord-industrialist-bureaucrat alliance was too weak in relation to the peasantry and the nascent proletariat which could be mobilized under the conditions of extreme pressure brought about by the World Wars and capitalist penetration. By the twentieth century, autonomous development required autarchy; politically the only base for securing such a policy was a mass one, requiring a disciplined party to overthrow the old elites. Moore sketches out the bones of this argument all too briefly:

> To a very limited extent these three types—bourgeois revolution culminating in the Western form of democracy, conservative revolutions from above ending in fascism, and peasant revolutions leading to communism—may constitute alternative routes and choices. They are much more clearly successive historical stages. As such, they display a limited determinate relation to each other. The methods of modernization chosen in one country change the dimensions of the problem for the next countries who take the step, as Veblen recognized when he coined the now fashionable term, "the advantages of backwardness." Without the prior democratic modernization of England, the reactionary methods adopted in Germany and Japan would scarcely have been possible. Without both the capitalist and reactionary experiences, the communist method would have been something entirely different, if it had come into existence at all. . . . Although there have been certain common problems in the construction of industrial

societies, the task remains a continually changing one. The historical preconditions of each major political species differ sharply from the others.

Gerschenkron's ideas have also found resonance in studies of Latin America. Albert Hirschman, in a well-known article on import-substituting industrialization, finds both parallels and differences between Latin America's "late late development" and the German-Japanese model: "lateness" may not correlate with vigorous growth, high concentration, and strong government in a linear way; in some respects, the curve is "backward-bending": after a certain point, lateness leads to sporadic growth, and erratic central direction. Drawing on Hirschman, Guillermo O'Donnell offers an explanation of the spread of dictatorship across Latin America. These "bureaucratic authoritarian" regimes, he suggests, derive from a crisis in the import-substituting strategy of developments whose failures induce diverse pressures which in turn provoke harsh political techniques for their control.

In some fascinating recent work on "Latin Europe," James Kurth makes a brilliant synthesis of Gerschenkronian reasoning and other concepts drawn from such diverse authors as Raymond Vernon (the product cycle), Joseph Schumpeter (the epoch-making innovation), and Max Weber (types of authority), in the service of speculations about the distinctive features of politics common to Portugal, Spain, Italy, Greece and the countries of Latin America. As with other "late developers," politics in each of these countries is strongly affected by the juxtaposition of preindustrial and industrial classes; the alternation between liberal and authoritarian forms derives in part from that mixture. Unlike the "earlier" late developers, the South European countries face an even more evolved international economic structure, one in which certain forms of industrial activity are sloughed off by the most advanced countries, or more precisely, by corporations seeking lower labor costs. The system whirls like a fast merry-go-round: Italy, Greece, Spain, or Portugal can leap on when certain types of manufacturing favor their mix of labor supply and organizational skills but they lack the matured strength to hold on for good, and consequently face the constant danger of being thrown off. This situation also constrains politics, pushing and pulling toward and away from liberalism.

For this group of authors with whom I am associating Gerschenkron's notion of late development, political outcomes within countries are strongly affected by the character of the world economy at the time in which they attempt industrialization. Because of competition and changes in technology, each entrant into the "industrialization race" faces a new game, with altered rules. For all these authors, however, the impact of each international situation cannot be determined without knowledge of the internal character of each society. Gerschenkron showed how certain characteristics of German and Russian society became advantages as the economy changed. Moore, Hirschman, O'Donnell, and Kurth all stress internal factors as well: the character of social development at the point at which the country is drawn into the international economy. This, among other points, differentiates them from the next group, the "dependencia" or "center-periphery" theorists.

Theories of Dependencia, Core-Periphery, and Imperialism

A second group of theorists attributes even greater importance to the international political economy in shaping political development than does what I have labeled the Gerschenkronians. This diverse set of writers (who will be called the dependencia theorists, even if they are more well known in association with some other rubric, such as imperialism or core-periphery theories) strives harder to avoid "reductionism" to the level of internal politics; indeed, they may be the only group to stay at the international system level, or to come close to doing so. Like the Gerschenkronians, the dependencia theorists stress the non-repeatable nature of development, the new rules for each follower, the importance of competition. In contrast with them, though less so than the liberals, the dependencia theorists attribute less weight to purely national, internal factors, such as specific historical traditions, institutions, economic forms, and politics. They are also gloomier about the possibilities and benefits of the process.

What the dependencia theorists stress is the matrix set up by the advanced capitalist countries, a system of pressures which sharply constrain, indeed, wholly determine the options available to developing countries. Since capital, organization technology, and military preponderance are in the hands of the core, the core countries are able to set the terms under which skill, capital, and markets will be provided to the periphery. The core forces others into subservience: suppliers of raw materials, purchasers of finished goods, manufacturers of whatever the core allows them to do. The developing countries are unable to allocate resources according to their internal needs, following some alternative vision of development. As a result they are locked into a structure where the benefits of growth accrue disproportionately to the core. Countries in the periphery develop dual economies: an expanding modern sector tied to the needs of the core, and a stagnant, miserable sector, irrelevant to the needs of international capitalism, hence abandoned and ignored.

The political consequence of this system for the periphery is some form of imperialism: outright colonialism for Lenin and Hobson, where the peripheries are ruled outright by the core powers; neocolonialism for Gunder Frank, where the peripheries have formal sovereignty but are in fact prisoners of a structure which they cannot affect.

None of the theorists speculates very far about how much variance in political form these relationships permit dependent regimes to have. They offer no explanations as to why some countries in the neocolonial position are more liberal than others, some more authoritarian, some civilian, some military. Generally they see a tendency toward authoritarianism in the neocolonial countries, but of two different types. Elite-based authoritarianism (with the elite of the comprador, or foreign-allied, foreign-dependent variety) suppresses popular pressure for a greater share of the wealth, or for a different type of development (Brazil, Chile, Argentina, Uruguay). Popular-based authoritarianism à la Cuba mobilizes the mass support needed to withdraw from the international capitalist economy altogether and pursue a socialist or communist development strategy.

Some of the authors in this group see political consequences for the core countries as well: Hobson and Lenin, of course, saw imperialism as the export of internal conflicts—falling profits and increasing worker pressure lead the capitalists to invest overseas. Hobson thought income redistribution could solve the problem of domestic demand but doubted that it could be realized. Lenin was certain that it could not. Again, the range of variance in political forms allowed core countries is not at all clear: neither Lenin nor Hobson derives from his theories of imperialism any systematic explanation of parliamentary vs. authoritarian development.

The most ambitious attempt to derive specific political forms from the international economy is that recently offered by Immanuel Wallerstein. While his argument thus far has been worked out in detail only for the period 1450–1650, Wallerstein intends to apply it through to the present and is at work on the subsequent volumes. Very briefly his argument is this: the development of capitalism in the fifteenth century entailed the formation of a core, semi-periphery, and periphery. Each pole had specific political requirements. Each country had therefore to generate the forms which corresponded to its place in the system. The core economies required strong states, the peripheries weak ones, while the semi-peripheries were hybrids. Thus France and England were strong as befits the core, while Poland and pre–Great Elector Prussia were weak as befits the periphery.

Wallerstein's treatment is complex: it has vices and virtues about which I and many others have written. For the purpose at hand, the importance of his discussion lies in his insistence on a "world-system" perspective. Wallerstein sees his work as a break with state-centered accounts of economic and political development. Commercialized agriculture, early manufacturing, and the factory system cannot be understood in disaggregated, national terms. From the beginning, national economies grew in interaction with each other. The analyst must seek therefore to understand the properties of the system as a whole. Differentiation is one of the central properties of that system, one which confirms the necessity of the world viewpoint since its effects can only be detected from such a perspective. For Wallerstein the very essence of capitalism lies in that sort of differentiation: the operation of market forces leads to the accentuation of differences, not their reduction. Rather slight differences at an early point may explain why one area or country rather than another takes a particular place in the system—why for example Western rather than Eastern Europe became the core. Once the system begins to articulate itself, it greatly magnifies the consequences of the early differences.

Also political differentiation must, for Wallerstein, be viewed from world system to country, not vice versa. The international system is the basic unit to be analyzed, rather than units of power which come into being from some process conceived of quite separately from the operation of the system.

States are the concrete precipitates from the system, not the component units of it. Perhaps it is not accidental that this argument has been enunciated by a sociologist, rather than by a political scientist or more particularly an international relations specialist. It amply partakes of Durkheim, as well as Marx, and not, as the international relations specialist would do, of Hobbes, Rousseau, and Kant. Durkheim derives the individual from society: he is as individually differentiated from others as the society allows, according to its division of labor. Similarly, Wallerstein derives the state from the system. The international division of labor determines how much variance in political forms is allowed the component units. Position in the division of labor determines the type of form: states at the core must be strong; states at the periphery must be weak.

Wallerstein wavers from this resolute application of the world-system framework at times. When he takes up the explanation of why "coreness" requires strength, he notes that the core states needed governments capable of defending themselves militarily against rivals, of imposing themselves on certain markets and sources of materials, and of creating large uniform markets internally. The reasoning is then circular: strong states led to a core position, not a core position to strong states. That there was interaction makes sense but reduces the explanatory leverage provided by the general argument. The explanation of strength can no longer be so cleanly connected to a system-level argument. Some exploration of internal dynamics becomes indispensable, which pushes us back to the Gerschenkronian camp. From the world-system point of view, it is hard to see why certain countries diverge politically: why, for example, Poland and Prussia become bywords for weak and strong states respectively while having very similar economic systems and similar positions in the international division of labor. And why Holland, Britain, and France were so different in the seventeenth century, when all were part of the core. Again, the answer directs us back to domestic politics. . . .

In order to dramatize the differences, I have focused on dependencia theorists who stress heavily international constraints. Not all writers associated with that school do so to an equal degree. To the extent that dependencia theorists pay attention to internal forces in explaining regime type and the Gerschenkronians stress external ones, the boundary between the two camps disintegrates. Ferdinand Enrique Cardoso perhaps best exemplifies the juncture of these two modes of reasoning.

READING #18   Imperialism, Dependency, and
World Capitalism: A Historical Outline
Anthony Brewer

We often imagine the world economy in terms of opposites: poverty and plenty, rich and poor, strong and weak. Political economy of uneven development is, indeed, a study of contrasts: Some regions advance and develop; others regress, remain stagnant, or suffer from atrophy. This stress upon polar opposites, signified by the concepts of core and periphery, is a basic characteristic of neo-Marxist theories of imperialism, dependency, and world capitalism. Anthony Brewer, in the reading that follows, reviews the fundamental structure of Marxist and neo-Marxist analyses of world political economy by examining its interpretation of the history of imperialism and several of its main analytical categories, including historical materialism, modes of production, social relations of production, structuralism, capitalism as a mode of production, capitalism as a world system, dependency, and uneven or underdevelopment.

According to Brewer, Marxist and neo-Marxist theories of imperialism envision poverty amidst plenty as but an outer shell of results produced by an inner structure of core and periphery. This core and periphery emerged historically in the course of Western imperialism. Incorporation of previously independent non-European regions into the colonial and, later, capitalist systems transformed them into peripheral zones of Western capitalism.

The relationship between core and periphery, however, continues even now to cause aggrandizement for a few and impoverishment for the many. Indeed, if core and periphery are to possess analytical significance, they must be understood to mean that the core could not exist in the modern world economy without the presence of the periphery.

The theoretical framework outlined by Brewer thus represents an attempt to portray uneven development as a *necessary* outcome of imperialism, dependency, and world capitalism. The periphery, from this perspective, is the direct consequence of the core; and uneven development or underdevelopment of the periphery is the other side of the overdevelopment of the core.

—E. W.

The last two or three hundred years have seen two interconnected developments that have totally transformed the world. Firstly, production and productivity have increased to levels that would previously have seemed not so much impossible as inconceivable, and the whole nature of industry and of many of the goods produced has altered beyond recognition. How could earlier generations have conceived of live colour television pictures from the moon, broadcast to a mass audience in their own homes? Secondly, inequalities of wealth and power between different parts of the world have grown to an equally unprecedented degree. American workers watch their colour televisions, while their African and Asian counterparts suffer malnutrition. These are facts that everyone knows, but we tend to take them

Anthony Brewer, *Marxist Theories of Imperialism.* Copyright © 1980 by Routledge & Kegan Paul Ltd. and Associated Book Publishers. Excerpt, pp. 1–18, reprinted with permission of Associated Book Publishers; endnotes deleted.

for granted and to ignore the extent to which they determine the whole character of the contemporary world. They can only be understood and analysed by looking at the historical process by which they have evolved, on a world scale and over a period of centuries.

The same period has been marked by a third, less obvious, development: the rise to dominance of the capitalist mode of production. In this form of economic organisation, production is carried out by many distinct, privately owned enterprises that sell their products on the market and employ wage workers. Capitalism has almost completely supplanted earlier forms of organisation (peasant agriculture, feudal estates, slave plantations) in the advanced countries. In the underdeveloped countries peasant agriculture still supports a large part of the population, but these areas have been drawn into a world market and a world-wide system of specialisation that has completely undermined traditional economic and social structures.

The colonial empires hacked out by European powers, and the whole system of European and American military and political dominance over the world, that reached its peak in the early twentieth century, can only be understood in the context of this process of uneven development. The basis for military supremacy was economic. Superior technology meant superior armaments and a capacity to transport armed men to any part of the world. Superior economic organisation made it possible to finance the overhead costs of military forces, and to deploy them to devastating effect. The motives for imperial expansion were also predominantly economic. Some historians now seek to deny this, but the men of the East India Company, the Spanish *Conquistadores*, the investors in South African mines and the slave traders knew very well what they wanted. They wanted to be rich. Colonial empires were exploited ruthlessly for economic gain as sources of cheap raw materials and cheap labour, and as monopolised markets. The romantic image of empire (flags fluttering over distant outposts, etc.) may be appealing, but a serious study must concentrate on more fundamental economic issues.

I am not arguing, nor has any sane Marxist ever argued, that every incident in the history of empire can be explained in directly economic terms. Economic interests are filtered through a political process, policies are implemented by a complex state apparatus, and the whole system generates its own momentum. Much of the history of the British empire, for example, pivots on the need to safeguard the route to India. British policy in, say, the Mediterranean should not be explained in terms of the economic gains to be made in that area alone, but in terms of the maintenance of the empire as a whole. The overall drive to imperial expansion must be explained as one element in the whole process of capitalist development.

Equally, the creation of formal empires, under a single flag and a single political authority, is only a part of the story, and perhaps not the most important part. Formal political independence, with a flag, an airline and a seat at the UN, does not guarantee real equality, though it may be a necessary precondition for real independence and development. Some countries have never been formally annexed, and most Latin American states have been formally independent for a century and a half, but they have been drawn into a system of inequality, exploitation and dominance almost as deeply as have areas subjected to direct colonial rule. Underdeveloped countries still participate on very unequal terms in a world system of trade and investment. . . .

I will give a very brief, selective, and inevitably inadequate outline of the historical record.

The fifteenth century is as good a starting point as any. At this time, Europe was not particularly rich or technically advanced compared with, say, India or China. The Arabic cities dominated what long-distance trade there was, controlling the trading links between Europe and Asia and the main Indian ocean routes. Certain parts of Europe had, however, a crucial lead in weaponry and shipbuilding, together with the ability and incentive to take advantage of it. This was the basis for the explosive expansion of the Spanish and Portuguese seaborne empires at the end of the fifteenth and the beginning of the sixteenth centuries.

During the first part of the 'mercantile period' (1500–1800), Spain and Portugal dominated. The Spanish empire was based on the mining of precious metals in Central America and the Andes; these were funnelled through Panama to Spain, running the gauntlet of piracy in the 'Spanish Main' on the way. The mines, and the agricultural estates that fed them, were worked by forced labour. The Portuguese empire was more a string of trading posts which controlled the traffic in spices and, later, in African slaves, leaving social systems and systems of production relatively untouched. At the same time the expanding mercantile cities of Western Europe came to depend on imports of grain produced by serf labour on the estates of Prussia and Poland, shipped from the Baltic ports.

In the seventeenth century, the emphasis shifted to the production of sugar in slave plantations in the Caribbean and Brazil, while Spain and Portugal progressively lost control of the seas and of key parts of their empires, first to the Dutch and then to the English and French. Labour was scarce in the areas suitable for sugar growing, and the 'Atlantic triangle' was born, with manufactured goods (especially guns) being shipped to Africa, slaves to the Americas, and sugar back to Europe. As the eighteenth century went on, the English, French and Dutch trading posts in Asia were being expanded into territorial possessions, and there were signs of the more profound changes in Europe that developed in the following century.

In the mercantile period, then, European commerce came to dominate much of the world, though the goods exchanged in intercontinental trade were still mainly luxuries (sugar, spices, tobacco, etc.) together with slaves and precious metals. The organisation of society and of production in South and Central America was totally and forcibly transformed, with whole populations being exterminated and replaced, while in Africa and Asia the impact of Europe was in general either superficial or wholly destructive (the slave trade, the looting of India).

How this pattern of trade and production should be described is controversial. [André Gunder] Frank and [Immanuel] Wallerstein . . . insist that it was a *capitalist* world system, while others such as [J.] Banaji, [Robert] Brenner and [P. P.] Rey . . . would describe it as a system of mainly *pre-capitalist* societies, linked by exchange, which contained an evolving capitalist centre in Europe. This disagreement is part of a larger debate over the definition of capitalism.

By the eighteenth century, capitalist relations of production, characterised by the employment of free wage labour in privately owned businesses producing for the market, were well established in England and, to a lesser extent, elsewhere in north-west Europe. Productivity was rising fairly rapidly (though not as rapidly as later), and was already well above levels in the rest of the world. One factor in this general technical advance was the development of science with state support. The seventeenth and eighteenth centuries were the period of the 'scientific revolution', which was very closely linked to military and mercantile needs. Astronomy and the measurement of time were critical to navigation, and these sciences were at the heart of the Newtonian revolution in physics, and thus of a wholly new view of nature.

The decades around 1800 are a critical turning point, separating the mercantile period from the classical epoch of capital development. In the political sphere, the American and, above all, the French revolutions created a new conception of politics. Britain supplanted France as a major colonial power and took effective control of India, which became the lynchpin of the British empire.

Even more significant, the industrial revolution, centered in Britain, marked the start of a new era. It was a protracted affair, but taken as a whole it must surely be regarded as about the most significant breakthrough in human history. Its short-run effects on the mass of the people were probably retrograde, but it was henceforth possible to conceive of the abolition of poverty and drudgery through the mechanisation of production. Marx's vision of the possibilities of socialism is based squarely on the potential created by industrialisation.

The industrial revolution happened when and where it did because of a conjunction of external and internal factors (whose relative importance is a matter of debate). The organisation of production in Britain was by this stage wholly capitalist, based on firms that were relatively large (by previous standards) but numerous, flexible and driven by fierce competition between themselves. These enterprises could recruit workers with the skills they needed from a substantial urban proletariat, and lay them off again equally quickly when market conditions changed or when labour-saving innovations made them redundant. Britain controlled the markets of the world; a vital advantage since the most important raw material, cotton, had to be imported, while a large part of the product was exported to markets abroad. The profits of empire contributed to the ready availability of funds for investment. This was a new kind of society, which the rest of the world regarded with amazement.

In a wider sense, the industrial revolution went on through much of the nineteenth century, a period of sustained capital accumulation and development in the main centres of capitalism. The new industrial methods were introduced into industry after industry, and at the same time they were spreading to other parts of Europe and North America. This was the context in which Marx wrote. By the end of the nineteenth century, Germany and the United States had emerged as major industrial rivals to Britain, and Japan had started on the process of industrialisation.

The case of Japan is important, since it is the only example of complete capitalist development outside Europe and areas of European settlement. Those who argue that it was subjection to Europe that was the cause of the failure of development elsewhere can point out that Japan was one of the few areas that remained outside European control, while those who argue that the success or failure of capitalist development depends primarily on internal social structures can point out that Japan started from a social structure that had much in common with European feudalism.

The area effectively integrated into the capitalist world economy expanded enormously during the nineteenth century. Most of Latin America achieved formal independence (with some British support), but came under informal British control. Asia, the largest and most populous continent, was opened up for capitalism. The British established effective control of the whole Indian subcontinent, and forced China, at gunpoint, to permit the import of opium. The French got Indo-China and the Dutch already controlled the East Indies. Russia was steadily pushing back its frontiers in Siberia and Central Asia. Parts of Africa were colonised, setting the scene for the scramble for the rest at the end of the century. North America was opened up (gold rushes, cowboys and so on) and so was Australasia.

It was in this period that the world was definitively divided into 'advanced' and 'underdeveloped' areas, and the basic patterns of the present world economy were established. A new pattern of trade emerged, replacing the trade in luxuries that characterised the mercantile period. The advanced capitalist centres exported manufactures in return for imports of food and raw materials. The physical bulk of goods traded expanded colossally, but the means of transport were able to cope, having themselves been revolutionised along with the rest of industry.

The end of the nineteenth century marks another major turning point, the beginning of what Lenin called the 'imperialist stage' of capitalism. Following his lead, many Marxists reserve the term 'imperialism' to describe the twentieth century, using other terms for the expansionism of earlier periods. . . .

At this time, there was a rapid increase in the size of firms and a very rapid spread of monopoly in the form of cartels, trusts and so on. The twentieth century is the period of 'monopoly capital'. There was also a large increase in the export of capital, augmenting rather than replacing trade in commodities, at first in the form of loans to governments and public utilities, but increasingly as 'direct' investment in productive enterprises. In the early twentieth century investment was mostly in resource-based industries and in related infrastructure. The natural resources of the whole planet were opened up for exploitation by the capitalist firms of the advanced capitalist centres.

At the same time there was a scramble for control of the few remaining areas not already brought under colonial control, especially in Africa. Latin America passed, more gradually, from the British to the American sphere. Once the division of the world was complete, any further territorial expansion had to be at the expense of rival colonial empires. There was a sharp increase in tension between the main powers, especially between Germany (the rising power) and Britain (with the largest empire), which culminated in two world wars.

That the rise of monopoly, the export of capital and the outbreak of inter-imperialist rivalry are connected is generally agreed among Marxists, though the exact nature of the connection is more disputable. . . .

The twentieth century has seen a number of developments. Firstly, the area covered by the world capitalist system has contracted as a result of the subtraction first of Russia, then of China, Cuba, much of southeast Asia and so on. In all cases these areas broke away as a result either of war or of violent internal struggles. The nature of the systems installed in these countries will not be discussed here, but the fact of their existence has had important effects on the world balance of power.

Secondly, international trade has grown more rapidly than total production, and (perhaps more important) international investment by major firms has grown even faster, and made them into 'multi-nationals' operating on a world-wide basis. Markets for liquid money capital have also been internationalised, particularly through the development of 'Euromarkets'. Within its reduced geographical territory, the world capitalist economy is much more tightly integrated than ever before, despite the achievement of formal independence by most underdeveloped countries. The system cannot possibly be understood by looking at particular nation states in isolation.

Thirdly, the capitalist world is very clearly divided into advanced and underdeveloped countries, which differ from each other not only in income levels, but also in almost every other aspect of their economic and social structure. There are, as in all previous periods, a few doubtful cases (semi-developed countries in southern Europe, and special cases like Israel and South Africa), but it is notable how small a fraction of the world's population they contain. In almost all cases there is no difficulty at all in assigning a country to one group or the other. This sharp cleavage is clearly a major structural feature of the world system.

The advanced countries (Europe, North America, Australasia, Japan) went through a bad patch in the two world wars and the depression of the 1930s, but then exprienced the 'long boom' of the 1950s and 1960s. Overall, levels of productivity have increased enormously over the century and the capitalist form of organisation has almost completely displaced others. Trade and investment flows within the advanced 'centre' have grown especially rapidly, so that trade with the underdeveloped 'periphery' is now a relatively small part of the total. The economy of a typical advanced country is dominated by a relatively large industrial sector, with a service sector which is also fairly large and organised on modern capitalist lines. Agriculture only employs a small fraction of the labour force, but uses modern capital intensive techniques. (In some cases, a peasant sector survives with the help of subsidies.) The majority of the population are wage earners, and trade union organisations, if they have not fundamentally altered the nature of capitalism, have at least ensured that the benefits of increased productivity have been shared with the working class. The institutions of 'bourgeois democracy' are well established with free elections and guarantees of personal freedom. The advanced countries contain the headquarters of the main multi-national companies and are the main centres of technological development.

These countries produce and export a very wide range of manufactured and primary products. Their imports from underdeveloped areas consist mainly of primary products, produced where natural conditions are most favourable, together with labour intensive products produced by cheap labour.

Turning to the underdeveloped world, there are important differences between the 'three continents' (Latin America, Asia, Africa). In Latin America indigenous societies were almost wholly destroyed centuries ago. White or creole ruling classes with a European culture have been established for an equally long time, and the institutions of the modern state were installed at almost the same time as in Europe. The larger Latin American countries have average income levels which are well above those of Africa and Asia, though equally far below those of Europe. At the same time, they have all the structural features of underdevelopment.

In Asia, major pre-capitalist civilisations were drawn into the capitalist orbit more gradually and at a later date. The larger Asian countries have well-established indigenous ruling classes, a considerable technological capacity, and industrial sectors which are quite large in absolute terms, though small relative to the size of the population. Average income levels, however, are very low, with an enormous mass of peasants and workers reduced to starvation level or below, and massive unemployment. Some smaller Asian countries, on the other hand, are relatively industrialised, and Japan is, of course, in another category altogether.

Africa suffered the destructive effects of the slave trade over several centuries, but actual European penetration into the larger part of the continent did not come until the 'imperialist' stage, much later than in Asia or Latin America. It is, in general, the least developed continent, with tiny industrial sectors and low levels of income.

Despite these differences, one can still talk of a 'typical' underdeveloped country, characterised by the small proportion of the population employed in modern industry, by permanent large-scale unemployment or underemployment, and by large, low-productivity agricultural and service sectors.

Wages and incomes are low (except for a small élite). Agriculture mainly consists of small peasant holdings, except where there are plantations producing for export. These peasant farms are no longer self-sufficient 'subsistence' holdings, but are integrated into the market system. Foreign trade generally accounts for a rather large fraction of total national income, with essential imports of capital goods, intermediate products and raw materials being paid for by exports of primary products or labour intensive manufactures. Export earnings also have to finance outflows of dividends, interest and royalties. Underdeveloped countries generally trade with advanced countries and not with each other. This pattern is clearly quite unlike that of an 'untouched' pre-capitalist economy, and is the result of incorporation into the world capitalist system.

The class structure of underdeveloped countries is also distinctively different both from that of a pre-capitalist society and from that of the advanced countries. The small scale of industry and its domination by foreign firms with labour-saving production methods mean that the industrial working class and local industrial capital, the principal forces in advanced countries, hardly exist. In their absence, the system is dominated by the local representatives and affiliates of multi-national companies, by trading interests and by landlords. The largest popular classes are the peasantry and the urban 'lumpenproletariat' of unemployed or casually employed workers.

Advanced and underdeveloped countries, then, are complementary halves of a very unequal world system, which is the product of a process of development that stretches back centuries. At different stages in its evolution, and in different areas, it has taken very different forms. A complete theory of imperialism must account for all of them. . . .

Imperialism must be explained in terms of the development of 'capitalism'. This approach derives, of course, from Marx, and in this section I will briefly summarise some of the elements of Marx's method, historical materialism.

Marx starts from the observation that production is always social; Robinson Crusoe is a myth. Seen from a technical, physical point of view (the *forces of production*) or in terms of the actual activity of work (the *labour process*), production is the activity of human beings working on the natural environment to modify it to meet their needs. As a social process, however, it also involves relations between people, the (*social*) *relations of production*, which govern access to the means of production and the use of the product. These relations are not a matter of deliberate choice; the organisation of production in, say, Europe today is not the result of a conscious decision that wage labour in capitalist factories is a better system than the serfdom of the middle ages or the slave system of antiquity. It is the product of a long process of historical evolution.

Marx argues that the analysis of society must start from this structure of social relations, and not from individual choices or motivations:

In the social production of their existence, men enter into definite, necessary relations, which are independent of their will, namely relations of production corresponding to a determinate stage of development of their material forces of production. The totality of these relations of production constitutes the economic structure of society, the real foundation on which there arises a legal and political superstructure and to which there correspond definite forms of social consciousness. The mode of production of material life conditions the social, political and intellectual life-process in general. . . .

Marx's assertion that the economic 'foundation' ultimately determines the 'social, political and intellectual life-process in general' is one of the most controversial aspects of his work. It does not seem to me to be useful to discuss it at a general level; the test is whether it can be justified by detailed analysis in particular cases. I propose to treat it throughout as a working hypothesis, adopted for purposes of argument, and to see how far we can get with an analysis which starts from the economic structure.

Marx insisted on the need for abstraction. Society is too complex to be grasped as a totality, an integrated whole, in a single step. Instead, we must isolate the simplest and most fundamental social relations and build up an abstract representation of how they work and how they fit together. The concepts developed in this way can then be used to construct an analysis of the real (or 'concrete') world.

However, a single set of abstract concepts will not serve for the analysis of all societies. Marx praised the 'classical' economists (of the late eighteenth and early nineteenth centuries, notably Smith and Ricardo) for recognising the need for abstraction, but criticised them for applying concepts appropriate to the analysis of the capitalist economies of their time to all periods of history, thus failing to recognise the historical specificity of capitalism. Different stages of development were characterised by particular, different structures, and a separate process of abstraction was necessary for each. A *mode of production*, in the abstract, is a simple, basic structure of social relations that is the starting point for the analysis of a particular stage of history. It is essential to Marx's approach that there are only a limited number of these basic forms.

Each mode of production (except the simplest, the primitive-communal, and the highest, the future communist mode) defines a pair of opposed *classes*, a class of producers and a non-producing class that exploits them. The relation between these two classes is the central, defining feature of the mode of production. At this level of abstraction, classes should not be thought of primarily as groups of people, but as opposing positions within a structure of social relations. In particular, a class cannot be conceived of in isolation, since it only constitutes a class by virtue of its relation to another class; there cannot be employers without employees, slave-owners without slaves, and so on.

Some words of caution are necessary here. Recent 'structuralist' interpretations of Marx seem to me to have lost contact with Marx's materialism. Although Marx places the primary stress on the objective structure of social relations, this does not mean that these structures are ghostly 'essences' manipulating their 'bearers'. They exist only in the relations between real, flesh and blood human beings, and modes of production, in their pure form, exist only in the mind of the analyst. If I say, as I will, that 'capitalism develops the forces of production' (or some similar formula), then this is shorthand for 'a social organisation of the sort described by the concept of the capitalist mode of production induces people to act in such a way as to bring about an increase in output and productivity'.

Marx's original idea was simple and elegant. The various modes of production were successive *stages* in the history of human society. Each had its own structure and was able to 'reproduce' itself, that is to maintain both the forces of production (by replacing used up means of production, etc.) and the relations of production (by perpetuating the subordination of one class to another). The mechanisms of reproduction differ, of course, between different modes. The stability of each mode, however, was only relative; each generated development of the forces of production and, in the process, brought about changes in its own functioning that led in the end to a breakdown of the existing structure and its replacement by the next in the sequence.

> At a certain stage in their development, the material productive forces of society come into conflict with the existing relations of production. . . . From forms of development of the productive forces these relations turn into their fetters. At that point an era of social revolution begins. . . . In broad outline, the Asian, ancient, feudal and modern bourgeois [capitalist] modes of production may be designated as progressive epochs of the socio-economic order. . . .

Society, according to this account, has evolved from a (rather nebulous) primitive-communal stage, through the ancient and feudal periods, into the capitalist societies of Marx's (and our) time, which will in turn be replaced by communism. The *ancient* mode is defined by the opposition between slaves and free, slave-owning citizens, while the *feudal* mode, in its classic form, involves production for local use by a class of unfree peasants or serfs who control their own subsistence plots, but are compelled, by extra-economic coercion, to support a class of feudal landlords.

The most frequently studied mode of production, and the only one that Marx analysed in detail, is the *capitalist* mode. This is characterised by generalised commodity production, production for the market by many distinct and unco-ordinated units of production, together with a polarisation of wealth, so that a class of owners of the means of production confronts a class of free but propertyless workers. Ownership of the means of production excludes non-owners (the workers) from production, except on terms acceptable to the owners. Workers have to sell their labour power (their capacity to work) to the capitalists in return for wages with which they buy the goods they need to live. . . .

Marx recognised that non-European history could not be fitted into this 'Eurocentric' succession of stages, and he introduced a distinct mode, the

'Asian' or 'Asiatic' mode . . . to deal with this problem. The point of the Asiatic mode is that it does not develop in a way that leads on to further stages, but tends to persist unless disrupted from outside. He also admitted that the succession of stages could be broken by outside influences, especially by conquest:

> In all conquests there are three possibilities. The conquering nation subjects the conquered nation to its own mode of production . . .; or it allows the old mode to remain and is content with tribute . . .; or interaction takes place, which gives rise to a new system, a synthesis. . . . In all cases the mode of production— whether that of the conqueror or of the conquered nation or the one resulting from the fusion of the two—is the determinant of the new distribution that occurs. . . .

What he insists on is the analytical primacy of the mode of production, not the inevitability of a certain succession of stages.

A real society cannot, in any case, be reduced to a single abstract mode of production. Marx argued that: 'In every social formation there is a specific kind of production that predominates over all the others, and whose relations therefore determine their rank and influence. It is a general illuminant tingeing all other colours and modifying their specific features'. . . . Relations characteristic of several modes of production may be combined in a 'social formation' with one of them predominating. This interpretation has been revived recently. . . . Among other advantages, it permits the inclusion of the *petty-commodity* mode of production, a mode which has never predominated, and which therefore does not appear in a list of stages. It is characterised by production for the market by independent producers who own their own means of production.

Once we regard modes of production as basic forms of organisation which can be combined and elaborated upon in many ways in different historical circumstances, the range of possibilities becomes almost infinite. A limited number of modes can be analysed carefully in (conceptual) isolation, and then the complications can be built in to analyse a rich variety of real situations. This is the scientific method; the discovery of simple ideas which can elucidate complex problems.

What Marx left, in short, was not a complete interpretation of history, but a fragmentary outline of European history, an analysis of the capitalist mode of production, and some tantalisingly brief indications as to how his analysis could be extended. It would be foolish to treat Marx's writings as holy writ. In the study of imperialism, a central problem is the analysis of interactions between initially very different societies, characterised by different dominant modes of production. Marx's few writings on India and Ireland . . . are not particularly helpful. The Marxist method, on the other hand, has proved very fruitful. . . .

Marxist theories of the development of capitalism on a world scale tend to fall into two groups. There are those that concentrate on the progressive role of capitalism in developing the forces of production, and conversely those that present capitalism as a system of exploitation of one area by another, so that development in a few places is at the expense of the 'development of underdevelopment' in most of the world. Capitalism, according to the first view, creates the material preconditions for a better (socialist) society, as well as the class forces that will bring it about, while on the second view it is precisely the failure of capitalism to generate economic development that makes revolution necessary. The historical record, however, suggests that there is an element of truth to both of these opposed views; capitalism has generated massive technological and economic advances and also enormous geographical disparities in economic development.

The first of these views is broadly that held by the 'classical' Marxists, from Marx himself to Lenin and his contemporaries. It has been strongly revived in recent years. According to this account, the development of each country is determined primarily by its internal structure, and specifically by the nature of the dominant mode of production. Capitalism, a system in which free wage workers are employed by competing firms, tends to generate economic development, while other modes do not. External forces have their effect primarily by altering the organisation of production.

Competition between capitals is at the heart of a classical Marxist analysis of capitalism. The largest, most efficient firms with the newest capital equipment are the most profitable, and can increase their lead, while weaker firms fall behind and the weakest are eliminated by bankruptcy or takeover. The threat of failure forces all firms to maximise profits, to plough profit back into expansion, and to seek out new methods of production, new markets, new sources of supply, and so on. In pre-capitalist modes of production, by contrast, the exploiting class must, above all, maintain the basis of the extra-economic coercion which they exercise over the producers. The result is relatively static systems dominated by custom, with the (potentially investable) surplus redirected into non-productive channels.

The expansion of capitalism constantly expands the demand for natural resources (minerals, land, etc.) and this is one motive behind the geographical expansion of capitalism. Even with a static demand, development of means of transport together with the search for cheaper sources of goods will tend to draw new areas into the capitalist orbit. Capital accumulation by itself tends to increase the demand for labour power as well, but the adoption of labour-saving methods tends to offset this. The search for cheap labour is another motive for geographical expansion.

In the classical Marxist account, grossly oversimplified, capitalism emerges first in a few centres and generates capital accumulation and development there, opening up a lead over the rest of the world without necessarily taking anything from it (though capital will always take anything it can get). Capitalism spreads, starting the same process in other areas. Different parts of the world can be regarded, very crudely, as runners in the same race, in which some started before others. Any advantage gained by one at the expense of others is incidental.

The alternative view has been developed since the Second World War, notably by Frank and Wallerstein, as a response to the failure of capitalist development in many parts of the world. In this view, the unit of analysis must be a *world system*, in which different geographical areas or nation states are merely component parts. Capitalism is not characterized by a specific relation between classes, but rather by production for profit within a world system of exchange and by the exploitation of some areas by others. The 'metropolis' or 'core' exploits the 'satellites' or 'periphery' by direct extraction of profit or tribute, by 'unequal exchange' . . . or through monopolistic control over trade. The state machines of the centre play a key role in this. In the periphery, ruling classes emerge which owe their position to their function as intermediaries in the system of exploitation, so that they have an interest in preserving it and in preserving the patterns of production that underlie it. Underdevelopment is not a state of original backwardness, but is the result of the imposition of a particular pattern of specialisation and exploitation in the periphery.

Within this world system, different forms of 'labour control' may be used, such as forced labour, wage labour, slavery, and so on. The class structure of different 'nations' and the particular forms of exploitation in production are merely results of the place of the areas concerned in the world system, rather than being the key determining factors (as they are in a classical Marxist analysis).

In this approach, oversimplified, capital accumulation is seen not as a precondition for genuine, qualitative advances in the level and methods of production, but rather as a redivision of a fixed magnitude, a transfer of resources from the exploited periphery to the centre. Development in some areas and the 'development of underdevelopment' in others are opposite sides of the same coin.

These two views involve quite different readings of history. In the classical Marxist view, capitalism started off in a few places and has since spread out geographically in a process of *internationalisation* of capital, and has also evolved through a succession of *stages*, with key turning points in the industrial revolution and at the date when large-scale export of capital (not goods) started (i.e. around 1900). According to Frank and Wallerstein, by contrast, capitalism as a world system dates from the sixteenth century, and the system has persisted essentially unchanged ever since. The classical Marxists see capitalism in dynamic terms, while their opponents see it as a basically static system of exploitation.

The contradictions between these two views should not be overstressed, though they are very real. The world economy is a complex whole in which relations of production and exploitation exist both within and between 'nations'. It may not matter very much whether we say that underdevelopment is the product of external influences (which also determine a certain class structure and organisation of production), or alternatively that underdevelopment is caused by a certain class structure and organisation of production (which may be in whole or part the result of external influences). When we get to a more detailed level of analysis there are many theories that cut across this simple classification. Nevertheless, I think it is a helpful preliminary way of ordering the material.

The definition of the term 'underdevelopment' differs according to the approach adopted. In the classical view, underdevelopment is synonymous with backwardness, with an earlier stage of development. Frank and his followers, on the other hand, would argue that an isolated country could not be called underdeveloped, and that underdevelopment is defined by incorporation into a world system in a subordinate position. Whichever definition is adopted, there is little doubt as to which category to put any particular country in (though there have been half-hearted attempts to label Canada as underdeveloped), so this is not likely to lead to confusion. I shall use the term descriptively; an underdeveloped country is one that shows the general structural features of underdevelopment. . . .

READING #19   Marxism and Dependency
V. Kubálková and A. A. Cruickshank

A sometimes bewildering array of theories and analytical interpretations attends the study of world political economy. Marxist-oriented approaches have been especially prolific in spawning a range of interpretations of poverty amidst plenty. V. Kubálková and A. A. Cruickshank, in the reading that follows, provide a clarifyingkl introduction to dependency theory. As they indicate, dependency theory stresses the linkages between internal and external forces in economic development. It thus represents a counterpart to the theory of relative autonomy of states that we encountered earlier.

Dependency theory, however, emphasizes the external influence of international economic forces upon the internal character of national socioeconomic growth—so much so, in fact, that some dependency theorists have been criticized for portraying economic development as if the periphery were no more than an analytical phantom of the core.

The presentation provided by Kubálková and Cruickshank demonstrates how some dependency theorists seek to avoid exaggerating the impacts of external forces upon the periphery by referring, in effect, to the **double injustice** of core and periphery. The logic behind this notion of double injustice revolves around the proposition that core and periphery exist doubly—that is, as a Core and Periphery (uppercase), representing zones of economic development between rich and poor countries in the world economy as a whole, and as a core and periphery (lowercase), representing rich and poor or strong and weak within specific national economies. The analysis offered by the theoretical frameworks created by dependency perspectives focuses upon the linkages between the world or transnational structure of Core and Periphery and that of core and periphery within the national economies of specific states or social formations.

The logic regarding the double injustice of dependency proceeds as follows:

1. The poor in peripheral countries suffer from two processes of exploitation, each of which reinforces the other. The first derives from relations between Core and Periphery as a transnational or world structure within the entire world political economy; the second stems from relations between a particular core and a particular periphery as an internal structure within the national economies of specific lesser developing countries.

2. Domestic elites in peripheralized lesser developing countries constitute a *comprador*, or clientele, class of military, agrarian, and state bureaucratic interests co-opted by the Core; thus they act in ways fundamentally inimical to the social development of their own societies.

3. The state is an instrumentality of class relations inasmuch as its purpose is to support and shield linkages between transnational and national class interests.

4. The rich in the Core and the rich in the Periphery tend to form alliances among themselves, whereas the poor in the Core and the poor in the Periphery tend to view themselves as rivals.

5. Economic growth in peripheral or lesser developing countries is linked to the demand structure of the Core and thus perpetuates an artificial process of development in poor countries that separates the growth or modernizing sectors of the economy from all others, especially rural agriculture.

6. This process of distorted growth, in which certain sectors become overdeveloped while others become underdeveloped, may be referred to as "disarticulation" in that economic growth in lesser developing countries gives expression to the "overdevelopment" of the Core.

7. A labor aristocracy forms within both Core and Peripheral social formations linked to transnational and capitalist modes of production, a process that brings about the marginalization of other segments of the labor force.

8. One of the major class functions of the state is to facilitate the accumulation and circulation of finance capital, but also to reinforce the immobility of labor by impeding the flows of surplus labor from one national economy to another.

9. Thus economic growth, however rapid, does not eliminate the class or structural positions between Core and Periphery or core and periphery but, rather, serves to reinforce them.

The concepts of core and periphery are not essentially geographical, although they are often signified by the terms *North* and *South*. Rather, they serve to represent the **structural positions** in which economies are located. These structural positions, according to neo-Marxist analysis of uneven development, produce and reproduce the disarticulated conditions of poverty amidst plenty while the economies of lesser developing countries grow. Consequently, dependency theorists conclude, the achievement of distributive justice becomes more rather than less difficult as economic growth occurs, precisely because such growth is disarticulated—a phenomenon attested to not only by neo-Marxist theories of uneven development but also by evidence from neoclassical liberal economic analysis, as previously noted by reference to the Kuznets thesis and to Lipton's analysis of urban bias in world development.

—E. W.

It is primarily the concept of *underdevelopment* that separates the Dependency approach from Marxism in general, and from Marxist theories of imperialism in particular. Thus it is understandable that much attention was paid, particularly in the first years of Dependency, to this concept. While obviously the term (once a synonym for *un*developed) pre-dates the Dependency school, the Dependency school separates the two terms and loads each with distinct and very different meanings. When Marx, with other Western economists, saw 'backward' societies as simply *un*developed he saw them in that original condition from which the path led onwards to capitalism and thence to the next, and final, stage of development—communism. Neo-Marxists and other Dependency authors use the Baran/Frank concept of *under*development: they no longer refer to the 'original condition' but perceive, as it were, a regressive, staged development (leading from 'backward' to still more backward or 'stunted') taking place in parallel, and with the concomitant development ('overdevelopment') of the metropolis countries. The conceptual possibility of development 'at the price of another'—of development ('overdevelopment') of the West at the cost of underdevelopment elsewhere—did not enter into Marx's reckoning. Jalée, too, speaks of making the Third World into 'capitalism's backyard', of retarding its development and bringing it to a place without exits: a cul de sac with no chance of 'development'. In an extreme formulation some authors (for instance Caldwell) have added that it is not only the Third World which is in the developmental cul de sac but *both* parties, and the only escape lies in the recognition and acceptance by the 'overdeveloped' that they had overshot the mark and must go into reverse. They must 'de-develop', 'deindustrialise', prepare for 'de-growth', because the turn-off point to a developed future (for the whole world) has been missed—and therefore only by going 'further back' can the destination still be reached.

By this stage it may have been appreciated that there do exist (or appear at first sight to exist) a striking number of similarities between Marxism and Dependency, to the extent that one is very often mistaken for the other. But of course not all Dependency theories are Marxist or neo-Marxist, any

V. Kubálková and A. A. Cruickshank, *International Inequality: Competing Approaches.* Copyright © 1981 by V. Kubálková and A. A. Cruickshank. Excerpt, pp. 104–114, reprinted with permission of St. Martin's Press, Inc.; endnotes deleted.

more than all Marxism or neo-Marxism is about Dependency (although much of Dependency terminology is Marxist—albeit often confusingly deployed or having undergone semantic change). There is also the familiar Marxist emphasis on history. This emphasis is to be seen particularly in the use by many Dependency authors of a periodisation approach to typologies (differing from one author to the next) to explain how changes in capitalism led to changes in the Third World. As with Marxism too, and unlike its own predecessor, the theory of modernisation, Dependency is essentially an economic theory. Like Marxism, it is also a macro-theory insofar as it argues that the part cannot be separated from the whole.

On closer examination, however, differences reveal themselves—just as much as attempts are made to smooth them over or explain them away. Such an attempt is made by, for example, Sutcliffe when he finds that there are essentially three stages of Marxist thinking on the subjects of imperialism, Dependency being the third such stage. The three stages, which purport to explain the differences between Dependency and Lenin's theory of imperialism, and between Dependency and classical Marxism are:

1. Marx and Engels' writing on imperialism, their regarding it as *plunder*, and the depreciation of the use of peripheral markets;
2. Lenin's ideas, and those of other Marxists, on the growth of monopoly and the extraction of raw materials from the periphery;
3. the post-colonial *Dependency* of the peripheral countries in which foreign capital (international corporations), profit repatriation and adverse balance in terms of trade (unequal exchange) all seem to play a part in distorting, or bringing to a halt economic development and industrialisation.

In these three sequential stages the role of the Periphery in the Centre's development is a further point of divergence: from primary accumulation in Stage 1, to its playing a part (in Stage 2) in a partial escape of a more mature capitalism from its own contradictions, to (in Stage 3) the method of exploitation—this latter being the least clear. In this respect it may help dispel confusion by tabulating points of similarity and difference.

The difference between the two orientations ('stages' to Sutcliffe) tabulated in Table [1] are substantial. Classical theories of imperialism centred around the problem of why and for what internal purposes powerful states behaved imperialistically. In other words, the theories of imperialism focused on an analysis of the 'predator', and attempted to answer such questions as whether, for example, it was inevitable that imperialist states should behave in a certain manner; or was their behaviour a function of a particular economic system which was within the states' power to modify. Preoccupied with such problems, classical theories of imperialism neglected to analyse the condition of the *victim*, and, if anything, assumed that the side effects were ultimately to his advantage—construed perhaps as a necessary evil. In the developed countries the revolutionary failure of these theories in

Table [1]. Summary of Differences between Classical Marxist Theories of Imperialism and Neo-Marxism and Dependency

	Classical Marxist theories of imperialism	Neo-Marxism and dependency
Focus	Eurocentrist	Third World centrist or global theories
Main impetus	'New Imperialism' of the nineteenth century, agressive behaviour of Western states	Economic plight of ex-colonies/poverty of the Third World
Type of relationship between Centre and Periphery i.e. in whose favour	Asymmetry: rich countries depend on poor for survival of capitalism	Asymmetry: poor countries depend on rich for their survival
Main concern	Effects on metropolis (prolongation of existence of capitalism)	Effects on Third World and how to undo damage
Driving force	Internal contradictions of modes of production	International aspects of exploitation
Economic consequences	Disposition of surplus export of capital	Underdevelopment
Key sociological group/ class	Labour aristocracy (corrupted and deflected from its revolutionary path)	'Lumpen-bourgeoisie' (Centre in Periphery) in a 'symbiotic' relationship with the Centre
General outlook	Optimistic	Pessimistic

Europe, in sharp contrast to their successes as revolutionary doctrine in the Third World, gave rise to a reversal of emphasis so that the main thrust of theories of Dependency aimed at a diagnosis of the victim's condition and concern for his immiserated state. Theories of Dependency as general macro-theories of world politics had their origin mainly in the micro-analysis of the Third World's ailing economies. From the analysis of the patient's symptoms in the micro-approach the Dependency approach soon turned its attention to the analysis of the metropolis (although at first it was neither a 'patient' nor on the 'sick list'—and certainly was not complaining). When joined together predator and victim brought into focus a macro-perspective which upon investigation revealed to the Dependency authors that the causes of the malaise were actually to be found in the relationship between the two. It was further found that, in the case of the metropolis in particular, the condition was pathological since, they argued, through its own deliberate actions the metropolis 'stunts' the colony's development and consciously brings to it 'underdevelopment'.

Apart from differences in origin, differences in approach (in the sense of perspective held by the two theories) reveal themselves. Following acceptance of the fact that both imperialism and Dependency conceive of the Centre-Periphery relationship as asymmetrical, and that both are theories of inequality, the divergencies are seen to far outnumber the shared features, and it becomes increasingly apparent that imperialism in the Marxist understanding is not a theory of dependence in the same sense as is Dependency.

Unlike other Marxist theorists (and Rosa Luxemburg in particular comes to mind) who saw the metropolis depending for its survival on outward expansion and exploitation of colonies, Dependency reverses the relationship to have the ex-colonies depend for their 'survival' on the developed countries. And there are refinements of these broad parameters of the relationship: Barratt Brown, for example, among others, whilst acknowledging the fact of the enrichment of the metropolis through colonialist exploitation, denies that this process is of any major importance to the 'torturer', even though the maiming of the victim continues—which is to say that whatever the relationship may once have been, it becomes no longer a zero-sum relation (B's loss in the long run being no longer necessarily the equivalent of A's gain). Perhaps the better way (and certainly the safer way) of summarising 'Dependency' and of retaining the suggestion of the lopsidedness of the relationship is the descriptor 'domination-dependence'.

Other important differences are to be found. For theorists of imperialism (including Hobson and Lenin) the strategy and 'mechanism' of imperialism consisted of the corruption of part of the proletariat and, by the creation therefrom of a labour aristocracy (itself a participant in some of the colonial superprofits) that traditionally revolutionary vanguard was deflected from its revolutionary purpose, whilst the mass of the proletariat continued to be oppressed. In contrast, whilst some Dependency theorists still subject the metropolis to sociological analysis and seek to isolate groups and identify their roles in the Dependency relationship, most do not. Inattention to the class structure of the Centre is of course of deliberate intent—to imply that the class structure of the Centre may be discounted as far as the exploitative relationship is concerned. As Emmanuel points out, 'socialism itself has become an internal affair. As such, it does not necessarily rule out exploitation and antagonism between rich nations and poor ones'. . . .

Hence, . . . for many Dependency writers states cannot in fact become 'socialist'. Some consider the possibility remote that change brought about within states could bring overall change to the system itself. In this connection T. Smith terms the assumption of Dependency that states possess very little autonomy or even opportunity to influence their own destiny the tyranny of the whole over its parts. This reaction too represents something of a contrast with most Western approaches which, by regarding development as achievement and attaching blame to the underdeveloped societies themselves, incline in the direction of the autonomy (not to say the tyranny) of the parts vis-à-vis the whole.

Whilst often oblivious to the class structure of the Centre, and no longer interested in a 'labour aristocracy', Dependency turns its attention to another class formation, one to be found this time in the Periphery. It is a formation for the description of which Gunder Frank quite aptly turned the phrase labour aristocracy, to become 'lumpenbourgeoisie'. Although not all writers on Dependency use this exalted description most incorporate into their version of the dependent relationship between Centre and Periphery (and even into their definitions thereof) an indigenous elite which they see as a most important Trojan horse introduced within imperialism's (the victim) own walls.

Thus in this respect does Dependency part company with those Marxists (including those of the contemporary Soviet and Chinese persuasions) who see a possible progressive role for the Centre in the Periphery. Whilst a Trojan horse might be the analogy for Dependency, for Marx, the agency (he referred to as the national bourgeoisie) performed a positive role, and in company with other indigenous (but pre-capitalist in nature) classes, such as the feudal, fought to expedite the transition to capitalism.

General Characteristics of Dependency: An Overview

We have now reached a point where, having dealt with the origins and evolution of the school and having surveyed briefly the differences between Dependency and Marxist and Leninist orientations, we can proceed to review those characteristics regarded by writers on the subject of Dependency as essential features—many of which would already have suggested themselves to the reader. In this context we observe first of all that:

(1) Dependency focuses neither on an analysis of interstate relations nor is it a sociology of domestic society: it is essentially a *sociology* of *world politics*. Dependency writers see as purely derivative the importance traditionally allocated to the state as the unit of analysis, and it is therefore neglected in their approach, or at best, 'unwrapped', that is, in the sense that its internal structure is subjected to scrutiny and its components (class among them) are either elevated to the level of or assumed to have a role above that of states. In this process the domestic circumstances of states are regarded as having replaced the important role once occupied in traditional thinking by the state itself—and indeed these circumstances are taken as determinants of the state's own situation within the global context. In other words, this perspective 'confronts global politics in terms of the vertically arranged hierarchies that run across geographic boundaries'. Possibly as a result of the neglect of history and economics by its predecessor (modernisation theory) the starting point for the Dependency approach is that of the economy, and proceeding from a historical survey it 'fastens upon the fact of global classes derivative of modern modes of industrial production, distribution and exchange and the universal dissemination of industrial culture'. All of these authors, to include even such ideological 'neutrals' as

Galtung, by conceiving not only of such groupings of states as Centre-Periphery (or Core-Periphery, Metropolis-Satellite, or North-South) and by carrying the imagery over to the description of the inner structure (centre and periphery) of the Centre and the Periphery, would seem to share this common characteristic.

(2) We come now to the perception of the essential duality (Centre-Periphery) which according to all Dependency authors is reproduced in the Periphery. Recognition of the link between a corrupt bourgeois or semi-bourgeois indigenous (Periphery) elite with the Centre is in most Dependency writing the essential characteristic and operative mechanism of the Dependency relationship. Some authors, including Galtung, see also a centre and a periphery of the Centre—a subdivision not generally accepted but shared incongruously enough (if for different reasons) by the Soviets and the Chinese. Most Dependency authors, however, treat the Centre as a totality to suggest the participation of the whole Centre in the exploitative relationship. It is something of a paradox when we consider Emmanuel's concept of 'unequal exchange', which, although in the conceptual tradition of a corrupted labour aristocracy in theories of imperialism, leads to the conclusion that all the elements of the Centre, including the proletariat, are guilty of partaking in the exploitative spoils. The Soviet approach . . . does not commit itself so far as to regard the indigenous elites as necessarily negative—or at least not so negative as to deny them 'assistance'. Indeed, in the Soviet view, and commensurate with the attitude of these elites towards the Soviet Union, it becomes possible to see in them positive possibilities: according to tactical requirements, to 'lure' the elite from that *symbiotic* relationship with the Centre that is central to much of the Dependency position.

Thus the connection of centre and Centre will vary in nuance from the mild position we have outlined above to the extreme view of a symbiosis where the threat of withdrawal on the part of the centre in the Periphery, implied in writings on Dependency, is to be added to the list of symbiotic binding agents. Some authors add yet another, third pole, an agency that would seem partially to defuse (mediate or offset) the antagonistic socio-political situation: 'In a system of unequal exchange the semi peripheral country stands in between in terms of the wage levels and profit margins it knows. Furthermore, it trades or seeks to trade in both directions; in one mode with the periphery and in the opposite with the core.' This concept of 'semi-periphery' directly parallels the Chinese concept of the Second World, and indirectly the Soviet 'socialist system'. Whilst 'socialist system' has by no stretch of the imagination a dual nature it is seen to assist the resolution of the Centre-Periphery conflict by assuming, as it were, responsibility for the class conflict so that it (the socialist system) rather than the Periphery becomes the major opponent of the Centre (capitalism).

(3) The relationship between the Centre and the Periphery is *asymmetrical*, an asymmetry that is reproduced within the Periphery—and, as explained above, for some authors, *also* in the Centre [see Figure (1)]. It is asymmetrical in terms of favouring one of the parties (the Centre), and of that party's deriving greatest benefit for at least most of the time.

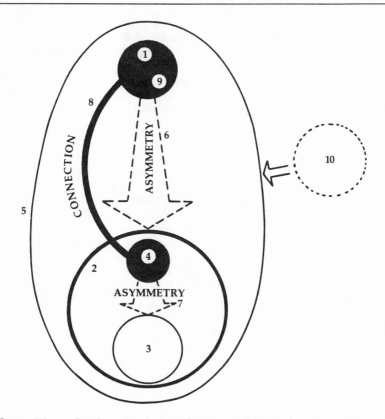

1. Centre (Metropolis, Core, North, capitalist, imperialist, Developed) countries.
2. Periphery (Satellite, South, non-communist, developing, LDCs, Third World) countries.
3. periphery in the Periphery
4. centre in the Periphery   class structure of the Periphery
   (indigenous bourgeois or
   semi-bourgeois elites)
5. Predicament of 'parts'—a consequence of the whole structure of the international system.
6. Asymmetrical, unequal, exploitative relationship favours mainly the Centre.
7. Asymmetrical, unequal, exploitative relationship reproduced within the Periphery.
8. 'Symbiotic' connection between the Centre and centre in Periphery.

'Optional' features:
9. Analysis of the (class) structure of the Centre.
10. Addition to the model of another 'unit' in different positions diluting, mediating or offsetting the main relationship with corresponding changes to the remaining parts of the model, as for example (a) semi-periphery; (b) 'Second World' (in the Chinese model); (c) 'socialist bloc' excluded from the Dependency relationship and capable of assisting the Periphery (Third World) in breaking out of the relationship.

Figure [1]. Rudiments of Dependency

Thus the Dependency relationship is defined as the dominance of the industrial nations within the international system, and the constraints which are operative in consequence over the internal development of the less developed economies. To many of the writers Dependency is understood as a *conditioning* context—the resultant, as it were, of the existence and functioning of certain types of internal and external structures. The structures condition the situation that causes underdeveloped countries to be both backward and exploited. The development of capitalism is believed invariably to lead to the combined and unequal development of its constituent parts: 'unequal' insofar as the development of parts of the system occurs at the cost of the underdevelopment of other parts; and 'combined' in that it is the combination of inequalities in conjunction with the transfer of resources from underdeveloped to developed countries that explains inequality, reinforces it and transforms it into a necessary and structural element of the world economy. The chief culprit throughout is the international system, the matrix within which Dependency operates and the context in which it is to be viewed. Underdevelopment and development are partially interdependent processes and structures within the global system, with the interconnected duality of dominant and dependent actors who are not simply at different *stages* of their development but are locked into their separate positions for the performance of certain *functions* within an overall international structure of reproduction and distribution. As Smith so aptly puts it, the dependent (underdeveloped) part is hooked, as it were, onto the dominant (developed) one: it cannot exist without dependence, and nor can it exist with it since it lacks the autonomous capacity for change and growth. Whilst the Centre revels in its military power the Third World shrivels to impotence. In the Periphery, the Centre's developed communications networks are paralleled by primitive lines at best, and at worst none. The cultural flowering at the Centre is mirrored in pale reflection at the Periphery. The Centre is assertive and self-reliant, the Periphery is dependent on and submissive to the whims and vagaries of foreign interest.

(4) The asymmetry derives not only from the unequal distribution of wealth but also from the perceived exploitative relationship that allows one party to grow at the expense of the other. The way in which this is done, however, is not made entirely clear and its analysis differs from one author to the next. Indeed, there is 'as much variety of opinion and analysis within it as could be found among the bourgeois development theories that Marxists so trenchantly criticised'. The spectrum of opinion is wide on this point: whilst the Marxist Geoffrey Kay argues that the crux of the matter is that the Centre *did not exploit the Periphery enough*, owing to the unduly prolonged dominance of the Third World by merchant capital (giving rise to wide in-depth differences in underdevelopment), such authors as Frank, at the other end of the spectrum, argue to the contrary that the Periphery was subjected to too much exploitation, and that contact with the Centre 'blocked transition', or any possibility thereof. Hence Frank's well known dictum 'development of underdevelopment' and the active process of 'appendagisation' and distortion. To correspond with this variety in viewpoints, conclusions dealing

with the possibility of Third World growth reflect a similar range, from the unequivocal position of Frank that sees immiseration as the end result of Dependency, through the middle position of (early) Furtado, Sunkel and Dos Santos, to the mild reformism of, for example, Cardoso, who conceives of some growth as still possible but that dependent countries will always remain committed to a subservient or 'marginalised' role.

(5) The asymmetrical mechanisms vary also in their explanation. Whilst authors such as Galtung point to the different nature of exchanged commodities, and consequently the unfavourable (to the Periphery) division of labour, most Dependency writers agree with Arghiri Emmanuel that the essence of unequal exchange does not lie exclusively, nor even primarily, in the nature of the commodities but chiefly in the differences in the *relative level of processing* of the commodities exchanged. To Emmanuel the key factor of unequal exchange is the difference in wage rates between rich and poor countries, and thus '[t]he worsening of the terms of trade for primary products is an optical illusion. It results from a mistaken identification of the exports of manufactured goods and the exports of poor countries with the exports of primary products.' Although the claim is made that the theory of unequal exchange derives from Marx's theory of surplus value, the consequences of Emmanuel's unequal exchange would seem to be contrary to the main thrust of classical Marxism in respect of its 'de-proletarianisation' of Marx's cherished Western proletariat. The belief that the major beneficiary of unequal exchange are workers in the Centre is difficult to reconcile with the classical Marxian terms of reference, since it makes absolute even Lenin's concept of a labour aristocracy and redefines 'class' so as to place the emphasis on external and international rather than on internal factors. In more specific terms, class is now defined by reference to an international division of labour. Thus the theory of unequal exchange leads its proponents to an absolute globalisation of class conflict insofar as the whole of the Centre becomes class-homogenised: once class is defined internationally in terms of the position of groups with respect to the international division of labour, the actual ownership of the means of production—so implicitly for Marx (and explicitly for Lenin) a sine qua non of class—suffers a loss of meaning.

READING # 20   Dependency Theory and Modern World Systems: A Liberal Critique
Robert Gilpin

Robert Gilpin, in the following reading, provides a critical analysis of dependency and modern world systems (MWS) by attributing economic performance in lesser developing countries primarily to factors relevant to their domestic economic efficiency. He thus rejects, in a fashion suggestive of neoclassical liberal analysis, conceptual frameworks based on theoretical notions of core and periphery.

The portrayal of poverty amidst plenty by neoclassical liberal analysis of political economy is different from that of neo-Marxist perspectives. Liberals tend to reverse the emphasis from poverty to plenty by claiming that plenty can be produced in a world of scarcity or poverty.

An abiding faith in the capacity of markets to accomplish the aims of distributive justice while preserving individual liberty sets liberals apart from theorists who envision international exchange as the mechanism of injustice. Liberals tend to oppose the political rhetoric and policy recommendations associated with the norms and values of distributive justice. (For further elaboration of this point, see Reading #28 by Miriam Camps, with Catherine Gwin.)

The logic of economic liberalism is as follows:

1. Authoritative attempts to redistribute benefits in society are not only morally wrong but also literally and practically counterproductive.
2. Efficient economic growth based on the dynamics of supply and demand in competitive markets alone provides the keys to achieving equitable social development.
3. Thus, efficiency serves as a socioeconomic priority over distributive justice, and increasing productivity is the optimal way of eliminating poverty.

Gilpin recognizes the importance of wealth and financial power in shaping development, but he refers to the emergence of newly industrialized countries as a prime example of what efficiency can do to reduce poverty. He implies that the concepts of core and periphery are no longer valid as units of analysis in world political economy, since the Third World may no longer be correctly conceived as a single formation.

The import of Gilpin's analysis is that lesser developing countries should strive to attract more, not less, capital and financial investment from advanced industrial societies by creating efficient domestic economies capable of competing effectively in world markets. The policy strategies advanced by liberal perspectives as best suited to achieving the aims of distributive justice and equity are thus market formulas. "The capacity of the state to order its priorities and its willingness to let loose market forces," Gilpin concludes, "have been the most important factors in those countries that have successfully developed their economies."

—E. W.

Although the study of economic development has failed to produce a body of developmental theory accepted by the whole fraternity of liberal economists, there is general agreement on several points.

Robert Gilpin, *The Political Economy of International Relations.* Copyright © 1987 by Princeton University Press. Excerpt, pp. 83–85, 263–269, and 288–290, reprinted with permission of Princeton University Press; endnotes deleted.

Liberalism maintains that an interdependent world economy based on free trade, specialization, and an international division of labor facilitates domestic development. Flows of goods, capital, and technology increase optimum efficiency in resource allocation and therefore transmit growth from the developed nations to the less developed countries. Trade can serve as an "engine of growth" as the less developed economy gains capital, technology, and access to world markets. This is a mutually beneficial relationship since the developed economies can obtain cheaper raw materials and outlets for their capital and manufactured goods. Because the less developed economies have smaller markets, opening trade with advanced economies is believed to benefit them relatively more than it does the developed economies. Moreover, since the factors of production flow to those areas where they produce the highest rewards, a less developed economy with a surplus of labor and a deficit of savings can obtain infusions of foreign capital that accelerate growth.

This theory of economic growth believes that many factors required for economic development are diffused from the advanced core of the world economy to the less developed economies in the periphery. The rate and direction of this spread effect are dependent upon a number of factors: the international migration of economic factors (capital, labor, knowledge); the volume, terms and composition of foreign trade; and the mechanics of the international monetary system. Although liberals recognize that economic progress is not uniform throughout the economy (domestic or international), they do believe that over the long term the operation of market forces leads toward equalization of economic levels, real wages, and factor prices among nations and regions of the globe. . . .

To support this thesis regarding the growth-inducing effects of international trade, liberal economists contrast the amazing economic success of the "export-led" growth strategies of the Asian NICs with the failure of the "import substitution" strategy of most Latin American countries. . . . Liberal economists find the basic obstacles to economic development within the less developed countries themselves: . . . the preponderance of subsistence agriculture, a lack of technical education, a low propensity to save, a weak financial system, and most important, inefficient government policies. They believe that once such bottlenecks are removed and a market begins to function efficiently, the economy will begin its escape from economic backwardness.

Most liberals consider that the key to economic development is the capacity of the economy to transform itself in response to changing conditions; they believe that the failure of many less developed countries to adjust to changing prices and economic opportunities is rooted in their social and political systems rather than in the operation of the international market system. . . . As Arthur Lewis has put it, any economy can develop if it has three simple ingredients: adequate rainfall, a system of secondary education, and sensible government. For the liberal, therefore, the question is not why the poor are poor but, as Adam Smith phrased it in *The Wealth of Nations,* why certain societies have overcome the obstacles to development, have transformed themselves, and through adapting to changing economic conditions have become rich. The answer given is that these successful societies have permitted the market to develop unimpeded by political interference. . . .

Failure to develop is ascribed to domestic market imperfections, economic inefficiencies, and social rigidities. Political corruption, a parasitic social and bureaucratic structure, and the failure to make appropriate investments in education, agriculture, and other prerequisites for economic development restrain these nations. Improper public policies such as high tariff barriers and overvalued currencies harmful to export interests are fostered by burdensome bureaucracies, urban bias, and economic nationalism. Although the advanced economies can indeed hinder the progress of the less developed economies by such restrictive practices as protectionist policies against Third World exports and could accelerate their development through foreign aid, liberals believe that each country bears its own responsibility for achieving meaningful change.

Accelerated capital accumulation is one vital foundation for development; this requires an increase in the domestic rate of saving. Although the advanced economies can and perhaps should assist in the process of capital formation through loans, foreign investment, and international assistance, the task rests with the less developed nations themselves. An unwillingness to suppress domestic consumption and to save is frequently considered to be the most serious retardant of economic growth. As Lewis, a sympathetic student of the LDC problems, has argued, "no nation is so poor that it could not save 12 percent of its national income if it wanted to," . . . and this amount is sufficient to put it firmly on the path of economic development.

Defending this position, proponents point out that the most successful economies among the less developed countries are precisely those that have put their own houses in order and that participate most aggressively in the world economy. They are the so-called Gang of Four: Hong Kong, Singapore, South Korea, and Taiwan. Although these newly industrializing countries have received great infusions of capital and technology from the advanced countries, they have mainly helped themselves and have established flourishing export markets. The least integrated economies, such as Albania and Burma, are among the most backward. Meanwhile, in the 1980s, even Communist China has realized its need for Western assistance, and Eastern Europe, along with the Soviet Union itself, seeks Western capital and advanced technology.

Beyond the general agreement on the primacy of internal factors, liberal development theories differ profoundly among themselves on the appropriate strategy for a less developed economy. In the first place, they disagree on the role of and the extent to which the advanced countries can or should assist the less developed ones; some advocate massive assistance programs in order to break what is called "the vicious cycle of LDC poverty"; other more conservative economists regard such outside efforts as wasteful or counterproductive. They also differ among themselves about whether a series of rather definable stages exists through which a developing economy must progress, or whether there are as many routes to development as national experiences. Some may stress balanced growth as the proper means for breaking out of historic poverty; others stress unbalanced growth. They vary regarding the emphasis given to agriculture or to industrial development. They also take different positions on the issue of efficiency versus equity in the process of economic development and on the role of the state in achieving one or the other. . . .

In summary, in the absence of a commonly accepted body of theoretical ideas, the debate among liberal economists over economic development is focused on strategic choices and alternative routes to economic development, that is, the determination of economic policies to achieve an efficient market economy. They share the conviction that the two foremost causes of international poverty are inadequate integration of the less developed countries into the world economy and irrational state policies that impede the development of a well-functioning market. For most liberal economists, then, the poor are poor because they are inefficient.

Liberal theory, however, tends to neglect the political framework within which economic development takes place, yet the process of economic development cannot be divorced from political factors. The domestic and international configurations of power and the interests of powerful groups and states are important determinants of economic development. The liberal theory is not necessarily wrong in neglecting these elements and focusing exclusively on the market; rather this theory is incomplete. For example, economic flexibility and the capacity of the economy to respond to changing economic opportunities are highly dependent upon the social and political aspects of a society. How else can one explain the remarkable economic achievements of resource-poor Japan and the troubles of resource-rich Argentina? Or, to take another issue, it is certainly correct to focus attention upon the crucial role of increased agricultural productivity in the economic development of Western Europe and the "lands of recent settlement" such as North America, Argentina, and South Africa. However, the fact that these fertile temperate lands were acquired by Europeans through the use of military force is also important to understanding the racial dimensions of the North-South division. In short, economic factors alone will not explain success or failure in economic development. . . .

The emphasis of the theory of the Modern World System on "the historical structure of the world political economy" also makes a valuable contribution to our understanding of the dynamics of the international political economy. . . . The setting of ideas, technology, and social forces within which state and market operate creates opportunities and constraints on political and economic behavior. The state could not exist, in fact, without the supporting ideology of nationalism; nor could the market survive without liberalism. This theory, however, is flawed by its economic determinism and its static conception of the international political economy.

According to this theory, the international political economy must be viewed as an integrated structure of core and periphery. The primary nexus of this system is the hierarchical international division of labor, which determines the place of a society in the system. The structure of the world economy is responsible both for the external relations and the internal characteristics of individual societies. The essential structure of the Modern World System, this theory argues, was put into place in the sixteenth century and has not been substantially altered over the succeeding three centuries.

The argument that the pluralist European state system was a necessary condition for the rise of a market economy is an important insight. Every state has a powerful disposition to attempt to gain control over economic activities and to make them serve its ends. The sufficient conditions for the rise of a world market economy, however, were the economic, institutional, and technological developments stressed by the dual economy theorists. One cannot, for example, reduce the development and subsequent evolution of science, which has so profoundly transformed the modern world, to the propositions advanced by supporters of the MWS theory. Nor can one account for the dynamics of the international system, as this position tends to do, solely in terms of the evolution of market forces.

Although the argument of the MWS theory that the world economy should be understood in hierarchical and structural terms is a necessary corrective to the emphasis . . . on an egalitarian and disaggregated market, it errs in several important particulars. First, although the economic structure does significantly influence the policies of powerful states, it is equally influenced by them. Second, the nexus among states is primarily political and strategic rather than economic, and political relations provide the framework for economic activities. Third, whether a state is "soft" or "hard" (for example, Argentina and Japan, respectively) is basically a function of internal social and political factors. Fourth, as the Japanese today and the Germans before them have proven, more than anything else it is the nature of the society and its policies that determine its position in the international division of labor. Fifth, the structure of the international market has changed dramatically over the past several centuries due to the evolution of the international division of labor and the changing position of economies in the system.

The argument that the structure of the world economy has been static is patently wrong. The market economy, as Marx pointed out, develops the world. It is an evolutionary system that over time has incorporated more and more of the world. The colonial empires of the early modern period integrated a very small fraction of Asia, Africa, and the New World into the so-called Modern World System; the largest segment of the world's periphery of traditional economies . . . lay outside the system. Until the end of the nineteenth century, in fact, Europe remained relatively self-sufficient in food and raw materials. It could feed itself and possessed most of its required industrial raw materials, especially coal and iron. . . . Only with the second phase of the Industrial Revolution and the huge growth of population late in the century did the European core require commodity imports; these came, however, mainly from the "lands of recent settlement" in the temperate zones and a few tropical entrants into the system. . . . What the MWS theorists call the periphery remained marginal until quite recently.

In truth, the modern world system in its present form did not really come into existence until the decades immediately preceding the First World War, when the dominant industrial economies emerged. The same countries that were important prior to the First World War were still the core economies in the post-1945 period. Most of the lands that Wallerstein and others would later assign to the periphery have been largely ignored by traders and investors until relatively recently (except for slaves and precious metals). The contemporary international division of labor between the industrialized Northern core and the nonindustrialized Southern periphery actually took shape in the closing decades of the last century. As Arthur Lewis . . . has shown, the modern world system is less than a hundred years old.

Contrary to the views of the MWS theorists, the modern world system was a consequence of the development of the North rather than the cause of its development. It has been the rapid development of the core and its need for food and raw materials that has led to the integration of the periphery into the system and the subsequent growth of those peripheral economies that could take advantage of this fact. As one Marxist economist has argued, modern capitalist economies have not been dependent upon exploitation of the periphery for their development, and the growth of the capitalist economies was due to the achievement of internal efficiency. . . . The Northern core has served as an engine of growth for the South throughout this history. The world economy diffuses rather than concentrates wealth.

Although it is appropriate to view the world economy as a hierarchical structure or system composed of core and periphery, it should be noted that the geographic locus of the core and the global distribution of economic activities have shifted continuously over the past three centuries, from the Mediterranean to the North Atlantic and, in our own age, toward the Pacific. The emergence of new industrial powers in Asia and Latin America is transforming the international division of labor and has resulted in profound changes in the leadership and nature of the international political economy. Providing a better understanding of the causes and consequences of this dynamic process is a major challenge. . . .

The crux of the dependency argument is that the world market or capitalist international economy operates systematically to thwart the development of the Third World. Therefore, evidence that individual countries have been exploited is not sufficient to support the theory. Although it is undeniable that, in particular cases, an alliance of foreign capitalists and domestic elites has contributed to an economy's underdevelopment, for example, the Philippines of Ferdinand Marcos, the charge of a systematic and functional relationship between capitalism and underdevelopment cannot be supported.

It should be noted that a single independent variable—the functioning of the international economy—is being used to explain three quite distinct types of phenomena found in the Third World: underdevelopment, marginalization, and dependent development. . . . From a simple methodological point of view, something is wrong with any theory in which a single independent variable is used to explain three mutually exclusive outcomes. Dependency theory is replete with ad hoc hypotheses and tautological arguments intended to account for these very different phenomena.

The general argument that the LDCs as a group have remained commodity exporters, have been exploited, and have been kept undeveloped is simply not true. Although many examples of this type of dependency relationship continue to exist in the late twentieth century, the overall argument cannot be sustained. By the late 1980s, only the countries of south Saharan Africa and a few others remained impoverished commodity exporters. Although the terms of trade for commodities have shown no secular tendency to decline, the business cycle is very damaging to those less developed countries that have failed to transform their economies. On the other hand, with the important exception of Japan, the LDCs as a group have grown faster in recent years than the advanced countries. . . . In brief, little evidence supports the charge that the international economy operates systematically to the disadvantage of the LDCs.

The charge of underdevelopment and dependency theorists that the world market economy has neglected and bypassed many countries in the Third World is correct. The process of global economic integration that began in the latter part of the nineteenth century and has expanded trade and investment among developed and less developed countries has been a highly uneven one. The simple fact is that both nineteenth-century imperialism and the operations of twentieth-century multinational corporations have left many of the world's traditional economies untouched because they found too little there to be "exploited." This marginalization of destitute areas (the Fourth and Fifth Worlds) such as the Sahel and other parts of Africa, however, constitutes a sin of omission rather than one of commission. The most serious threat faced by much of the Third World, in fact, is not dependence but the likelihood of continued neglect and further marginalization. What has been lacking in the postwar world, as John Ruggie . . . has noted, is an adequate international regime whose purpose is global economic development. But this failing is not just that of the capitalist world; it is also a failing of the socialist bloc and the wealthy oil producers. It should be noted that the West has been far more generous than the socialist bloc or OPEC producers.

The claim that the dependent or associated development exemplified by the newly industrializing countries of Brazil, South Korea, and other countries is not "true" development is, of course, largely normative. . . . However, even if one accepts the position that the objective of development ought to be national independence, social welfare, and autonomous industrialization, the evidence in support of the above contention is mixed. Many present-day developed and independent countries previously followed the road of dependent development. As those Marxist writers who incorporate Marx's own views on the subject appreciate, dependent development in a growing number of less developed countries has begun a process of sustained industrialization and economic growth. . . . In fact, the success of the NICs may be partially attributable to the legacy of Japanese imperialism. . . .

Bill Warren, writing in the tradition of Marx, Lenin, and other classical Marxists, has provided a clear assessment of what is taking place among the less developed countries: "If the extension of capitalism into non-capitalist areas of the world created an international system of inequality and exploitation called imperialism, it simultaneously created the conditions for the destruction of this system by the spread of capitalist social relations and productive forces throughout the non-capitalist world. Such has been our thesis, as it was the thesis of Marx, Lenin, Luxemburg and Bukharin." . . . However, it must be added that economic development will not occur unless the society has put its own house in proper order. As liberals stress, economic development will not take place unless the society has created efficient economic institutions.

The available evidence suggests that neither integration into the world economy nor economic isolation can guarantee economic development. The former can lock a country into an export specialization that harms the overall development of its economy. High export earnings from a particular commodity and powerful export interests can hinder diversification; export overdependence and fluctuating prices create vulnerabilities that can damage an economy. On the other hand, economic isolation can cause massive misallocations of resources and inefficiencies that thwart the long-term growth of an economy. What is important for economic development and escape from dependence is the capacity of the economy to transform itself. This task is ultimately the responsibility of its own economic and political leadership. As Norman Gall . . . has cogently shown, too many of the less developed countries have suffered the consequences of poor leadership. . . .

However elaborate and sophisticated it might appear, every theory of poverty and of escape from it can be reduced to one or a combination of the following formulations: (1) that the poor are poor because they are inefficient (essentially the position of economic liberalism) and therefore must create an efficient economy; (2) that the poor are poor because they are powerless or exploited (the argument of most contemporary Marxists and dependency theorists) and therefore must acquire national power; or (3) that the poor are poor because they are poor, that is, they are caught in a vicious cycle of poverty from which they cannot escape (the view of traditional Marxists and present-day structuralists) and therefore somehow this cycle must be broken. The development strategy advocated for the less developed countries is largely dependent on which interpretation one believes to be correct.

CHAPTER FIVE

The New Transnationalism: Toward a Political Economy of Transnational Modes of Production

---

READING #21   The Multinational Corporation and the Law of Uneven Development

Stephen Hymer

Several mechanisms for coordinating economic activities have emerged in modern times, including states, markets, and transnational business enterprises. The relationships among them point to the very foundations of the world economy. The following reading by Stephen Hymer contributes to our understanding of the specific character of transnational business enterprises.

But even more than this, Hymer's analysis, originally published in 1972, represents a pioneering effort to examine transnational business enterprise and transnational modes of production in a manner relevant to world political economy, hence to uneven development, and, ultimately, to distributive justice. For all that has been written about the transnational business enterprise, few analyses have been as significant within the context of political economy. Hymer's presentation, in effect, provides a political economy of transnational business enterprise. He begins by examining the transformation of business enterprises from pre-capitalist family firms to modern transnational conglomerates and proceeds to explore the connection between transnational business and uneven development. It is this emphasis throughout Hymer's analysis of the processes of production and the control of international finance by transnational business enterprise, on the one hand, and the social impacts of such economic power especially within developing countries, on the other, that renders the following reading a political economy of transnational business enterprise.

A transnational business enterprise may be characterized as a firm operating for profit within or across two or more societies or sovereign jurisdictions in order to enhance profits and reduce costs during production, marketing, and distribution of commodities and services. Transnational business enterprises carry with them a "package" of investment capital, managerial expertise, and technological know-how that often gives them a competitive edge over smaller or nationally based firms. Thus they can and often do dominate international trade and production by helping to create oligarchic market structures in which a few sellers or suppliers provide goods or services for many buyers in a wide range of product lines.

A transnational business enterprise may be privately or publicly owned and operated. It is usually composed of a head office in one country and branches or subsidiaries in several others. Although these firms function in many countries, they tend to be financially and administratively based in one country. As Hymer observes, transnational business enterprises are managed at the top by individuals usually of the same nationality. Thus, a single economy, such as that of the United States or Japan, but even that of a lesser developing country, more often than not provides the major proportion of financial assets and the primary research base for a transnational business enterprise.

In this sense, the term *multinational corporation* is misleading. Although transnational business enterprises do function in many countries, they tend to be directed and financed from one country in particular. But they are not, as Hymer makes clear, identical to traditional "corporations" in the sense of a single body or corporate entity. Transnational business enterprises are composed of many subsidiary enterprises and branch-plants owned outright or proportionately by means of direct investments rather than "portfolio shares."

The basic features of a transnational business enterprise thus often include single home-country origins, multiple subsidiary facilities or branch-plants, specialized kinds of production in several host-countries, and coordination and policy control over global strategy by centralized management. Moreover, the transnational business enterprise represents transnational modes of production that cut both vertically and horizontally across the economies of many states in the form of vertical centralization of management and horizontal diffusion of production tasks across many countries and many plant facilities.

Hymer's essential argument is that transnational business enterprise fosters uneven or underdevelopment by means of such vertical and horizontal divisions of labor. Vertical divisions of labor measure the distance between home office and subsidiary or branch-plant. This "vertical" distance may be calculated geographically—that is, in terms of the space separating capital or managerial cities such as New York, London, and Tokyo from cities that host branch-plant facilities, mostly in East Asia and Latin America. But vertical divisions of labor are more accurately judged by distances separating levels of managers from each other. Within capital cities, for example, senior managers direct the flow, or circulation, of financial investment and technology throughout the transnational enterprise. Thus they "manage the managers," who, in turn, manage the lower echelons, who direct specified production activities or local distribution and marketing campaigns.

Vertical integration of the transnational enterprise and its conglomerate, as well as the consequent transnational penetration of several subordinate economies, leads to a horizontal division of labor involving not only the dispersion of industrial branch-plants but also the creation of branch-plant sectors or enclaves within lesser developing economies. Such sectors, in Hymer's analysis, represent conceptual equivalents of "the core within the periphery" described in Reading #19.

As Hymer demonstrates, one great advantage of transnational business enterprise is its capacity to control flows of investment capital from one country or region to another and to direct research, development, and the circulation of technology within the world economy. Consequently, it can create horizontal forms of division of labor in which certain sectors of developing economies specialize in specific kinds of production geared to the overall objectives of transnational enterprise.

Horizontal divisions of labor thus involve *delocalization of industry.* Branch-plants are established within growth- or Core-oriented capitalist enclaves that have little or nothing to do with the demand structure of the host economy. Workers make running shoes that they do not want and will never wear, or they produce silicon semiconductor chips that their economy cannot absorb. Industry linked to the Core but located in the Periphery is, in this sense, delocalized.

To be sure, much of the investment of transnational business enterprise from within the Core has flowed back into it. American conglomerates tended in the 1960s and 1970s, for example, to invest in European transnational business enterprises, just as Japanese investments in the 1980s have tended to flow into the United States. To the extent that transnational investments have circulated from advanced to lesser developing countries, however, they have promoted, at least in terms of the following analysis, vertical and horizontal divisions of labor between capital-intensive, high-wage, high-productivity economies and labor-intensive, low-wage, low-productivity economies, all in the name of corporate efficiency and global economies of scale.

—E. W.

The settler's town is a strongly-built town, all made of stone and steel. It is a brightly-lit town; the streets are covered with asphalt, and the garbage-

Excerpt, pp. 113–129, reprinted with permission of Macmillan Publishing Company from Stephen Hymer, "The Multinational Corporation and the Law of Uneven Development," in J. W. Bhagwati, ed., *Economics and World Order.* Copyright © 1972 by Macmillan Publishing Company. Endnotes deleted.

cans swallow all the leavings, unseen, unknown and hardly thought about. The settler's feet are never visible, except perhaps in the sea; but there you're never close enough to see them. His feet are protected by strong shoes although the streets of his town are clean and even, with no holes or stones. The settler's town is a well-fed town, an easy-going town, its belly is always full of good things. The settler's town is a town of white people, of foreigners.

The town belonging to the colonized people, or at least the native town, the Negro village, the medina, the reservation, is a place of ill fame peopled by men of evil repute. They are born there, it matters little where or how; they die there, it matters not where nor how. It is a world without spaciousness: men live there on top of each other, and their huts are built one on top of the other. The native town is a hungry town, starved of bread, of meat, of shoes, of coal, of light. The native town is a crouching village, a town on its knees, a town wallowing in the mire. It is a town of niggers and dirty Arabs. The look that the native turns on the settler's town is a look of lust, of envy . . .

—Fanon, *The Wretched of the Earth*

We have been asked to look into the future towards the year 2000. This essay attempts to do so in terms of two laws of economic development: the Law of Increasing Firm Size and the Law of Uneven Development.

Since the beginning of the Industrial Revolution, there has been a tendency for the representative firm to increase in size from the *workshop* to the *factory* to the *national corporation* to the *multi-divisional corporation* and now to the *multinational corporation*. This growth has been qualitative as well as quantitative. With each step, business enterprise acquired a more complex administrative structure to coordinate its activities and a larger brain to plan for its survival and growth. The first part of this essay traces the evolution of the corporation stressing the development of a hierarchical system of authority and control.

The remainder of the essay is concerned with extrapolating the trends in business enterprise (the microcosm) and relating them to the evolution of the international economy (the macrocosm). Until recently, most multinational corporations have come from the United States, where private business enterprise has reached its largest size and most highly developed forms. Now European corporations, as a by-product of increased size, and as a reaction to the American invasion of Europe, are also shifting attention from national to global production and beginning to "see the world as their oyster." If present trends continue, multinationalization is likely to increase greatly in the next decade as giants from both sides of the Atlantic (though still mainly from the U.S.) strive to penetrate each other's markets and to establish bases in underdeveloped countries, where there are few indigenous concentrations of capital sufficiently large to operate on a world scale. This rivalry may be intense at first but will probably abate through time and turn into collusion as firms approach some kind of oligopolistic equilibrium.

A new structure of international industrial organization and a new international division of labor will have been born.

What will be the effect of this latest stage in the evolution of business enterprise on the Law of Uneven Development, i.e., the tendency of the system to produce poverty as well as wealth, underdevelopment as well as development? The second part of this essay suggests that a regime of North Atlantic Multinational Corporations would tend to produce a hierarchical division of labor between geographical regions corresponding to the vertical division of labor within the firm. It would tend to centralize high-level decision-making occupations in a few key cities in the advanced countries, surrounded by a number of regional sub-capitals, and confine the rest of the world to lower levels of activity and income, i.e., to the status of towns and villages in a New Imperial System. Income, status, authority, and consumption patterns would radiate out from these centers along a declining curve, and the existing pattern of inequality and dependency would be perpetuated. The pattern would be complex, just as the structure of the corporation is complex, but the basic relationship between different countries would be one of superior and subordinate, head office and branch plant.

How far will this tendency of corporations to create a world in their own image proceed? The situation is a dynamic one, moving dialectically. Right now, we seem to be in the midst of a major revolution in international relationships as modern science establishes the technological basis for a major advance in the conquest of the material world and the beginnings of truly cosmopolitan production. Multinational corporations are in the vanguard of this revolution, because of their great financial and administrative strength and their close contact with the new technology. Governments (outside the military) are far behind, because of their narrower horizons and perspectives, as are labor organizations and most non-business institutions and associations. (As John Powers, President of Charles Pfizer Corporation, has put it, "Practice is ahead of theory and policy.") Therefore, in the first round, multinational corporations are likely to have a certain degree of success in organizing markets, decision making, and the spread of information in their own interest. However, their very success will create tensions and conflicts which will lead to further development. . . .

I. The Evolution of the Multinational Corporation

The Marshallian Firm and the Market Economy

Giant organizations are nothing new in international trade. They were a characteristic form of the mercantilist period when large joint-stock companies, e.g., The Hudson's Bay Co., The Royal African Co., The East India Co., to name the major English merchant firms, organized long-distance trade with America, Africa and Asia. But neither these firms, nor the large mining and plantation enterprises in the production sector, were the forerunners of the multinational corporation. They were like dinosaurs, large in bulk, but small in brain, feeding on the lush vegetation of the new worlds (the planters and miners in America were . . . *Tyrannosaurus rex*).

The activities of these international merchants, planters and miners laid the groundwork for the Industrial Revolution by concentrating capital in the metropolitan center, but the driving force came from the small-scale capitalist enterprises in manufacturing, operating at first in the interstices of the feudalist economic structure, but gradually emerging into the open and finally gaining predominance. It is in the small workshops, organized by the newly emerging capitalist class, that the forerunners of the modern corporation are to be found.

The strength of this new form of business enterprise lay in its power and ability to reap the benefits of cooperation and division of labor. Without the capitalist, economic activity was individualistic, small-scale, scattered, and unproductive. But a man with capital, *i.e.*, with sufficient funds to buy raw materials and advance wages, could gather a number of people into a single shop and obtain as his reward the increased productivity that resulted from social production. The reinvestment of these profits led to a steady increase in the size of capitals, making further division of labor possible and creating an opportunity for using machinery in production. A phenomenal increase in productivity and production resulted from this process, and entirely new dimensions of human existence were opened. The growth of capital revolutionized the entire world and, figuratively speaking, even battered down the Great Wall of China.

The hallmarks of the new system were the *market* and the *factory*, representing the two different methods of coordinating the division of labor. In the factory entrepreneurs consciously plan and organize cooperation, and the relationships are hierarchical and authoritarian; in the market coordination is achieved through a decentralized, unconscious, competitive process.

To understand the significance of this distinction, the new system should be compared to the structure it replaced. In the pre-capitalist system of production, the division of labor was hierarchically structured at the *macro* level, *i.e.*, for society as a whole, but unconsciously structured at the *micro* level, *i.e.*, the actual process of production. Society as a whole was partitioned into various castes, classes, and guilds, on a rigid and authoritarian basis so that political and social stability could be maintained and adequate numbers assured for each industry and occupation. Within each sphere of production, however, individuals by and large were independent and their activities only loosely coordinated, if at all. In essence, a guild was composed of a large number of similar individuals, each performing the same task in roughly the same way with little cooperation or division of labor. This type of organization could produce high standards of quality and workmanship but was limited quantitatively to low levels of output per head.

The capitalist system of production turned this structure on its head. The macro system became unconsciously structured, while the micro system became hierarchically structured. The market emerged as a self-regulating coordinator of business units as restrictions on capital markets and labor mobility were removed. (Of course the State remained above the market as a conscious coordinator to maintain the system and ensure the growth of capital.) At the micro level, that is the level of production, labor was gathered under the authority of the entrepreneur capitalist.

Marshall, like Marx, stressed that the internal division of labor within the factory, between those who planned and those who worked (between "undertakers" and laborers), was the "chief fact in the form of modern civilization, the 'kernel' of the modern economic problem." Marx, however, stressed the authoritarian and unequal nature of this relationship based on the coercive power of property and its anti-social characteristics. He focused on the irony that concentration of wealth in the hands of a few and its ruthless use were necessary historically to demonstrate the value of cooperation and the social nature of production.

Marshall, in trying to answer Marx, argued for the voluntary cooperative nature of the relationship between capital and labor. In his view, the *market* reconciled individual freedom and collective production. He argued that those on top achieved their position because of their superior organizational ability, and that their relation to the workers below them was essentially harmonious and not exploitative. "Undertakers" were not captains of industry because they had capital; they could obtain capital because they had the ability to be captains of industry. They retained their authority by merit, not by coercion; for according to Marshall, natural selection, operating through the market, constantly destroyed inferior organizers and gave everyone who had the ability—including workers—a chance to rise to managerial positions. Capitalists earned more than workers because they contributed more, while the system as a whole provided all its members, especially the workers, with improved standards of living and an ever-expanding field of choice of consumption.

The Corporate Economy

The evolution of business enterprise from the small workshop (Adam Smith's pin factory) to the Marshallian family firm represented only the first step in the development of business organization. As total capital accumulated, the size of the individual concentrations composing it increased continuously, and the vertical division of labor grew accordingly.

It is best to study the evolution of the corporate form in the United States environment, where it has reached its highest stage. In the 1870s, the United States industrial structure consisted largely of Marshallian type, single-function firms, scattered over the country. Business firms were typically tightly controlled by a single entrepreneur or small family group who, as it were, saw everything, knew everything and decided everything. By the early twentieth century, the rapid growth of the economy and the great merger movement had consolidated many functions over many regions. To meet this new strategy of continent-wide, vertically integrated production and marketing, a new administrative structure evolved. The family firm, tightly controlled by a few men in close touch with all its aspects, gave way to the administrative pyramid of the corporation. Capital acquired new powers and new horizons. The domain or conscious coordination widened and that of market-directed division of labor contracted.

According to [A.] Chandler the railroad, which played so important a role in creating the national market, also offered a model for new forms of business organization. The need to administer geographically dispersed operations led railway companies to create an administrative structure which distinguished field offices from head offices. The field offices managed local operations; the head office supervised the field offices. According to [A.] Chandler and [F.] Redlich, this distinction is important because "it implies that the executive responsible for a firm's affairs had, for the first time, to supervise the work of other executives."

This first step towards increased vertical division of labor within the management function was quickly copied by the recently-formed national corporations which faced the same problems of coordinating widely scattered plants. Business developed an organ system of administration, and the modern corporation was born. The functions of business administration were sub-divided into *departments* (organs)—finance, personnel, purchasing, engineering, and sales—to deal with capital, labor, purchasing, manufacturing, etc. This horizontal division of labor opened up new possibilities for rationalizing production and for incorporating the advances of physical and social sciences into economic activity on a systematic basis. At the same time a "brain and nervous system," *i.e.*, a vertical system of control, had to be devised to connect and coordinate departments. This was a major advance in decision-making capabilities. It meant that a special group, the Head Office, was created whose particular function was to coordinate, appraise, and plan for the survival and growth of the organism as a whole. The organization became conscious of itself as [an] organization and gained a certain measure of control over its own evolution and development.

The corporation soon underwent further evolution. To understand this next step we must briefly discuss the development of the United States market. At the risk of great oversimplification, we might say that by the first decade of the twentieth century, the problem of production had essentially been solved. By the end of the nineteenth century, scientists and engineers had developed most of the inventions needed for mass producing at a low cost nearly all the main items of basic consumption. In the language of systems analysis, the problem became one of putting together the available components in an organized fashion. The national corporation provided *one* organizational solution, and by the 1920s it had demonstrated its great power to increase material production.

The question was which direction growth would take. One possibility was to expand mass production systems very widely and to make basic consumer goods available on a broad basis throughout the world. The other possibility was to concentrate on continuous innovation for a small number of people and on the introduction of new consumption goods even before the old ones had been fully spread. The latter course was in fact chosen, and we now have the paradox that 500 million people can receive a live TV broadcast from the moon while there is still a shortage of telephones in many advanced countries, to say nothing of the fact that so many people suffer from inadequate food and lack of simple medical help.

This path was associated with a choice of capital-deepening instead of capital-widening in the productive sector of the economy. As capital accumulated, business had to choose the degree to which it would expand labor proportionately to the growth of capital or, conversely, the degree to which they would substitute capital for labor. At one extreme business could have kept the capital-labor ratio constant and accumulated labor at the same rate they accumulated capital. This horizontal accumulation would soon have exhausted the labor force of any particular country and then either capital would have had to migrate to foreign countries or labor would have had to move into the industrial centers. Under this system, earnings per employed worker would have remained steady and the composition of output would have tended to remain constant as similar basic goods were produced on a wider and wider basis.

However, this path was not chosen, and instead capital per worker was raised, the rate of expansion of the industrial labor force was slowed down, and a dualism was created between a small, high wage, high productivity sector in advanced countries, and a large, low wage, low productivity sector in the less advanced.

The uneven growth of per capita income implied unbalanced growth and the need on the part of business to adapt to a constantly changing composition of output. Firms in the producers' goods sectors had continuously to innovate labor-saving machinery because the capital output ratio was increasing steadily. In the consumption goods sector, firms had continuously to introduce new products since, according to Engel's Law, people do not generally consume proportionately more of the same things as they get richer, but rather reallocate their consumption away from old goods and towards new goods. This non-proportional growth of demand implied that goods would tend to go through a life-cycle, growing rapidly when they were first introduced and more slowly later. If a particular firm were tied to only one product, its growth rate would follow this same life-cycle pattern and would eventually slow down and perhaps even come to a halt. If the corporation was to grow steadily at a rapid rate, it had continuously to introduce new products.

Thus, product development and marketing replaced production as a dominant problem of business enterprise. To meet the challenge of a constantly changing market, business enterprise evolved the multidivisional structure. The new form was originated by General Motors and Du Pont shortly after World War I, followed by a few others during the 1920s and 1930s, and was widely adopted by most of the giant U.S. corporations in the great boom following World War II. As with the previous stages, evolution involved a process of both differentiation and integration. Corporations were decentralized into several *divisions*, each concerned with one product line and organized with its own head office. At a higher level, a *general office* was created to coordinate the division and to plan for the enterprise as a whole.

The new corporate form has great flexibility. Because of its decentralized structure, a multidivisional corporation can enter a new market by adding a new division, while leaving the old divisions undisturbed. (And to a lesser extent it can leave the market by dropping a division without disturbing the rest of its structure.) It can also create competing product-lines in the same industry, thus increasing its market share while maintaining the illusion of competition. Most important of all, because it has a cortex specializing in strategy, it can plan on a much wider scale than before and allocate capital with more precision.

The modern corporation is a far cry from the small workshop or even from the Marshallian firm. The Marshallian capitalist ruled his factory from an office on the second floor. At the turn of the century, the president of a large national corporation was lodged in a higher building, perhaps on the seventh floor, with greater perspective and power. In today's giant corporation, managers rule from the tops of skyscrapers.

U.S. corporations began to move to foreign countries almost as soon as they had completed their continent-wide integration. For one thing, their new administrative structure and great financial strength gave them the power to go abroad. In becoming national firms, U.S. corporations learned how to become international. Also, their large size and oligopolistic position gave them an incentive. Direct investment became a new weapon in their arsenal of oligopolistic rivalry. Instead of joining a cartel (prohibited under U.S. law), they invested in foreign customers, suppliers, and competitors. For example, some firms found they were oligopolistic buyers of raw materials produced in foreign countries and feared a monopolization of the sources of supply. By investing directly in foreign producing enterprises, they could gain the security implicit in control over their raw material requirements. Other firms invested abroad to control marketing outlets and thus maximize quasi-rents on their technological discoveries and differentiated products. Some went abroad simply to forestall competition.

The first wave of U.S. direct foreign capital investment occurred around the turn of the century followed by a second wave during the 1920s. The outward migration slowed down during [the] depression but resumed after World War II and soon accelerated rapidly. Between 1950 and 1969, direct foreign investment by U.S. firms expanded at a rate of about 10 percent per annum. At this rate it would double in less than ten years, and even at a much slower rate of growth, foreign operations will reach enormous proportions over the next 30 years.

Several important factors account for this rush of foreign investment in the 1950s and the 1960s. First, the large size of the U.S. corporations and their new multidivisional structure gave them wider horizons and a global outlook. Secondly, technological developments in communications created a new awareness of the global challenge and threatened established institutions by opening up new sources of competition. For reasons noted above, business enterprises were among the first to recognize the potentialities and dangers of the new environment and to take active steps to cope with it.

A third factor in the outward migration of U.S. capital was the rapid growth of Europe and Japan. This, combined with the slow growth of the United States economy in the 1950s, altered world market shares as firms confined to the U.S. market found themselves falling behind in the competitive race and losing ground to European and Japanese firms, which were growing rapidly because of the expansion of their markets. Thus, in the late 1950s, United States corporations faced a serious "non-American" challenge. Their answer was an outward thrust to establish sales production and bases in foreign territories. This strategy was possible in Europe, since government there provided an open door for United States investment, but was blocked in Japan, where the government adopted a highly restrictive policy. To a large extent, United States business was thus able to redress the imbalances caused by the Common Market, but Japan remained a source of tension to oligopoly equilibrium.

What about the future? The present trend indicates further multinationalization of all giant firms, European as well as American. In the first place, European firms, partly as a reaction to the United States penetration of their markets, and partly as a natural result of their own growth, have begun to invest abroad on an expanded scale and will probably continue to do so in the future, and even enter into the United States market. This process is already well under way and may be expected to accelerate as time goes on. The reaction of United States business will most likely be to meet foreign investment at home with more foreign investment abroad. They, too, will scramble for market positions in underdeveloped countries and attempt to get an even larger share of the European market, as a reaction to European investment in the United States. Since they are large and powerful, they will on balance succeed in maintaining their relative standing in the world as a whole—as their losses in some markets are offset by gains in others.

A period of rivalry will prevail until a new equilibrium between giant U.S. firms and giant European and Japanese firms is reached, based on a strategy of multinational operations and cross-penetration. We turn now to the implications of this pattern of industrial organization for international trade and the law of uneven development.

II. Uneven Development

Suppose giant multinational corporations (say 300 from the U.S. and 200 from Europe and Japan) succeed in establishing themselves as the dominant form of international enterprise and come to control a significant share of industry (especially modern industry) in each country. The world economy will resemble more and more the United States economy, where each of the large corporations tends to spread over the entire continent and to penetrate almost every nook and cranny. What would be the effect of a world industrial organization of this type on international specialization, exchange, and income distribution? The purpose of this section is to analyze the spatial dimension of the corporate hierarchy.

A useful starting point is Chandler and Redlich's scheme for analyzing the evolution of corporate structure. They distinguish "three levels of business administration, three horizons, three levels of task, and three levels of decision making . . . and three levels of policies." Level III, the lowest level, is concerned with managing the day-to-day operations of the enterprise, that is, with keeping it going within the established framework. Level II, which first made its appearance with the separation of head office from field office, is responsible for coordinating the managers at Level III. The functions of Level I—top management—are goal-determination and planning. This level sets the framework in which the lower levels operate. In the Marshallian firm, all three levels are embodied in the single entrepreneur or undertaker. In the national corporation a partial differentiation is made in which the top two levels are separated from the bottom one. In the multidivisional corporation, the differentiation is far more complete. Level I is completely split off from Level II and concentrated in a general office whose specific function is to plan strategy rather than tactics.

The development of business enterprise can therefore be viewed as a process of centralizing and perfecting the process of capital accumulation. The Marshallian entrepreneur was a jack-of-all-trades. In the modern multidivisional corporation, a powerful general office consciously plans and organizes the growth of corporate capital. It is here that the key men who actually allocate the corporation's available resources (rather than act within the means allocated to them, as is true for the managers at lower levels) are located. Their power comes from their ultimate control over *men* and *money* and although one should not overestimate the ability to control a far-flung empire, neither should one underestimate it.

> The senior men could take action because they controlled the selection of executive personnel and because, through budgeting, they allocated the funds to the operating divisions. In the way they allocated their resources—capital and personnel—and in the promotion, transferral and retirement of operating executives, they determined the framework in which the operating units worked and thus put into effect their concept of the long term goals and objectives of the enterprise. . . . Ultimate authority in business enterprise, as we see it, rests with those who hold the purse strings, and in modern large-scale enterprises, those persons hold the purse strings who perform the functions of goal setting and planning.

What is the relationship between the structure of the microcosm and the structure of the macrocosm? The application of location theory to the Chandler-Redlich scheme suggests a *correspondence principle* relating centralization of control within the corporation to centralization of control within the international economy.

Location theory suggests that Level III activities would spread themselves over the globe according to the pull of manpower, markets, and raw materials. The multinational corporation, because of its power to command capital and technology and its ability to rationalize their use on a global scale, will probably spread production more evenly over the world's surface than is now the case. Thus, in the first instance, it may well be a force for diffusing industrialization to the less developed countries and creating new centers of production. (We postpone for a moment a discussion of the fact that location depends upon transportation, which in turn depends upon the government, which in turn is influenced by the structure of business enterprise.)

Level II activities, because of their need for white-collar workers, communications systems, and information, tend to concentrate in large cities. Since their demands are similar, corporations from different industries tend to place their coordinating offices in the same city, and Level II activities are consequently far more geographically concentrated than Level III activities.

Level I activities, the general offices, tend to be even more concentrated than Level II activities, for they must be located close to the capital market, the media, and the government. Nearly every major corporation in the United States, for example, must have its general office (or a large proportion of its high-level personnel) in or near the city of New York because of the need for face-to-face contact at higher levels of decision making.

Applying this scheme to the world economy, one would expect to find the highest offices of the multinational corporations concentrated in the world's major cities—New York, London, Paris, Bonn, Tokyo. These, along with Moscow and perhaps Peking, will be the major centers of high-level strategic planning. Lesser cities throughout the world will deal with the day-to-day operations of specific local problems. These in turn will be arranged in a hierarchical fashion: The larger and more important ones will contain regional corporate headquarters, while the smaller ones will be confined to lower level activities. Since business is usually the core of the city, geographical specialization will come to reflect the hierarchy of corporate decision making, and the occupational distribution of labor in a city or region will depend upon its function in the international economic system. The "best" and most highly paid administrators, doctors, lawyers, scientists, educators, government officials, actors, servants, and hairdressers, will tend to concentrate in or near the major centers.

The structure of income and compensation will tend to parallel the structure of status and authority. The citizens of capital cities will have the best jobs—allocating men and money at the highest level and planning growth and development—and will receive the highest rates of remuneration. (Executives' salaries tend to be a function of the wage bill of people under them. The larger the empire of the multinational corporation, the greater the earnings of top executives, to a large extent independent of their performance. Thus, growth in the hinterland subsidiaries implies growth in the income of capital cities, but not *vice versa*.)

The citizens of capital cities will also be the first to innovate new products in the cycle which is known in the marketing literature as trickle-down or two-stage marketing. A new product is usually first introduced to a select group of people who have "discretionary" income and are willing to experiment in their consumption patterns. Once it is accepted by this group, it spreads, or trickles down to other groups via the demonstration effect. In this process, the rich and the powerful get more votes than everyone else; first, because they have more money to spend, second, because they have more ability to experiment, and third, because they have high status and are likely to be copied. This special group may have something approaching a choice in consumption patterns; the rest have only the choice between conforming or being isolated.

The trickle-down system also has the advantage—from the center's point of view—of reinforcing patterns of authority and control. According to Fallers, it helps keep workers on the treadmill by creating an illusion of upward mobility even though relative status remains unchanged. In each period subordinates achieve (in part) the consumption standards of their superiors in a previous period and are thus torn in two directions: If they look backward and compare their standards of living through time, things seem to be getting better; if they look upward they see that their relative position has not changed. They receive a consolation prize, as it were, which may serve to keep them going by softening the reality that in a competitive system, few succeed and many fail. It is little wonder, then, that those at the top stress growth rather than equality as the welfare criterion for human relations.

In the international economy trickle-down marketing takes the form of an international demonstration effect spreading outward from the metropolis to the hinterland. Multinational corporations help speed up this process, often the key motive for direct investment, through their control of marketing channels and communications media.

The development of a new product is a fixed cost; once the expenditure needed for invention or innovation has been made, it is forever a bygone. The actual cost of production is thus typically well below selling price and the limit on output is not rising costs but falling demand due to saturated markets. The marginal profit on new foreign markets is thus high, and corporations have a strong interest in maintaining a system which spreads their products widely. Thus, the interest of multinational corporations in underdeveloped countries is larger than the size of the market would suggest.

It must be stressed that the dependency relationship between major and minor cities should not be attributed to technology. The new technology, because it increases interaction, implies greater interdependence but not necessarily a hierarchical structure. Communications linkages could be arranged in the form of a grid in which each point was directly connected to many other points, permitting lateral as well as vertical communication. This system would be polycentric since messages from one point to another would go directly rather than through the center; each point would become a center on its own; and the distinction between center and periphery would disappear.

Such a grid is made *more* feasible by aeronautical and electronic revolutions which greatly reduce costs of communications. It is not technology which creates inequality; rather, it is *organization* that imposes a ritual judicial asymmetry on the use of intrinsically symmetrical means of communications and arbitrarily creates unequal capacities to initiate and terminate exchange, to store and retrieve information, and to determine the extent of the exchange and terms of the discussion. Just as colonial powers in the past linked each point in the hinterland to the metropolis and inhibited lateral communications, preventing the growth of independent centers of decision making and creativity, multinational corporations (backed by state powers) centralize control by imposing a hierarchical system.

This suggests the possibility of an alternative system of organization in the form of national planning. Multinational corporations are private institutions which organize one or a few industries across many countries. Their polar opposite (the antimultinational corporation, perhaps) is a public institution which organizes many industries across one region. This would permit the centralization of capital, *i.e.,* the coordination of many enterprises by one decision-making center, but would substitute regionalization for internationalization. The span of control would be confined to the boundaries of a single polity and society and not spread over many countries. The advantage of the multinational corporation is its global perspective. The advantage of national planning is its ability to remove the wastes of oligopolistic anarchy, *i.e.,* meaningless product differentiation and an imbalance between different industries within a geographical area. It concentrates *all* levels of decision making in one locale and thus provides each region with a full complement of skills and occupations. This opens up new horizons for local development by making possible the social and political control of economic decision making. Multinational corporations, in contrast, weaken political control because they span many countries and can escape national regulation.

A few examples might help to illustrate how multinational corporations reduce options for development. Consider an underdeveloped country wishing to invest in education in order to increase its stock of human capital and raise standards of living. In a market system it would be able to find gainful employment for its citizens within its *national boundaries* by specializing in education-intensive activities and selling its surplus production to foreigners. In the multinational corporate system, however, the demand for high-level education in low-ranking areas is limited, and a country does not become a world center simply by having a better educational system. An outward shift in the supply of educated people in a country, therefore, will not create its own demand but will create an excess supply and lead to emigration. Even then, the employment opportunities for citizens of low-ranking countries are restricted by discriminatory practices in the center. It is well-known that ethnic homogeneity increases as one goes up the corporate hierarchy; the lower levels contain a wide variety of nationalities, the higher levels become successively purer and purer. In part this stems from the skill differences of different nationalities, but more important is the fact that the higher up one goes in the decision-making process, the more important mutual understanding and ease of communications become; a common background becomes all-important.

A similar type of specialization by nationality can be expected within the multinational corporation hierarchy. Multinational corporations are torn in two directions. On the one hand, they must adapt to local circumstances in each country. This calls for decentralized decision making. On the other hand, they must coordinate their activities in various parts of the world and stimulate the flow of ideas from one part of their empire to another. This calls for centralized control. They must, therefore, develop an organizational structure to balance the need for coordination with the need for adaptation to a patch-work quilt of languages, laws, and customs. One solution to this problem is a division of labor based on nationality. Day-to-day management in each country is left to the nationals of that country who, because they are intimately familiar with local conditions and practices, are able to deal with local problems and local government. These nationals remain rooted in one spot, while above them is a layer of people who move around from country to country, as bees among flowers, transmitting information from one subsidiary to another and from the lower levels to the general office at the apex of the corporate structure. In the nature of things, these people (reticulators) for the most part will be citizens of the country of the parent corporation (and will be drawn from a small, culturally homogeneous group within the advanced world), since they will need to have the confidence of their superiors and be able to move easily in the higher management circles. Latin Americans, Asians, and Africans will at best be able to aspire to a management position in the intermediate coordinating centers at the continental level. Very few will be able to get much higher than this, for the closer one gets to the top, the more important is "a common cultural heritage."

Another way in which the multinational corporations inhibit economic development in the hinterland is through their effect on tax capacity. An important government instrument for promoting growth is expenditure on infrastructure and support services. By providing transportation and communications, education and health, a government can create a productive labor force and increase the growth potential of its economy. The extent to which it can afford to finance these intermediate outlays depends upon its tax revenue.

However, a government's ability to tax multinational corporations is limited by the ability of these corporations to manipulate transfer prices and to move their productive facilities to another country. This means that they will only be attracted to countries where superior infrastructure offsets higher taxes. The government of an underdeveloped country will find it difficult to extract a surplus (revenue from the multinational corporations, less cost of services provided to them) from multinational corporations to use for long-run development programs and for stimulating growth in other industries. In contrast, governments of the advanced countries, where the home office and financial center of the multinational corporations are located, can tax the profits of the corporation as a whole, as well as the high incomes of its management. Government in the metropolis can, therefore, capture some of the surplus generated by the multinational corporations and use it to further improve their infrastructure and growth.

In other words, the relationship between multinational corporations and underdeveloped countries will be somewhat like the relationship between the national corporations in the United States and state and municipal governments. These lower-level governments tend always to be short of funds compared to the federal government which can tax a corporation as a whole. Their competition to attract corporate investment eats up their surplus, and they find it difficult to finance extensive investments in human and physical capital even where such investment would be productive. This has a crucial effect on the pattern of government expenditure. For example, suppose taxes were first paid to state government and then passed on to the federal government. What chance is there that these lower level legislatures would approve the phenomenal expenditures on space research that now go on? A similar discrepancy can be expected in the international economy with overspending and waste by metropolitan governments and a shortage of public funds in the less advanced countries.

The tendency of the multinational corporations to erode the power of the nation-state works in a variety of ways, in addition to its effects on taxation powers. In general, most governmental policy instruments (monetary policy, fiscal policy, wage policy, etc.) diminish in effectiveness the more open the economy and the greater the extent of foreign investments. This tendency applies to political instruments as well as economic, for the multinational corporation is a medium by which laws, politics, foreign policy, and culture of one country intrude into another. This acts to reduce the sovereignty of all nation states, but again the relationship is asymmetrical, for the flow tends to be from the parent to the subsidiary, not *vice versa*. The United States can apply its antitrust laws to foreign subsidiaries or stop them from "trading with the enemy" even though such trade is not against the laws of the country in which the branch plant is located. However, it would be illegal for an underdeveloped country which disagreed with American foreign policy to hold a U.S. firm hostage for acts of the parent. This is because legal rights are defined in terms of property-ownership, and the various subsidiaries of a multinational corporation are not "partners in a multinational endeavor" but the property of the general office.

In conclusion, it seems that a regime of multinational corporations would offer underdeveloped countries neither national independence nor equality. It would tend instead to inhibit the attainment of these goals. It would turn the underdeveloped countries into branch-plant countries, not only with reference to their economic functions but throughout the whole gamut of social, political, and cultural roles. The subsidiaries of multinational corporations are typically amongst the largest corporations in the country of operations, and their top executives play an influential role in the political, social, and cultural life of the host country. Yet these people, whatever their title, occupy at best a medium position in the corporate structure and are restricted in authority and horizons to a lower level of decision making. The governments with whom they deal tend to take on the same middle management outlook, since this is the only range of information and ideas to which they are exposed. In this sense, one can hardly expect such a country to bring forth the creative imagination needed to apply science and technology to the problems of degrading poverty.

READING #22   Dependent Development and the Product Cycle
Peter Evans

One of the central features of modern economic growth is technological innovation. Within the world economy, technology has become as important as standard factors of production, such as land, labor, and capital, in promoting prosperity. Traditionally, technological progress was organized by and for specific national economies. Consequently, technology has tended to be immobile—that is, more like land or labor than like capital—as a result of both the security and the economic self-interests of states. The rise of transnational business enterprises operating in many countries and the subsequent emergence of the product cycle, however, have challenged the premises of a nationally based technology.

Thus, the transformations of the world political economy (described by Hymer in the previous reading) have been driven by transnational circulations of technology. This process, originally depicted by Raymond Vernon in a study entitled *Sovereignty at Bay*, is designed to reduce costs of production by means of economies of scale generated through the product cycle.

In the reading that follows, Peter Evans grafts an explanation of uneven development onto the basic design of product cycle theory. According to his analysis, the product cycle, in combination with horizontal diffusions of investment and technology and divisions of labor, leads to *dependent development*. Dependent development represents a special kind of underdevelopment. In the course of dependent development, economic growth, such as that of newly industrialized economies, does occur, but it *articulates*, or gives expression to, the technologies and demand structures of the advanced industrial world and the need for cost reduction on the part of transnational business enterprises.

The concepts of core and periphery now become further deepened by introducing the elements of product cycle and the transnational circulation of technology. The "managers who manage managers," described by Hymer, now appear to maintain the polarities of core and periphery by controlling transnational flows of research, development, and distribution of technology. The product cycle, from this perspective, becomes the vector of dependent development.

In particular, the product cycle involves stages in the research, development, production, and marketing of any major commodity or service. The product cycle proceeds according to the following logic:

1. All manufactured products and their technologies undergo a "natural cycle" of at least three phases: the *innovation* phase, consisting of research, development, and introduction of the product within home markets; the *standardization* phase, which involves the wide distribution of the product through extensive marketing at home, but also through export abroad; and the *maturation* phase, during which the product is manufactured abroad for purposes of reexport and consumption at home.
2. Input costs vary with each phase of the life cycle, from the high costs of capital investment required by research and development to the low labor costs made possible by allowing developing economies with excesses of cheap labor to manufacture mass-produced or maturing products.
3. Horizontal diffusions of investment and technology from economy to economy allow a corporation to shift production and assembly of goods to those societies and plants able or willing to sustain the least expensive moments of manufacturing and marketing at each and every phase of the product cycle.
4. Thus, transnational business enterprises seek to reduce input costs in production by manufacturing products "horizontally" in many economies in accordance with the logic of transnational cost reduction throughout the life cycle of a product.

Evans suggests that product cycles reflect transnational modes of production and divisions of labor. The core engages in capital-intensive forms of production, whereas labor-intensive forms of industrial production become situated in the periphery in order to service the demands and the profit margins of capital from the core. The resultant patterns of exploitation are characterized by capital-intensive research and development in the core and labor-intensive production in the periphery, resulting in savings within the core and extension of low-wage labor in the periphery; consequent reductions of production costs of businesses organized by the core; increased profits and savings in the core as a result of dependent development in the periphery; and capital-intensive research and product development, thus initiating the product cycle all over again.

The case presented by Evans leads to a dismal set of conclusions not unlike those delineated by Hymer:

1. The economic growth experienced by newly industrializing economies, especially those in Latin America, represents a form of dependent development that promotes *more* rather than *less* dependence upon the core.
2. Economic growth, when it takes the form of dependent development, separates core-oriented or "modernizing" growth sectors of the economy from "traditional" sectors, particularly rural agriculture.
3. Consequently, growth in one economic sphere does not foster growth in others, as in the case in the economies of the advanced industrial world.
4. Economic growth reflective of dependent development perpetuates unjust conditions of exploitation and underdevelopment.

Evans thus establishes a basis for assessing the extent to which distributive justice and equity can result from economic growth within the newly industrializing economies, particularly the forms of growth that reveal the dynamics of the product cycle and the structural constraints of transnational modes of productions.

—E. W.

The starting point is still relations with the external world. A dependent country is one whose development is "conditioned by the development and expansion of another economy." . . . Dependent countries are classically those whose histories of involvement with the international market have led them to specialize in the export of a few primary products. While the income from these few products is absolutely central to the process of accumulation in the dependent country, for the center each product represents only a tiny fraction of total imports, and can usually be obtained from several different sources. The development of the dependent country, however, requires the continued acceptance of its products in the center. Therefore, economic fluctuations in the center may have severe negative consequences for the periphery, whereas an economic crisis in the periphery offers no real threat to accumulation in the center.

Complementing and often underlying dependence based on trade relations is dependence based on foreign ownership of the productive apparatus of the dependent country. When the principal aspect of dependence is that key sectors of the local productive apparatus are integral parts of capital

Peter Evans, *Dependent Development: The Alliance of Multinational, State, and Local Capital in Brazil.* Copyright © 1979 by Princeton University Press. Excerpt, pp. 26–30, reprinted with permission of Princeton University Press; endnotes deleted.

that is controlled elsewhere, then accumulation in the dependent country is externally conditioned more by the "development and expansion of center-based capital" . . . than by the "development and expansion of another country." The asymmetry is there nonetheless.

Dependence is then defined most simply as a situation in which the rate and direction of accumulation are externally conditioned. Curiously, however, while external relations are the starting point for the analysis of dependence, most of the emphasis of dependency theorists is on the internal class relations of dependent countries. As [Fernando H.] Cardoso and [Enzo] Faletto . . . say, ". . . there is no such thing as a metaphysical relation of dependency between one nation and another, one state and another. Such relations are made concrete possibilities through the existence of a network of interests and interactions which link certain social groups to other social groups, certain social classes to other classes."

Dependence includes a wide range of disparate situations. OPEC and the oil crisis provided a powerful reminder that exporting primary products does not universally entail having a weak position in international trade. Even more important, saying that a country is "dependent" does not indicate that its relation to the international economic system is immutably fixed. It means rather that the historic process of accumulation in that country exhibits certain distinctive features that are shared by other countries of the periphery and set it apart from the nations of the center.

Contemporary dependency theorists see the international division of labor as shifting substantially on the surface while continuing to have the same fundamental effect. Curiously, the most carefully elaborated theoretical underpinning for this view comes not from within the dependency tradition itself but rather from the latest version of the theory of comparative advantage, known as the "product life cycle model." . . . According to the product life cycle model, new products are likely to be first produced and sold in the center, later produced in the center and exported to the periphery, and finally produced in the periphery. Over time, more and more products will be manufactured in the periphery, but these products will continue to share certain characteristics.

Production moves to the periphery only after the technology involved has become routinized. At this point uncertainties are small and savings from cheap labor make a difference. Thus, the Schumpeterian "windfall profits" associated with new products always remain the prerogative of the center. In addition, the periphery is forced to rely on the low cost of its labor for its comparative advantage in the international market, making low living standards the basis of dependent development.

The introduction of manufacturing on the periphery also lacks the traditional "multiplier effect" associated with manufacturing investments in the center. Peripheral economies are "disarticulated," that is, firms on the periphery are not connected to each other in the same way as firms in an autocentric economy. Firms in dependent countries buy their equipment and other capital goods from outside, so that the "multiplier effect" of new investments is transferred back to the center. Increases in the output of export sectors, dramatic as they may be, do not feed back into the peripheral economy in the same way that they would feed back into an autocentric economy. As [Samir] Amin . . . puts it: "When the iron ore of Lorraine is eventually worked out this may create a difficult reconversion problem for the region, but it will be able to overcome these difficulties, for an infrastructure has been formed on the basis of the mineral, which could be imported from elsewhere. But when the iron ore of Mauritania is worked out, that country will go back to the desert."

Disarticulation between technology and social structure reinforces the economy's lack of integration. Celso Furtado . . . speaks of the importation of technology as contributing to a "structural deformation" of the peripheral economy. Productive technologies imported from the center are not designed to absorb the huge reserves of underemployed agricultural labor. Products developed in the center and assimilated by the periphery are luxury products in the context of the periphery. Their production uses scarce resources and results in a "distortion in the allocation of resources in favor of those products and to the detriment of mass consumption goods." . . .

For the elite, disarticulation is an obstacle to self-sustained, autocentric accumulation, but for the mass its consequence is exclusion. Because accumulation depends primarily either on exports or on goods beyond their means, the mass of the population can be excluded as consumers. Capital intensive technologies in the modern sector make it possible to marginalize them as producers. Because they are effectively barred from economic participation, to allow them political participation would be disruptive. Social and cultural exclusion follow from political and economic exclusion.

Exclusion, like disarticulation, is a constant feature of dependency. The gross gap between elite and mass that characterized classic dependence was expected to diminish once a domestic manufacturing sector was established. But the record of the sixties shows increasing inequality. . . . On the political level, populism has not proved an enduring strategy. As [Guillermo] O'Donnell's . . . pessimistic but convincing comparative analysis of Latin American countries shows, the ruling groups in the more advanced peripheral societies have discovered that the kind of economic development they need to sustain their own lifestyles requires the increasing political exclusion of the mass of the population.

READING #23   The Global Factory: Foreign Assembly in International Trade
Joseph Grunwald and Kenneth Flamm

Joseph Grunwald and Kenneth Flamm, in effect, update the observations made in previous readings concerning the new transnationalism, transnational modes of production, and the product cycle. The product cycle has, in recent years, given way to a full-fledged global assembly line now operating within the world economy. Transnational modes of production organized vertically by transnationally integrated business enterprises have turned the clock forward on industrial organization such that diffusions of technology and investment by means of a horizontal proliferation of "delocalized" branch-plant facilities have become unified in the process of foreign assembly. Moreover, the degree of horizontal specialization among various branch-plant facilities around the globe has significantly increased.

The significance of the global assembly line can be measured by changes in the product cycle. The aim of transnational business investment in lesser developing economies is no longer simply to establish branch-plants in peripheral or lesser developing countries that manufacture the same or nearly identical products, but at later stages relative to those manufactured within home economies. On the contrary, the global assembly line extends the concept of economy of scale to include a fully integrated transnational mode of production.

This global assembly line entails component or specialized forms of manufacture and assembly in factories located throughout the Third World. These are often owned or operated by *different* firms, but under contract through a process often referred to as **out-sourcing.** The outputs of some plants become the inputs of others. Components are produced and assembled in host as well as home countries in a series of stages and steps that defy the automatic routines of the product cycle. This process, in turn, requires a tightening of vertical coordination and control by centralized management, which works to expand economies of scale by taking advantage of cost discrepancies in different economies as they develop virtually on a week-to-week basis.

As a result, corporate-guided intrafirm trade has increased enormously as a percentage of world trade. Transnational business enterprises, as never before, can pick and choose among national economies in which to invest according to their tax structures and tariff codes; for example, the extent to which domestic or host-country laws permit semifinished products to enter duty-free, or the degree to which national host-country regulations require goods assembled abroad for domestic consumption to include components produced at home.

Marketing strategies often demand the partnership of domestic firms, whereas the advancing pace of technological innovation requires even transnational firms to share costs. Thus, interconglomerate alliances, often leading to joint ventures within several national jurisdictions, have become the order of the day, thus replacing emphasis upon wholly owned subsidiaries.

A complex cluster of alliances among transnational business enterprises is the result. These involve joint ventures, cross-licensing of technology, off-shore production schemes, and "outsourcing" of components through subcontractual arrangements between conglomerates and locally based firms. Together these and similar developments characterize the rapid transformation of the world political economy in ways that go far beyond the standard interpretations of both liberalism and Marxism.

In the following reading, Grunwald and Flamm examine the transnational reorganization of production in the world economy, sector by sector, country by country. In particular, they outline the impacts of these developments upon labor relations and distributive justice in newly industrializing countries. The political implications of the global assembly line have hardly been realized during its advance through the back doors of state sovereignty. In its wake, governments may become increasingly beholden to privatized forms of transnational economic power and decisionmaking. Certainly, domestic labor relations within both advanced and lesser developing countries are increasingly influenced by external decisions taken by foreign business managers competing for domestic market shares within national economies.

—E. W.

The International Reorganization of Production

In present-day discussions of the changing international division of labor, manufacturing industries are often divided into those using stable, widely understood technology to make relatively simple products—traditional industries—and those using rapidly developing technology to make a continuous stream of quickly obsolete new products—high-tech industries. The traditional industries have generally been associated with fairly labor-intensive technologies and, because of the persistence of low wage rates in the third world and the relatively low development cost of establishing a production capability in these older products, these industries have been the leading edge of the burgeoning exports of manufactures produced in developing countries.

The high-tech industries, on the other hand, depend for their success on access to the specialized resources required for research and development and highly complex production processes. These industries have therefore been located in the industrial countries. As products mature, technology diffuses, high-tech products eventually become traditional products, and production moves to more competitive locations abroad. This is roughly the product-cycle description of international trade first advanced by Raymond Vernon in 1966.

While production overseas to serve local markets—stimulated by protection and transport costs and, in some instances, lower production costs—has long been a feature of direct foreign investment by U.S. producers of

Joseph Grunwald and Kenneth Flamm, *The Global Factory: Foreign Assembly in International Trade.* Copyright © 1985 by The Brookings Institution. Excerpt, pp. 2–3, 5–8, excluding tables, 217–219, 222–224, and 226–228, reprinted with permission of The Brookings Institution; endnotes deleted.

manufactures, volume manufacture in foreign locations for reexport to the home market or other export markets is a qualitatively new feature of foreign manufacturing operations that emerged in the late 1960s. In developing Asia, more than a quarter of sales of U.S. affiliates went to the United States in 1977, up from less than 10 percent in 1966. In electrical machinery, in particular, some 70 percent of output was shipped back to the United States in 1977. . . .

A similar phenomenon appears to have taken place in Japanese multinationals. Japanese data for 1975 . . . show a significant share of sales as exports to Japan from Asian affiliates, though at a smaller proportion than exports to the United States from U.S. affiliates. When not investing abroad in order to secure material resources, Japanese firms seemed more inclined than U.S. firms to use their foreign affiliates as low-cost platforms for exports into markets other than Japan.

European firms, by way of contrast, showed relatively little propensity to serve their home markets through exports from affiliates located in low-wage areas. There were a number of possible explanations for their reluctance to move abroad: high European Community (EC) tariffs and other barriers to trade had considerable effect in inhibiting foreign production; a strong, well-organized trade-union movement possibly also exercised considerable influence in restraining firms from relocating; and the important fact of significant state participation in ownership of many European multinationals, particularly in the electronics industry, may have placed further political constraints on exports to the home market from foreign locations. Nevertheless, large outflows of European direct investment continued throughout the 1960s and 1970s into the establishment of numerous foreign subsidiaries for the purpose of penetrating protected foreign markets.

The growing participation of foreign affiliates of national firms in exports of manufactures from developing countries to markets in industrial countries probably also served to reduce political resistance to these imports. . . . Imports of manufactures into the industrial markets increased in relation to total consumption of manufactures. . . .

The movement abroad was not restricted exclusively to large U.S. multinationals. There are many smaller firms involved in these trade links from the United States and other countries. The small firms, in fact, tend to stick closer to home—U.S. firms to Mexico and the Caribbean, Japanese firms to Taiwan and Korea, and Western European firms to Eastern Europe and the Mediterranean. In familiar nearby areas with which communication links are good, and where a considerable overhead investment in learning the local ways is not necessary, even small firms can afford to move out of the country—and they may be forced to do so by their competition.

Thus, those observers who claim that the 1960s and 1970s marked a new stage in the evolution of the world capitalist system appear to be correct, insofar as the operations of U.S. multinational firms seem to have switched, on a fairly large scale for the first time, to overseas production of manufactured exports for the home market. Asia and Latin America became the primary locations for these operations and electrical machinery the principal product.

One way to regard the phenomenon of production abroad is as a system of production geared to retaining competitiveness for firms in developed countries after a product has entered the down side of the product cycle. That is, the firms that developed the product continue to produce economically by eventually relocating or subcontracting assembly production facilities in low-wage developing countries. They must generally have some other competitive cost advantage, such as access to capital, marketing, administration, or technology, for this strategy to work, since an indigenous firm producing a standard product in its native business environment presumably could do so at no greater—and possibly at lower—cost. Also, production processes must permit such a division of labor, and transportation costs should not be excessive.

Production of more traditional products such as textiles and apparel, radio and television receivers and, to a certain extent, automobiles has been integrated vertically across national boundaries in response to foreign competition for some time. But production abroad is even more important in certain high-tech electronics industries, where the products are anything but traditional. Semiconductors alone account for about 40 percent of the value of U.S. components reimported into this country after overseas assembly, and more than 80 percent of U.S. semiconductor production is probably assembled abroad.

The technical characteristics of the product that determine transport cost, the separability of labor-intensive operations from other steps in production, and the capital intensity of assembly operations are critical to the decision whether to produce abroad. High value-to-weight ratios of apparel and electronics reduce transport costs as a barrier to trade, and production operations are easily separated into distinct steps—manufacture of components, assembly, testing, and packaging—that do not require physical contiguity. All these products require relatively small inputs of capital and large inputs of unskilled labor in the assembly stage, when labor-intensive methods are used.

While assembly abroad is important in the U.S. economy—in 1981 perhaps 15 percent of U.S. imports of manufactures, 22 percent of those from developing countries, and very much higher percentages of imports of certain items of apparel and electronics were assembled abroad—the amount of controversy generated by such production arrangements gives them a disproportionate prominence. To critics in the third world they symbolize not only a development strategy concentrated on export promotion, "industrialization by invitation," and the continued deepening of external links to a fluctuating world economy, but also, since they are often under the control of foreign investors, a strategy guaranteed to extend the power of multinational corporations as a political and economic pressure group within the host state. Considerable debate often surrounds the questions how much employment these activities generate, what its quality is, what their net contribution to the balance of payments of the host country is, what kinds of technology are transferred, whether industrialization is fostered, how much economic instability is caused by dependence on export markets, and what the social effects of this type of development are. Proponents of production sharing as part of an industrialization policy generally claim that the net balance is positive.

Production sharing also generates considerable friction within the industrial countries. Labor groups view with alarm a presumed "export" of jobs, although assembly abroad can increase the use of domestically produced components and stave off competition from low-cost foreign imports, thereby avoiding the departure of the entire industry. The workers displaced in industries in which assembly production is moved out of the country, it is argued, are especially vulnerable to adjustment problems. Some fear the loss of U.S. competitiveness through the leakage of technology used in foreign plants or the deterioration of the balance of payments in important industries.

Two factors seem to guarantee that overseas production arrangements will remain for some time a significant issue in foreign economic policy discussions in the industrial countries. First, in many of the industries in which import penetration has been most pronounced and trade policy most highly charged with political pressures—sectors such as apparel, electronics, and automobiles—firms have reorganized their operations to use assembly abroad as an integral part of their strategy for survival. Second, in apparel as in electronics, the constant cycle of change and obsolescence has been an obstacle to automation. Automation, because it generally requires large fixed investments, is normally economical only when large production runs are guaranteed. In electronics, rapid innovation and continuous technological change have posed a barrier to automation, while in apparel, the principal barrier has been the frequent and unpredictable changes in fashions and styles.

Transferring assembly abroad has been the cutting edge of continued growth in the foreign investments of transnational industrial enterprises. U.S.-owned assets in foreign manufacturing subsidiaries, for example, increased faster in overseas assembly areas than in other regions of the world between 1966 and 1977. . . .

The international reorganization of production . . . is an essentially reactive strategy of firms in industrial countries that face competition from low-cost imports. In an attempt to defend domestic markets against international competition, rather than as an aggressive move against competitors at home, producers have transferred abroad production processes in which they have lost their international competitive advantage. The value of such a strategy depends on the relative costs of labor, transport, and communications, the importance of quality, the risks to investment, and the economic costs of the principal alternative to labor-intensive assembly—automation. It has been on the whole a successful way for threatened firms in industrial countries to retain competitiveness and for developing countries to exploit their own comparative advantage.

Assembly production abroad, therefore, is a sharp manifestation of the North-South dichotomy: capital-intensive, high-technology production in industrial countries; low-skilled, labor-intensive production in developing countries. The system produces global benefits as well as serious misgivings. In the North, the movement abroad creates adjustment problems for large pockets of the unskilled that remain in manufacturing industry; in the South, the growth of assembly production for export raises the specter of a trap that will perpetuate a low-grade labor force and rudimentary production activities. The southern perception is nurtured by the absence of strong linkages of assembly activities to the rest of the economy, particularly in the larger developing countries.

Assembly activities are concentrated in two types of manufacture: electronics and apparel. In both, the value-to-weight ratios are high and transport costs are therefore low. Both can be manufactured in sequential operations that can be separated in time and space without affecting the quality of the product. They are goods with relatively short life cycles, as fashions and technologies change. Both types of product require extensive routine assembly operations, which can be performed either by unskilled labor or by sophisticated machines. An ample supply of low-wage labor can keep production costs internationally competitive. Automation as an alternative to manual assembly generally requires a large fixed-capital investment. Its attractiveness will therefore depend on the relative cost of capital and the size of the production flow that can repay the capital charges.

In all countries, subcontracting between independent firms appears to be the principal mode of having assembly done abroad in the apparel industry. In electronics, however, such operations are usually carried out by subsidiaries of multinational enterprises. In complex, high-technology industries it can be risky for a U.S. company not to control all manufacturing processes: valuable technology may leak to competitors, and independent subcontractors may not have the skills and techniques to undertake precision operations to the exacting standards for which the U.S. firm must bear responsibility to its customers.

Assembly of the same type of product can be found in many countries and a single firm often maintains similar production facilities in several locations abroad. Because wage levels in these locations are widely divergent and the costs of transport and communications are different, the return on investment abroad varies substantially from one place to another. Country risks, such as potential political and economic disturbances, also have a significant influence on decisions on the location of assembly operations for the home market. Diversifying production among countries is therefore an explicit strategy for reducing these risks, which loom large in the generally poor low-wage countries.

The trade-off between risk and economic return available in a particular assembly location will depend on both the technological characteristics of the product and the wage rates of the country in question. . . .

Production Abroad and the Industrial Countries

The transfer of labor-intensive operations to locations abroad affects the industrial countries by lowering the costs of assembled goods to their consumers. It alters the relative availability of labor and capital, the wages, and the profit rates in the domestic economy and fosters the equalization of factor prices internationally.

The traditional trade-theory view of these matters is often that struggles over import competition pit the incomes of specific workers against the general level of economic welfare. If workers whose incomes are reduced as a consequence of imports were offered a suitable system of transfers, the economy as a whole would benefit. The extra income created by trade will more than pay for the transfers required by the workers affected, so liberalization of trade leaves everyone better off. Underlying these arguments is the assumption that a system of perfectly competitive markets guarantees the employment of all resources, including labor, in the economy. When this assumption does not hold, policies other than free trade may also be required to ensure improvements in social welfare. . . .

The workers who suffer most in the two industries most strongly affected by foreign production, apparel and electronics, especially in the least-skilled assembly jobs, are women. Empirical studies tend to show that adjustment costs for displaced female workers are greater than for male workers of the same ages and skill levels. Periods of unemployment of displaced women workers, for example, seem to be much longer than those of male workers, at all ages. Assembly abroad is thus likely to cause acute problems of employment displacement. It seems inequitable for unskilled working women to bear costs that are more than compensated for by lower costs to consumers.

Because certain vulnerable segments of the U.S. labor force have borne the brunt of retrenchment, the importance in total employment of the more highly skilled segment remaining in the United States has increased. Since skilled workers are less likely to be laid off in response to a down-turn, fluctuations in total employment in an industry may have decreased. This seems to have been the case in the semiconductor industry.

Production abroad, then, has wrought permanent change in the composition of the demand for labor in that part of the industry left behind. The least skilled and the marginally employed—those for whom displacement is most costly—are those most strongly affected. Ironically, though, the demand for assembly workers seems to increase with the technological changes in design that increase the use of electronic components. Savings in cost realized through movement abroad, in turn, may have helped stimulate those design changes.

Long-Run Prospects for the Unskilled

Concern for the effects of changes in patterns of production and trade on the demand for unskilled labor in the industrial countries is not unique to the industries that engage in coproduction abroad. Nonetheless, an analysis of the mix of skills in U.S. industrial employment reveals that those industries which use much more than the average amount of unskilled labor coincide closely with the assembly industries examined here. . . . More than half the unskilled workers in U.S. manufacturing in 1978 were in these labor-intensive industries, and more than a third were in electrical and electronic equipment, apparel and textile products, and motor vehicles. If only assemblers are considered, 97 percent were in manufacturing, 68 percent in the labor-intensive industries, and 53 percent in electronics and motor vehicles. Thus, in the United States, unskilled manual labor in general and assembly labor in particular is largely concentrated in manufacturing, and within manufacturing it is found in precisely those industries that have tended to shift assembly operations to other countries.

In the aggregate, this may not seem to be a critical issue. Unskilled operators, excluding those in transport, made up about 8 percent of U.S. employment in 1978. But these occupations are highly concentrated in assembly industries: a quarter of employment in all U.S. manufacturing, nearly a third of employment in electronics, and roughly two-thirds of employment in apparel. And even if services remain sheltered from low wages in the third world, it is difficult to imagine the 60 percent expansion of service employment that would be required to absorb the continued and steady displacement of all the unskilled in manufacturing. (There were about 8 million unskilled nontransport operators in the U.S. economy in 1978 and about 13 million service workers.) Since these service jobs generally pay substantially less than jobs in manufacturing, the continued displacement of the unskilled will mean the end of their relatively high incomes in Western industrial societies.

Traditional trade theory predicts that wages, as well as other factor prices, will be equalized across countries. Because the underlying assumptions are often violated, one does not always expect to observe this equalization. But the assembly industries in many ways do approximate those assumptions, and a process leading to equalization of wages seems to be under way. Continued downward pressure on real wages of the unskilled manufacturing worker seems likely.

Assembly Production and Developing Countries

The benefits of assembly production to host countries are significant. In economies with large unemployed or underemployed resources, assembly activities offer opportunities for low-cost employment and the creation of income. In most countries with important assembly operations, net foreign exchange earned from assembly contributes significantly to the external balance. Experience in Mexico and Haiti seems to indicate that capacity utilization and hours worked are higher in assembly than in the rest of the economy. In addition to the smaller capital requirements per job than in other sectors, most of the workers in these activities were previously not in the labor force, were not employed, or were engaged in occupations in which their productivity was substantially lower.

Employment

A feature that seems to characterize all assembly activities is a predominantly female work force. A great many ills, ranging from the disruption of the family to exploitation of the workers, have been attributed to this fact. The wages of women have been generally lower than those of male workers in assembly plants, as in other economic activities, but the comparison cannot be controlled for occupation and other factors. In apparent contrast to those in the developed countries, an overwhelming proportion of the female workers are young and unmarried, with the upper age limit at roughly the mean age of marriage for factory women in their local societies. Many of these young women participate formally for the first time in the labor force as export assembly-plant workers, and critics charge that rather than eradicating unemployment, this may actually induce it by encouraging groups that might otherwise not do so to join the labor force.

The fact is that women predominate in certain assembly operations everywhere in the world; developing countries are not unique in that respect. What is new, however, is that the introduction of assembly production into developing countries has accelerated the entrance of women into the labor force. This may also have accelerated the disruptions and the adjustment problems that usually appear as the proportion of women gainfully employed increases in the course of economic development.

In large countries, assembly activities have not been extensive enough to employ a significant share of the labor force. Of all developing countries, Mexico has the largest employment in assembly production for the U.S. market, yet assembly jobs constitute less than 1 percent of the total Mexican labor force. Their effect is concentrated in the towns along the northern border, where they make up about half of manufacturing employment.

Around the world, assembly for foreign manufacturers probably did not employ more than about 1 million workers in the mid-1970s, while total open unemployment in the third world was estimated to be 33 million. Yet it is a critical source of employment in certain small countries, particularly in the Caribbean basin, such as Barbados and Haiti, and it is fairly important in some countries in Asia, including Singapore and Hong Kong and, to a lesser extent, South Korea and Taiwan.

With respect to migration, the effect on Mexico is limited by the fact that assembly for export has created much of its own labor force there by bringing in primarily young women from urban areas who were formerly not active economically. Most of the undocumented workers in the United States have tended to be males from rural areas. If this trend continues, an increase in assembly employment will have little effect on Mexican migration to the United States. In the small countries of the Caribbean basin, however, where assembly operations constitute a significant part of employment and where in the poorest countries, such as Haiti, female participation in the labor force has traditionally been high, the pressures to emigrate would probably be greater without such activities.

   As noted in case studies on Mexico and Haiti, wages in assembly plants in those countries tend to be at or above the legal minimum. Since evasion of minimum wage requirements seems widespread in both countries, the wages paid there to assembly workers are probably significantly higher than a market wage.

   Because they tend to be more visible and their environment more closely regulated than those of other firms, working conditions in assembly plants are generally thought to be somewhat better than in firms of similar size in the rest of the country, though undoubtedly they are unsatisfactory by developed-country standards. On the other hand, special concessions to limit the rights of workers have been granted to assembly firms in some countries.

READING #24   The Core-Periphery Structure of Production and Jobs: The Internationalizing of Production
Robert W. Cox

The *New York Times* of September 8, 1987, featured an article written by James LeMoyne entitled "In Long-Suffering Central America, the Workers Suffer Most." This title summarizes the socioeconomic processes leading to widespread despair on the part of those able and willing to work throughout the region. The article states:

> With inefficient and inegalitarian land use, a growing population, continued migration to the cities and stagnant economies, there is a vast pool of unemployed workers that is a bonanza for businessmen and plantation owners, most of whom have not had to pay a raise in real terms in the last decade.
>
> For the workers, especially the vast majority who do not have the protection of a union, the consequence is salaries, work hours and working conditions that are equivalent to those in Europe and the United States at the turn of the century.
>
> Child labor is common. . . . Unions are regularly repressed and broken. There is seldom guaranteed retirement income. Strikes are almost inevitably declared illegal.

The elements that combine to create these tragic conditions of worker repression include vast numbers of marginalized jobless, inadequate forms of compensation and labor protection, substandard working conditions, insufficient opportunities and varieties of work, and highly concentrated forms of employment. Any combination of these is brutalizing; but when they all appear together, as they so often do in the case of dependent peripheral economies, the impact is devastating.

   Robert W. Cox, in the reading that follows, concludes our discussion of the political economy of uneven development by focusing on the nature of work within a *world* economy characterized by transnational modes of production, as opposed to work within an *international* economy oriented toward trade between economies in which factors of production remain immobile. In lucid fashion, he reveals the processes by which transnational modes of production and business enterprises—or what he calls "transnational production organizations"—have changed the essential structure of work on a global scale.

Cox redefines the concepts of core and periphery to accommodate the basic thrust of his analysis: Core and periphery are neither geographical designations nor economic zones as such; rather, they refer to categories of work. In a world economy featuring transnational modes of production, core and periphery represent the differing roles of labor within any national economy, rich as well as poor. According to Cox, cheap, semi-skilled, temporary, labor-intensive forms of work reveal the periphery—wherever and however it appears—in both advanced and lesser developing economies. Core forms of work and employment occur within the immediate vicinity of peripheral labor since the gaps between the two are theoretical and conceptual, not geographic.

Transnational modes of production create peripheralized labor forces in advanced economies as well as in lesser developing countries. In the United States, for example, new jobs in the lowest paying sectors are serviced by peripheralized segments of the work force representing various ethnic communities, both indigenous and newly arrived. As a consequence, many of the symptoms of peripheralization are beginning to appear in the United States. These include rapid increases in the number of families living below the poverty line, sweat shops, child labor, foreign worker ghettoes, urban slums, inadequate housing, and structural or positional declines in the earning power of workers.

Cox concludes his analysis with an incisive description of the underground economy that arises as a manifestation of peripheralized labor and/or structural declines in core-type employment. The existence of such an underground economy reflects the efforts of a peripheralized labor force to stave off the pressures of advancing poverty amidst plenty.

—E. W.

The Internationalizing of Production

The Pax Americana created a world hegemonic order in which a *world* economy of international production emerged within the existing *international* economy of classical trade theory. The international-economy model connects national economies by flows of goods, capital, and specie. Where the international-economy model focuses on exchange, the world-economy model

Robert W. Cox, *Production, Power, and World Order.* Copyright © 1987 by Columbia University Press. Excerpt, pp. 244–249, 318–326, reprinted with permission of Columbia University Press; endnotes deleted.

focuses on production. It consists of transnational production organizations whose component elements are located in different territorial jurisdictions.

Each of these transnational production organizations produces for the world market. Each takes advantage of differences in costs and availabilities of factors of production in deciding about the location of its component elements.

Knowledge, in the form of technology and market information, is the principal resource in the world economy, especially knowledge in its dynamic form as the capacity to generate new technologies and to market new products. Money can be tapped where it is to be found by those who have knowledge assets, e.g., in local capital markets or in international credit. The nature of international trade changes. Arms-length intercountry exchanges are characteristic of the international economy. Intracorporate transfers become more important in the world economy.

Transnational production organizations take advantage of the differences between the factor endowments of countries in the international economy, especially differences in labor costs. They internalize these differences, making use of them to minimize overall production costs. The world economy promotes a homogenization of consumer habits, social values, and productive technologies, but it does this on the basis of existing differences, which affect relative costs of production and access to markets. Accumulation takes place through a hierarchy of modes of social relations of production linked within transnational production organizations. Some of these modes of social relations of production generate more surplus than others. Struggles take place over the proportions of the surplus to be captured by the central decision makers of the transnational production organization and by the political authorities of the different jurisdictions in which it functions. The crucial problem for transnational production organizations is continually to increase the surplus through higher productivity and to lower production costs.

Production costs are determined by (1) the cost of producer goods, (2) the cost of raw materials, (3) the cost of labor, (4) the cost of externalities such as environmental degradation insofar as the producing organization is required to bear them, and (5) the combinations in which (1), (2), (3), and (4) are put together.

Most research and development has taken place in the advanced capitalist countries and most of that in the United States. Very little of it has been located in the less developed countries. A great deal of this research has been done by large corporations or by government agencies working on projects from which large corporations could benefit (e.g., nuclear and space research). Advance in productive technologies was concentrated in core-country headquarters of transnational production organizations. These organizations have been in a position to maintain a lead in the productivity of industrial processes.

Access to cheap raw materials, especially energy, but also other minerals, was a major initial goal of the postwar expansion of U.S. corporations and those of some other advanced capitalist countries. There is little question but that raw materials exported from less developed countries as inputs to advanced-country industries were cheaper than similar raw materials extracted in the latter countries, though the exact extent of the cost difference was obscured by the fact that prices were controlled by advanced-country-based multinational corporations (MNCs). Nevertheless, from 1969 to 1974 all raw materials prices (including but not confined to the price of oil) rose, signifying a major readjustment in international accumulation.

Cheaper labor was available either by employment of immigrants from poor countries or by relocating plants from rich to poor countries. Japanese firms, for cultural reasons, never encouraged immigration and preferred to locate subsidiaries or use subcontractors in South Korea, Taiwan, and other countries with cheaper labor, while countries of Western Europe resorted to immigration on a large scale and with corresponding social and political costs. U.S. industries have used both immigrant labor and foreign location as means of tapping cheaper labor. Often these methods have been used in sequence: French-Canadian labor was imported to man the textile plants of New England before these plants were relocated, first in the southern states, then abroad. The future expansion of European industries seems more likely to take place through relocation in less developed countries than by any recurrence of the massive immigration of cheap labor that took place in the 1960s and 1970s.

Somewhat similar to the search for cheaper labor has been the impact of environmental controls imposing cleanup or anti-pollution costs on industries. Such regulations proliferated in the rich countries from the 1970s as public awareness of environmental degradation became aroused. Poor countries offered sites that did not impose such costs.

Transnational production organizations can maximize cost advantages by combining these various factors in complex hierarchical systems. Inputs to the production process organized by dominant firm A can be provided by (1) foreign-located dependent firm B, which produces raw materials, or (2) foreign-located dependent firm C, which produces components by employing labor cheaper than is available to A in its home country and/or which pollutes the environment in ways not allowed in A's country. Thus part of A's profits are derived from cheaper raw materials, the degradation of nature, and cheaper labor in the countries of B and C. In fact, A may not derive any profit from the workers it directly employs in its own country. These are highly skilled and well paid and enjoy considerable job security and benefits. They are necessary to maintain the sophisticated technology at the core of this transnational production organization and to do the nondirectly productive work of research and development, market research and promotion, and financial operations crucial to the planning of the transnational organization. Labor costs at the core of the industrial process have, in fact, been absorbed into the fixed capital costs of the organization. The difference between sales and costs comes rather from the dependent units in the production organization and thus ultimately from the differences in social relations of production prevailing among them.

An illustration can be had from one of the most recent industries, microchip information technology. Microchip manufacturing began in 1971 and grew rapidly during the 1970s, peaking in 1974 and then declining as there was more competition and growing capacity, leading to a crisis of overproduction in 1981. Initially, computers were made by male electrical engineers in core installations; as the industry grew, chips made in Silicon Valley, California, were sent to Far East assembly plants to be placed in their carriers by semiskilled enterprise-labor-market women using microscopes. As industrial capacity became surplus, some of these women were sent back to the rural communities from which they had been recruited. The labor costs to the manufacturer of expanding and then contracting production were thus minimized. The poor-country enterprise-labor market became the buffer for economic downturn.

The formal institutional, legal, or proprietary relationships involved in transnational production organizations may be of many different kinds. These include the internalizing of a dual labor process within firm A by the recruitment of an immigrant labor force alongside a core skilled labor force of national origin; outright ownership by A of foreign subsidiaries B or C; supply of A by foreign joint venture firms using capital subscribed in part by A and in part by nationals and states of countries in which they are situated that use technology supplied by A; subcontracting by A to foreign firm D; leasing of patented technology by A to foreign firm D; compensation agreements through which A provides technology, and foreign firm D or E repays with part of its production of goods (used as components by A); and ad hoc commercial agreements worked out by A with a variety of foreign firms on the basis of its superior information about the sourcing of required inputs throughout the world. Any or all of these arrangements constitute aspects of the internationalizing of production.

Preferences differ in the choice among these various techniques for putting together transnational production organizations. Internalizing of dual labor processes and outright ownership of subsidiaries was the preference of MNCs, especially in the first phase of expansion. Subcontracting was extensively used by Japanese corporations in their overseas movement. Joint ventures were urged on MNCs by the governments of industrializing Third World countries and some socialist countries as a means of enhancing local participation. Compensation agreements are associated with the relationships between capitalist-country-based MNCs and socialist-country enterprises. Electronic information processing has been applied by Japanese firms to put together deals for the acquisition of components and other inputs in a variety of countries.

Political pressures can influence within limits the distribution of power in transnational production organizations. The success of OPEC in capturing a larger share of petroleum rents is an outstanding case of a successful political coalition redistributing surplus. Neomercantilist states have successfully pressured MNCs to undertake more research and development locally, to do more processing of raw materials, and to manufacture more for export. Governments can intervene to contest administrative pricing by MNCs so as to maximize their fiscal take from corporate activities. The limits within which political influences can be effectively exerted on foreign capital are the points beyond which capital loses its incentive to invest. A less-developed-country location presents a balance of advantages and disadvantages to the decision-making centers of transnational production organizations. This balance is calculated in terms of access to raw materials, market opportunities, the preempting of competitors, political security, and so forth. The range of what is acceptable to foreign capital may be fairly wide. It may include changes in formal ownership; indeed, the transnational decision-making center may turn the nationalization of a peripheral subsidiary to advantage if it becomes a means of acquiring capital infusions from the peripheral country government and giving that government an interest in the profitability of the transnational production organization as a whole. What is negotiable concerns the relative shares of the surplus. What is not negotiable concerns the goals and direction of the development process itself. Actions by peripheral country governments that would disrupt the accumulation process, e.g., by default on debts, rather than accept new terms for rescheduling, or that would redirect production toward meeting local basic needs rather than maximize profits on the world market, invite either a severance of economic relations or the political riposte of destabilization. . . .

The Core-Periphery Structure of Production and Jobs

In order to grasp whether and in what way the global accumulation process may be changing, it is necessary to ascertain the mutations taking place in the relationships among different technologies of production and the modes of social relations associated with them. These mutations can be observed only as tendencies that are still fluid. The patterns that ultimately emerge will be shaped both by social power relations and the technological solutions that are available. States will orient the choices made, thereby reinforcing certain social forces, and state actions will in turn be influenced by international competition, military and economic. It is unlikely that the total process of change in production and jobs will prove to be reducible to any single factor and futile to look for such a determining factor. It will be more to the point to consider the variety of factors underlying observable changes so as to try to estimate their relative weight in different situations and therefore the probabilities of alternative futures.

The more capital-intensive phases of production and the innovation of more sophisticated technologies through research and development take place in the core. The more labor-intensive phases and standardized technologies shift to the periphery. The core concentrates increasingly on software while the periphery takes a growing share of hardware production. The hardware production of the periphery, however, usually remains technologically dependent on the softwares of the core.

This differentiation in production organization corresponds to differences in labor supply. Labor for the capital-intensive, technologically sophisticated phases of industry is high-cost labor, but because of the capital-intensity of the production process, labor costs are a lesser proportion of total production costs than they are with standardized labor-intensive technologies. Managements accordingly seek to retain in their service the core workers in whom they have made an investment in training and whose skills and dedication are necessary for the continuing flow of production by high-cost equipment. Managements also seek to find for the labor-intensive phases workers who are quickly trainable, readily disposable, docile, and cheap.

While it is relatively simple to describe these characteristics of core and periphery, it is more difficult to give the terms *core* and *periphery* generalizable concrete points of reference. The terms originated with a geographical connotation that they still retain. The core was first located in the leading industrial countries and the periphery in the economically less developed countries. Yet it is quite possible to note shifts in industrial leadership within the geographical core (from the United States to Japan for certain aspects of electronics), as well as instances of conventional core-type industry in certain less-developed countries (e.g., steel in Brazil and South Korea). Similarly, within so-called core countries, there exists a core-periphery division within industries between the principal centers of innovation and development, on the one hand, and regional or provincial production units of a lower technological level, on the other. Geographical shifts of the core have also taken place within countries, the most recently celebrated being that from the northeast to the southwest of the United States. Although the functional characteristics of core and periphery remain analytically valid, their association with specific geographical positions must be considered to be a matter of perhaps transitory circumstance, not of immutable destiny.

Similarly, the association of core and periphery with sectors of industry, i.e., that large-scale corporate industry constitutes the core and small- to medium-scale industries the periphery, has been and remains questionable. The difficulties of the automobile industry illustrate those of large corporate multinational enterprises that have some of the features of periphery production: relatively labor-intensive and standardized technology. At the same time, some of the breakthroughs in innovative technology have been made by relatively small enterprises.

As regards labor supply, two strategies have been followed with opposite geographical consequences in the search for cheap and disposable labor. One lay in the design of plant, which would combine a reduced proportion of high-cost, high-skill labor with a higher proportion of low-skill, quickly trainable labor. The European automobile industry followed this route. Immigrants from the Mediterranean countries provided the cheap labor. There was, however, a limit to the tolerance of societies for immigrants and their ability to absorb and provide them with services. Xenophobic reaction ensued. Another answer was to transfer plant into geographically peripheral zones either within the same country or abroad. Within countries this usually means shifting away from centers of strong trade-union organization to tap a new labor force of former farmhands, immigrants, and women workers lacking a tradition of trade-unionism. In movement abroad, countries that had extended primary education to a large part of the population and that have strong regimes ready and able to control or suppress unions have had the advantage. Taiwan, South Korea, and Singapore are preeminent examples. This movement provoked a response in the form of pressure for state policies to counteract "deindustrialization."

Although the geographical and industrial-sector connotations of core and periphery have become increasingly confused, the analytical validity of the differentiation between core and periphery has been strengthened by the economic crisis since the mid-1970s. The basis for the distinction, however, needs to be redefined so as to avoid tying it too closely to these factors of geography and industrial sector.

The combination of heightened international competition for market shares in a nonexpanding world economy with the existence of surplus capacity in already installed technologies has oriented new investment toward cutting production costs. This takes two directions: the introduction of automation, robotics, and analogous methods of displacing labor by equipment, and the more systematic use of cheap labor. At the same time market demand has become more differentiated, particularly the effective demand of the elite markets that pull forward the process of innovation in capitalist development. Thus, in tandem with cost cutting, enterprises seek greater flexibility in adjusting production to this differentiated demand. The knell is sounding for the mass production of standardized articles made possible by Fordism. The consequences of this search for cost-cutting and diversification of output as the keys to competitiveness are to be found in the variety of divergent tendencies now observable in contemporary production processes.

A general pattern underlies these various tendencies. Employers under competitive pressure have been very sensitive to labor costs, fiscal burdens, and costs imposed by regulation (for example, antipollution controls). They have sought to stabilize their work forces at as low as possible a level consistent with continuous production. They have also sought to achieve with this work force the maximum versatility to meet changing market demands. As regards increases in demand, they have tried to meet this either by investing in more highly productive equipment or by using sources of labor that involve no long-term employment commitments and in some cases that facilitate evasion both of fiscal controls and administrative regulations.

Employers are now tending to envisage their work forces as composed of fixed and variable elements. At the core of the enterprise is a group of full-time career employees engaged directly in the production process and in managerial, financial, and marketing work. This core group does not vary with fluctuations in the enterprise's level of activity. It has long-term security of employment. For this group, management emphasizes flexible utilization made possible by training, retraining, and redeployment within the enterprise. The skills of the members of the group become increasingly polyvalent but also increasingly specific to the enterprise. Their security and their knowledge bind them to it.

Next to this core group is a peripheral category of full-time employees who have few opportunities of career development and less job security. Many of these are semiskilled workers or else downgraded skilled workers who did not make it into the core group. Management tolerates or encourages a relatively high turnover among this group so as to facilitate adjustments to market-dictated changes in output. Most conflict is likely to arise from within this group, particularly on the part of downgraded workers who look to their trade unions for protection.

A further peripheral category consists of employees of the enterprise on contracts of a type that allow for adjustment of employment levels to demand changes. These include part-time and short-term contracts and also work-sharing arrangements.

Finally, employers make increasing use of outwork and externally contracted services. This includes contracting for certain operations within the plant, such as maintenance and cleaning services, and also contracting for work done outside the plant either by self-employed individuals or by subcontracting enterprises.

The more stable and permanent jobs are those with the best working conditions and prospects of advancement. Low-paid, dangerous, dirty, or polluting work and work for which there is a more variable demand are relegated to the technologically peripheral category for subcontracting, etc. An international extension of the subcontracting practice is a most likely development, whereby Third World enterprises would contract to undertake the most energy-consuming and most polluting early stages of industrial processes, reserving the cleanest, most sophisticated stages for the core installations in their home countries. Such a differentiation between categories of tasks and terms of employment was pioneered in Japanese industry. Now all major world industries, from their cores outward, are undergoing a process of Japanization.

Through such strategies, employers are able to shift the burden of uncertainty from themselves and the core group to the various peripheral groups. The cumulative consequences of these strategies can be observed in a declining proportion of securely employed, relatively highly paid, and enterprise-integrated workers, together with a growing proportion of less securely employed, low-paid, peripheral workers segmented into several distinctive groups having little cohesion with one another. . . .

These changes in the social relations of production in the advanced capitalist countries are particularly marked since the onset of the economic crisis in the mid-1970s. In the United States, it has been observed that new jobs created have been predominantly in the low-skill, low-pay category, and mainly in services (of which temporary clerical work and fast-food restaurants are preeminent examples). In West Germany, before the crisis, labor market segmentation into isolated categories was not significant; there was a general mobility flow from less to more attractive jobs within enterprises, and where workers were displaced by technology, they were rapidly reemployed elsewhere. Since the crisis, boundary lines have become visible separating (1) a core labor force with secure employment, (2) a secondary labor force of more precariously employed workers vulnerable to economic cycles and doing the less attractive work, and (3) a marginal category of the more or less permanently unemployed. At the same time as these changes are increasing social vulnerability for a large section of the labor force and for those excluded from the labor force, the fiscal crisis of the state leads to a reduction of social services.

The trend toward a declining proportion of core jobs and an increasing proportion of peripheral jobs in the advanced capitalist countries, accelerated by the economic crisis, can be described as the peripheralization of the labor force. The structure of employment in these countries begins to take on some of the features hitherto associated with industrializing countries of the Third World. The trend has also been perceived as a regression to the heroic age of competitive capitalism in the nineteenth century.

Peripheralization takes both legal and extralegal or illegal forms. The legal avenues include part-time and temporary employment and subcontracting. The extralegal forms, i.e., avoidance of legal regulations and nonobservance of legal norms, and the illegal forms, i.e., those involved in the activities of criminal organizations, together comprise what has been called the underground or submerged economy, a counterpart in many ways to what in Third World countries has been described as the informal sector.

The underground economy covers a multitude of different forms of work and of social relations of production. Most underground activities are very poorly paid, a few are highly rewarded. There is work by undeclared workers: some work as outworkers in their homes, others in clandestine workshops often removable so as to avoid state inspectors. There is also undeclared work (and therefore untaxed income) by workers who hold legally declared jobs. Some of this takes the form of unreported overtime paid outside the official pay envelope. Often it takes the form of a worker having two jobs, one legally regulated and declared, the other undeclared and unregulated. Different kinds of people typically enter into these different kinds of illicit production relations. Women and children are commonly employed as outworkers. These groups are joined by illegal immigrants in clandestine workshop employment. Skilled male workers are more commonly practitioners of double employment. A further form of exchange in the underground economy is barter, for example, of services among higher income professionals. The only common features among these various forms of work in the underground economy are that no taxes are paid on the transactions, and legal norms and regulations are ignored.

These various forms of underground production have been noted in the United States. Illegal work is prevalent in agriculture, hotels and restaurants, cleaning services, and the clothing industry. Most striking has been the revival of sweatshops in the garment industry in New York City, employing many illegal immigrants from the Caribbean. But the underground economy is implicated also in the shift of industry toward nonunionized sites in the Southwest and in the expansion of domestic outwork. Among Western European countries, the phenomenon of the underground economy has been most pronounced in Italy and may have comparable dimensions also in Spain. In these countries, it is well represented in construction, clothing, shoes, gloves, hotels and restaurants, mechanical maintenance and electronics, agriculture, and domestic services but is present to some extent in virtually every branch of economic activity. In Naples alone, it is estimated that more than 100,000 persons are engaged in clandestine work, whole neighborhoods being organized for the production of gloves, shoes, and articles of clothing. In Prato, near Florence, a town noted for its booming small-scale textile manufacture, the vast majority of enterprises employ illegal workers. Double employment is particularly common among government employees in Italy. It has been estimated that about one-third of the shoe production in one region of Spain is either in clandestine workshops or by undeclared outworkers, the latter about 70 percent women and 25 percent children.

The underground economy is not separated from the regular economy. The two are closely interconnected. Factories that operate to a degree within the law also employ illegal workers; some may declare a few workers but employ in practice many more, others pay undeclared overtime to their declared workers. Clandestine factories subcontract to supply large-scale enterprises of the regular economy. Self-employed workers enter into undeclared contracts with legally recognized enterprises. Individuals, holding two jobs, divide their time between the regular and the underground economy. The underground economy is clearly an extension of the regular economy, symbiotically linked to it. The two make a functional whole.

PART THREE

THE POLITICAL ECONOMY OF STATES IN THE LIBERAL INTERNATIONAL ECONOMIC ORDER

The Conflicting Pulls of State Sovereignty and the New Transnationalism

The discussion in Part One of political economy of development focused on domestic patterns of national economic growth. Our aim was to determine how poverty amidst plenty could be explained by comparing the developmental experiences of different societies. Certain general features emerged within this conceptually confined analytical framework, including impoverishment of the rural sectors, expansions of inequalities in income, declines in urban employment, and worsening living conditions among the relatively poor. Some societies revealed less severe forms of inequality than others, however, and some policy strategies were clearly better designed than others to fulfill the requirements of the poor. Thus differences do arise among economies. Moreover, they represent important factors in assessing internal economic growth from the normative perspective of distributive justice.

Political economy of development establishes the linkages, therefore, between analytical and normative investigations of poverty amidst plenty within a theoretical perspective circumscribed by the political jurisdictions of specific civil societies. For it is within concrete societies that most economic activity occurs and policy strategies for social change appear to be most readily available.

Comparisons of individual societies alone, however, do not measure the internal impacts of relationships among them, nor do they take into account the domestic influences of structures and dynamics arising within the world economy as a whole. Nonetheless, as we discovered, domestic economic policies employ an array of major international instrumentalities. Governments do use the economies of other states as a means of pursuing their own national economic objectives.

International trade, in particular, is a policy area that is capable of significantly altering domestic economic conditions. This is especially true in the modern world economy, where international exchange has become increasingly dense in terms of sheer volume or quantity of goods, but also as measured by the complexity or quality of the services involved, as, for example, in information and finance. The influence of international trade is especially important in the modern world economy—so much the case that we found it necessary to investigate the role played by the world economy in determining the political character as well as the economic policies of governments and, indirectly, in shaping the domestic relations between the rich and poor.

We were thus prompted to look beyond the realm of domestic society for an explanation of the relationship of poverty to plenty even within analytical contexts established by national economies. The political economy of development alone, though an essential element in evaluating the causes of poverty amidst plenty, proved inadequate for what it ignores as much as for what it includes. For this reason, we found it necessary to go beyond the comparative approach to construct in Part Two a theoretical framework appropriate to political economy of uneven development. We were finally able to survey poverty amidst plenty from a perspective that included both international as well as transnational global forces and structures.

As we saw in Part Two, the rise of sovereign states since the fifteenth century involved (1) expansions of international trade, (2) imperialist incorporation of non-Western regions into the Western economic orbit, and (3) the eventual establishment of a world economy based upon (4) the first liberal market forms of international exchange and capitalist modes of production. In modern times, related phenomena such as (1) complex divisions of labor, (2) transnational business enterprise and modes of production, and (3) structural or positional relations between core and periphery have introduced elements of the new transnationalism into the modern world economy. Although disagreements arise regarding the nature of its probable impacts, few would argue that the new transnationalism, linking sectors of national economies to each other in ways unimaginable even a few years ago, are irrelevant to poverty, plenty, and the concerns of distributive justice. But how the new transnationalism relates to the extensions of poverty and thus to issues of distributive justice does represent a matter of considerable debate. It is to this set of issues that we must now turn in Part Three.

What our combined investigations of the political economy of development and of uneven development demonstrated is that the world economy is caught between the conflicting pulls of state or political sovereignty, on the one hand, and functional or structural forms of divisions of labor, on the other. Whereas sovereignty points toward social and political autonomy, division of labor bespeaks an economic transnationalism fostered initially by international trade but more recently by transnational modes of production.

Sovereignty and transnationalism from the perspectives of political economy of development and uneven development thus involve contrasting assumptions regarding the applicability of the normative standards of distributive justice to the world economy. Whereas the values of sovereignty within the political economy of development favor considerations of distributive justice only in the context of domestic society and sovereign states, the effects of transnationalism within the framework of the political economy of uneven development present a case for the relevance of international and transnational or global standards. For if we speak of the new transnationalism in a world economy, as an argument often advanced within the perspective of political economy of uneven development declares, we must be prepared to consider world society as a singular normative order in which standards of distributive justice may be said to apply.

In an attempt to resolve these tensions, we must adopt a third perspective in political economy: the political economy of states in the liberal international economic order. This is the purpose of Part Three, which is divided into two chapters; one deals with the international society of states, and the other, with the Liberal International Economic Order.

The Nationally Poor as a Segment of the Globally Poor

The concept of an international society of states is grounded in a basic recognition of the legal status and political sanctity of sovereignty. Sovereignty, however, is viewed not merely as a characteristic of individual states but from the perspective of the entire collective order made up of states on the basis of their sovereignty. The concept of a Liberal International Economic Order recognizes the central significance of state sovereignty and political autonomy. But it also registers the fact that international economic policies and intergovernmental organizations exist in the world economy to advance the cooperative and mutual interests of states presumably on a fair and reciprocal basis.

Actual application of the standards of international distributive justice in the real world of international politics and international economic relations occurs, in any event, within contexts established by either the international society of states or the Liberal International Economic Order. For it is these terms that identify the political and social character of the modern world economy as it is generally understood.

Debates over the extent to which international distributive justice represents a normative standard appropriate to the international society of states revolve around disagreements over the normative weight to be conceded to sovereign jurisdictions within the international society of states, as opposed to those to be conceded to the world economy given the international role of markets, from commodities to finance, and the impacts of transnational modes of production, from the circulation of technology to the flows of finance.

A basic set of questions thus emerges:

1. Since poverty appears internally within national economies or civil societies, are the norms of distributive justice limited to *national* applications alone?
2. Does international trade require the application of *international* standards of distributive justice, given increasingly dense international economic exchange and its accelerating domestic socioeconomic impacts?
3. Does the new transnationalism involve socioeconomic structures relevant to *transnational* applications of distributive justice whereby the nationally poor become considered segments of a globally poor community—and if so, upon what grounds might such standards be based?

The readings in Chapter Six address these questions, but from quite varied political, analytical, and normative perspectives. Contrasts among the three authors represented here point to the problems of applying international or transnational normative standards in a world economy defined by rapid economic change, but also by continuities of state sovereignty and power. The analysis provided by each reading takes its place along a spectrum created by the polar value-tensions between state sovereignty, on the one hand, and the new transnationalism, on the other. This pattern of disagreement typifies the debates being waged over the political economy of states in the Liberal International Economic Order.

Terry Nardin, in Reading #25, for example, envisions the international society of states as a form of **practical association** based on the political autonomy of its members and on the pluralism in the objectives they pursue. The international society of states did not arise historically, nor does it continue to exist because states have agreed to achieve a particular set of common aims or purposes. On the contrary, sovereignty ensures that states will sustain a great variety in the goals they seek.

The dictates of political order must thus come before the claims of distributive justice. In a practical association based on the autonomy of its members, the only form of normative consensus possible is that regarding not the ends, but the means or the procedures by which members interact with each other, such as the agreements embodied in the canons of international law. Thus, Nardin concludes, international law and legal forms of justice governing processes of state interaction must lay claim to precedence over any substantive end, such as international distributive justice, however desirable it may be.

W. H. Smith, in Reading #26, attempts to defend a possible middle position between the state-centric view, which rejects the application of international distributive justice on anything but national grounds, and the transnational view, which insists upon the validity of global standards of distributive justice regardless of the national jurisdictions of states. Smith examines the normative implications of interstate cooperation grounded in voluntary acceptance of international obligations. Thus his analysis points toward the possibilities of international justice, one that would operate between national and global forms of distributive justice, through the cooperative efforts of states and intergovernmental enterprise devoted to specific aims.

Within this context, Smith reviews two recent examinations of the role of equity and distributive justice in society in order to see how these might be extended to embrace international society. The first, that of John Rawls, entails **contractarian** approaches to civil society, which emphasize **egalitarian** values; the second, that of Robert Nozick, advances **conventional** approaches, which emphasize **libertarian** values. Smith remains skeptical, however, that either can serve to provide a basis for normative standards in international society.

Charles Beitz, in Reading #27, does present a case for cosmopolitan and egalitarian standards applicable to all national jurisdictions involved in the dynamics of international economic exchange and transnational modes of production. Poverty amidst plenty within one economy is but the reflection of global structures and dynamics. Thus domestic consequences of international and transnational processes must be properly judged according to global egalitarian standards.

At the heart of the argument developed by Beitz resides a concern for people as persons. The domestic impacts of transnational economic processes most readily subject to normative judgment are those that create disparities among persons in the name of aggregate or national economic growth. Accordingly, within the context of the international society of states, Beitz provides an argument against bias in world development comparable to that posited earlier by Lipton in the context of the political economy of development.

The basic thrust of the cosmopolitan argument in favor of distributive justice thus seems clear: However socioeconomic distortion or disarticulation occurs, whether as a result of national policies, international processes, or transnational structures, the norms of distributive justice become relevant and directly applicable to persons across all civil societies regardless of political jurisdictions.

The Polar Values in the
Liberal International Economic Order:
Political Autonomy and Economic Reciprocity

Since the end of World War II, the consolidated efforts of states to enhance national economic growth and world economic productivity have occurred within a set of arrangements constituting the Liberal International Economic Order. The struggle for distributive justice in the coming years will be waged within this order, which most assuredly was established not for the purposes of equity, but through a series of agreements designed to protect the stability of international economic relations, especially with respect to trade and monetary management.

The Liberal International Economic Order, initiated by the Bretton-Woods agreement of July 1944, defined the political framework for the creation of two major intergovernmental organizations: the General Agreement on Tariffs and Trade (GATT) and the International Monetary Fund (IMF). Both institutions are composed of member-states and thus are based upon the precepts of sovereignty and political autonomy. Together they have sustained the normative principles and rules governing trade and finance within the world economy since their foundation. Hence they have also appeared at times to promote elements of reciprocity in the economic relations of states. It follows that they represent important factors in any examination of the future possibilities of distributive justice.

The focus of Chapter Seven results from these observations. We must inquire about the basic values incorporated within the Liberal International Economic Order in order to establish the degree to which it has promoted the cause of distributive justice. In addition, we must investigate how it regulates both international trade and monetary policies in order to identify its effects upon the plight of lesser developing countries in reducing the gaps between poverty and plenty.

In recent years, the impacts of the Liberal International Economic Order have become highly controversial. Many Third World countries, for example, accuse it of serving the interests of the advanced industrial economies or, at the very least, of preserving a game in which the cards are stacked in favor of the rich.

In addition, intellectual debates have been waged over whether the Liberal International Economic Order should be considered an **international regime**. Some authors, including Stephen Krasner and Robert O. Keohane in this volume, argue that it is. Their claim is based upon the observation that the intergovernmental institutions established by and operating within it, such as the GATT and the IMF, maintain norms, principles, and decisionmaking rules or procedures that serve to restrain the behaviors of member-states. Other authors, including Susan Strange, disagree on the grounds that the Liberal International Economic Order permits such broad latitudes of political autonomy with respect to economic policies that it can hardly be conceived as a regime governing what those policies should be. Each of the four readings in Chapter Seven attempts to contribute not only to this debate but also to our understanding of how the Liberal International Economic Order promotes or impedes advancement of distributive justice within the world economy.

In Reading #28, Miriam Camps, assisted by Catherine Gwin, outlines the fundamental values maintained by the Liberal International Economic Order and the tensions that arise among them. Their analysis portrays a compromise between the values of autonomy and equity that, in effect, is built into the GATT and other intergovernmental organizations. Upon the conclusion of this reading, however, one is left to determine personally just how satisfactorily this liberal compromise operates in ameliorating the conditions of the poorest of the poor.

Susan Strange, in Reading #29, analyzes the significance of two recent developments that violate the spirit of the Liberal International Economic Order and, indeed, the letter of the GATT regarding free and nonsubsidized trade. These are widely referred to as **strategic competition** and the **new protectionism**. Her analysis introduces important insights into the nature of the new protectionism and its impact upon newly industrializing economies and, indirectly, upon the future course of distributive justice.

Strange's analysis of protectionism in international trade reminds us that politics plays a crucial role in determining international economic policies and that the state is the basic political agent within the Liberal International Economic Order. In this context, Stephen Krasner, in Reading #30, argues that the quest for distributive justice is tainted by the political agendas of Third World governments.

Not only are the societies of lesser developing nations poor, Krasner suggests, but their governments are politically weak. And in their weakness, they seek, through the promotion of authoritative revisions of the Liberal International Economic Order, to obtain the power and, if possible, the wealth they feel cannot be acquired through the dynamics of market competition. Krasner concludes that Third World appeals for a New International Economic Order in the name of distributive justice represent an assault against the international regimes of the Liberal International Economic Order.

Richard E. Feinberg concludes the chapter with Reading #31. His analysis reverses Krasner's emphasis from one concentrating on how Third World states defy the norms of the Liberal International Economic Order to one focusing on how the Liberal International Economic Order prevents lesser developing countries from promoting distributive justice at home.

In particular, Feinberg investigates the impacts of IMF lending and adjustment policies upon the capacity of lesser developing nations to provide basic needs to the poorest among the poor. He evaluates the extent to which IMF "conditionality"—that is, the conditions imposed by the IMF upon countries seeking balance-of-payments adjustment assistance—actually impedes distributive justice. His analysis demonstrates, in the context of international monetary management, what the study by Lipton revealed in the context of domestic economic policy—namely, a bias toward industrial development, Western-oriented commercial sectors, and financial penetration of lesser developing countries by transnational banking and business enterprises. His conclusion is stark: "Considerable evidence suggests that under many IMF-supported stabilization programs the wealthy elites have fared better than the rest of the population, and significant sectors of the poor have suffered disproportionately."

CHAPTER SIX

States and Distributive Justice: The Search for Grounds

READING #25   Justice in the International Society of States

Terry Nardin

Terry Nardin, in the following selection, affirms the primacy of political order over the objectives of distributive justice. Arguments favoring distributive justice mistake the international society of states for an association dedicated to common aims, or what Nardin calls a **purposive association**. The international society of states, however, is not a world organization dedicated to the achievement of specific ends or social conditions. Rather, it represents a formal or procedural form of association, one Nardin describes as a **practical association**. In this type of association, participant-members can forge agreements, but only with respect to rules and procedures by which all purposes, goals, or objectives are realized.

In a sense, Nardin's argument validates the legitimacy of standards of equal opportunity as opposed to those of equality of condition. State sovereignty within international society parallels the notion of individual opportunity within domestic society. Procedures that are put into play in the name of distributive justice, Nardin implies, must do so to advance equal opportunity among states, not equality of the conditions within or between them—an aim that advocates of cosmopolitan forms of distributive justice sometimes overlook.

But is a state in international society equivalent to an individual within civil society? And what if political autonomy perpetuates conditions of unjust inequality within and between states? Nardin's answers remain unequivocal. The morality of states is the morality of process and procedure, not of ends or conditions, however desirable they may be. "A just world," he concludes,

"is a world in which distributive considerations are subordinated to moral
ones, not the reverse."

—E. W.

Justice among states has traditionally been understood as requiring conduct
according to the rules of the society of states reflected in international law
and international morality. Conspicuously missing from the perennial debates
concerning the character of this society and the adequacy of its rules was
the issue of whether the institutions of the states system should be responsible
for the social and economic well-being of its member states and their
inhabitants. It is only in the present century, as the states system has become
increasingly organized, that the idea of international society as an arrangement
for furthering the particular substantive ends of providing social and economic
benefits and redistributing global wealth has become significant. Before these
developments the issue of distributive justice in international relations scarcely
existed. Justice, in the classical system, meant conformity to "the law of
nations" understood broadly as encompassing both international custom
and natural law. Today, the discussion of international justice is dominated
by redistributive demands and attacks on international law, in part because
the states system has been transformed from a European into a worldwide
society of states whose many new members possess in various international
organizations a forum for the expression of their views. International justice
has come to be identified with reforms aimed at securing a more equal
distribution of wealth rather than with conduct according to the common
rules of international society.

It is important to understand, in assessing the implications of this shift,
that the demand for distributive justice in the society of states is not limited
to transfers of wealth from the developed states of the West to the less
developed states of the Third World. It also involves changes in the rules
and institutions of the society of states, especially, but not exclusively, those
most directly concerned with economic matters. One can find in the arguments
of those favoring redistribution some extreme rhetoric, although it is not
always clear how seriously it is intended. There is, for example, the charge
that the current regime of international law constitutes an exploitative order
of rules created by the Western states during the colonial period—a charge
that continues to be made after decades of participation by the new states
in the international practice upon which customary international law is
based, as well as in the renegotiation and codification of many important
areas of international law, including the law of treaties, diplomatic representation, armed conflict, human rights, and the law of the sea. There is

Terry Nardin, *Law, Morality, and the Relations of States*. Copyright © 1983 by Princeton University
Press. Excerpt, pp. 267–271, reprinted with permission of Princeton University Press; endnotes
deleted.

also the assertion that those who are disadvantaged by international law as it exists have no legal or moral duty to observe the limits it imposes, that unjust rules cannot create binding obligations.

To some extent these charges and claims are well founded, for to some extent it is accurate to characterize the institutions of the society of states as enterprises for the promotion of the interests of the rich and powerful. It is therefore understandable and reasonable that the disadvantaged should wish to use these institutions for their own purposes. Nor is it surprising or unreasonable that in these circumstances they should adopt an instrumentalist approach to the question of obligation. The attractions of instrumentalism grow when expressions like "civility" and "the rule of law" are invoked hypocritically to justify the pursuit of self-serving policies. Insofar as international institutions are indeed enterprises for the pursuit of particular purposes, judgments of their desirability and of the authority of their rules will appropriately depend upon instrumentalist considerations. The rationale of participation in a purposive association lies in the advantages to be derived from it.

But, as I have tried to show, it is a mistake to regard international society itself as an association of this kind. Although states may decide how they will interact with each other *within* it (by making treaties or becoming members of international organizations), they are members of the society of states as such whether they choose to be or not. A state may withdraw from the International Labor Organization, but not from international society. A state may seek to minimize its transactions with other countries, but no state can participate in international society entirely on its own terms. The idea of society is the idea of certain shared understandings, practices, and standards of conduct. Even the most isolated states cannot escape the rules defining statehood, sovereignty, and territorial jurisdiction, and it is hard to imagine any state succeeding for long in ignoring the rules governing treaties and diplomatic representation. A state, like an individual, may be impatient with the rules and duties of social existence, but it cannot escape them so long as there remains any regular contact with others.

There are certain principles of customary international law that are so basic that it makes sense to say that they reflect the requirements of society in the circumstances of international relations. These principles include the independence and legal equality of states, the right of self-defense, the duty of nonintervention, the obligation to observe treaties, and restrictions on the conduct of war. Although one may make the authority of a purposive arrangement, such as that of a treaty or international organization, contingent on whether or not it is successful in serving its assigned purpose, the authority of those rules that are constitutive of international society itself is independent of any such consideration. If there exists an international society, in the sense of a universal association of states within a common framework of rules, it follows that individual states are not at liberty to accept or reject these rules at will, or to insist on their own private understanding of what the rules require in particular situations. And this is so regardless of whether or not these rules are advantageous, fair, or otherwise desirable. To require that all states benefit from a rule as a condition of acknowledging its authority is to demand the unattainable and to make life according to rules impossible.

Deference to the limits defined by a common set of rules means more than abandoning the proposition that the pursuit of particular substantive goals, such as economic development and redistribution, should override even the most fundamental and morally significant principles of international association. It also means that, even if the desirability of these rules is carefully distinguished from the question of their authority and ideals of distributive justice brought forward only as a standard for the criticism and reform of international law and institutions, any proposed alteration must itself be evaluated according to the constitutional principles embodied in international law and morality. Foreign policy in the world as it is cannot ignore distributive considerations, for the states system rests in part upon purposive arrangements that are open to criticism in purposive terms. Furthermore, redistributive policies might indeed strengthen the foundations of a rule-based international order. But that a particular redistributive proposal violates acknowledged moral limits is a consideration that should tell decisively against it. A just world is a world in which distributive considerations are subordinated to moral ones, not the reverse.

Despite their occasionally extreme rhetoric, this seems to be generally understood by the advocates of international redistribution. The demand for a "new international economic order" is basically a demand that certain rules of international law regulating international economic relations be altered to advance the development and increase the autonomy of the non-Western nations. It is essentially a set of proposals for reform, and like all such proposals it presupposes the existence and continued viability of the institutions within which the desired changes are to be implemented. The demand, for example, that the new states have a significant voice in an International Seabed Authority assumes an effective authority whose legal powers will be generally recognized. The demand for trade preferences requires a legally binding structure of trade rules into which preferential tariffs can be incorporated. Even the demand for exemptions from the requirements of international law, which is often made by representatives of the new states in treaty negotiations, presupposes rules from which exemptions can be granted and which others are required to observe. None of the changes sought by the less developed states as part of a "planetary bargain" with the developed states can be realized except on the basis of an authoritative body of common rules. While it is usual to demand that international law serve as the instrument of some higher purpose such as economic development and redistribution and that the only rules anyone has a duty to observe are those that serve to further these ends, the actual conduct of states suggests widespread recognition that such a doctrine is in fact subversive of a common moral order.

READING #26   Three Levels of Justice: National, International, and Global
W. H. Smith

W. H. Smith seeks to identify the grounds for applying standards of distributive justice nationally, internationally, and transnationally. He thus points to three levels of analysis: national, international, and global. In the course of his analysis, he assesses the nature of economic relations *within* national economies, *between* them, and *among* or *across* them all. Smith finds, not surprisingly, that the most sturdy foundations of distributive justice rest within civil society, where the complexity of economic exchanges, the frequency of social interactions, and the willingness to conform to laws and authoritative practices reinforce habits of cooperation basic to all forms of justice.

Smith explores two interpretations of justice within civil society in order to evaluate their relevance to international or global society. The first is the **contractarian** approach presented by John Rawls, and the second is the **conventional** approach reflected in the work, among others, of Robert Nozick. The contractarian approach to justice judges the real or non-ideal world from a perspective informed by principles derived from an ideal world structured by a social contract. The conventional approach rejects this philosophical methodology by arguing that only the conventions of the real world can serve as the basis for determining the norms of distributive justice.

The debate between Rawls and Nozick regarding distributive justice constitutes an important element in Smith's analysis. Rawls argues that the primary objective of social order is to apportion basic rights, moral obligations, and social benefits in the most equal or fair manner possible. Without some acceptance of the principles of justice and in the absence of some measure of equality, social cooperation turns into bitter conflict. Ideally, those inequalities that do exist must work on behalf of the least disadvantaged. These observations, as Smith indicates, lead Rawls to assert two principles of justice: the principle of greatest equal liberty or fairness, and the principle of difference.

The conventional approach disavows contractarianism as a logical basis for normative judgment. Civil society in the real world does not originate with social contracts, real or ideal; rather, it reflects the historical evolution of conventions. These conventions define the entitlements and protections due individuals as they provide for themselves and others through their own efforts. Nozick's conventional approach thus counters the contractarianism of Rawls by suggesting that persons in society are entitled to the holdings they have acquired by means of their own initiatives so long as these do not involve criminal or immoral acts. Interference in the distribution of such holdings is never an act of distributive justice but one that involves the suppression of liberty. Nozick thus advances a **libertarian** perspective in contrast to the **egalitarian** approach of Rawls.

Smith evaluates the relevance of both the conventional and contractarian perspectives to international distributive justice and demonstrates that contractarianism may be the modern counterpart of a theory envisaging the international society of states as a **civitas maxima,** that is, a civil order based upon a contract among states, whereas the conventional perspective enjoys a long intellectual history stemming from the **natural law tradition.** Smith outlines some of the fundamental assumptions about international justice advanced by these traditions and, on this basis, examines modern arguments regarding international distributive justice, including those advanced by Charles Beitz in the subsequent reading.

In the end, Smith carves out a middle ground in his interpretation of the normative bases of international distributive justice. He rejects notions of global justice on a variety of grounds, both historical and philosophical, but he does envision an extended future role for the norm of international distributive justice—one that would mediate the claims of national justice with the demands for global justice. "Justice within the state is at once a contribution to global justice and a barrier to it," he writes. "But international justice cannot ignore the claims of mankind as a whole."

—E. W.

Traditionally justice has been regarded as a quality of politically autonomous institutions. Such an organisation holds final authority over the individuals and lesser groups within it, a sovereignty which is self-contained and exclusive of the authority of other organisations. It is in the state that problems of distribution perennially arise. The social and economic co-operation that facilitates the creation of goods of all kinds takes place largely within states. In many societies, moreover, the distribution of these goods is something which the central government can significantly influence. Government, in other words, offers one means of creating justice at least within its own boundaries.

The business of social co-operation is highly complex, giving rise to many rights and duties among those participating in the enterprise. These rights and duties are 'special' in the sense that they are held not by all individuals but by specific individuals by virtue of the association or connection between them. Each society, while perhaps accepting the idea of general rights, will determine for itself what particular rights and duties (as examples of goods in general) ought to be distributed and what rules of distribution ought to be adopted. As Hume observed in the *Inquiry Concerning the Principles of Morals*, the content of rights and duties varies

W. H. Smith, "Justice: National, International or Global," in Ralph Pettman, ed., *Moral Claims in World Affairs.* Copyright © 1979 by Croom Helm Ltd. Excerpt, pp. 92–114, reprinted with permission of Croom Helm Ltd.; endnotes deleted.

from society to society and the fact that they exist at all is not a necessary but merely a contingent fact. Only when men come together for some purpose does the possibility of justice arise and then it is limited to that specific group.

It is the stuff of political philosophy to speculate on the nature of political association among men. Explanations are, in the broadest terms, based either on a social contract or on convention. Both approaches seek to account for the fundamental principles which govern a society and must therefore find a place for concepts of justice. This is not the occasion to go over the classical theories, although I shall refer to some of them here and there. I shall instead look at two contributions to the theory of justice—one based on contract, the other on convention—which are of recent date and might be expected to throw some light on the more contemporary issues.

The first work is John Rawls's A Theory of Justice which, in the author's words, 'generalizes and carries to a higher level of abstraction' traditional contract theories. For Rawls justice is 'the first virtue of social institutions.' . . . It is concerned with 'the way in which the major social institutions distribute fundamental rights and duties and determine the division of advantages from social co-operation.' . . . Rawls envisages the basic principles of justice being chosen by free and rational individuals who are willing to co-operate yet concerned for their own interests. In this 'original position' the parties are equal in terms of bargaining power but, most importantly, ignorant of the position which each will occupy in the social structure for which they are drawing up rules. From behind this 'veil of ignorance' two principles are said to emerge. The first states the requirement of equality in apportioning basic rights and duties; the second holds that inequality is justified only if it produces benefits for the whole society, in particular for those least favourably placed. This latter principle Rawls terms the 'difference principle' and adds to it provisions concerning equality of opportunity to enjoy whatever privileges do prove necessary.

Rawls's theory is far richer than this summary might suggest. Two important qualifications which Rawls makes need to be noted here. The first is that justice is not the only prerequisite for a viable society since problems of co-ordination, efficiency and stability must also be solved. . . . Secondly, Rawls assumes a society which is more or less self-sufficient. . . . It is not altogether clear what Rawls means by this. A community that is self-sufficient both economically and politically certainly fits the description. The whole notion of a contract suggests political autonomy but the consequences of extensive foreign relations and interdependence are not spelled out (though it is only fair to observe that Rawls does not see his theory as complete).

In the tradition of contract theorists Rawls demonstrates the crucial connection between social co-operation and the possibility of justice. Each society requires some notion of justice for without it conflict and coercion will prevail over co-operation. But the creation of justice is necessarily something that sets one group of individuals, the parties to the contract, apart from the rest of humanity. And by uniting with some, as Rousseau has it, we become enemies of mankind. Rawls's theory is also a tribute to the long tradition in Western philosophy which has sustained a vision of the perfectly just society and has thereby provided standards by which to measure existing societies. It is also typical of the Greek inheritance which tends to relegate foreign relations to an afterthought. Rawls's attempt in this direction will be considered in a later section.

The alternative approach to political association relies not on a contract, real or notional, but on the historical fact that groups of human beings have come together for common purposes and have developed through custom and convention principles to govern their relations. This approach bestows the blessing of history rather than of reason on the connection between society and justice. It begins by noting that in no society was there any initial distribution of goods in the sense of a deliberate parcelling out of rights and benefits. Men come together possessed of all kinds of resources and talents, some well endowed, some barely endowed at all. There is no call to justify this state of affairs, however randomly Nature or God might appear to have dealt out the good things of the world. Personal worth or merit has no significance for these initial holdings.

Individuals, furthermore, are free to use or dispose of their resources as they wish: to employ them, for example, to create more resources or to give them away to anyone they choose. The crucial provision governing such changes in holdings is that they do not take place in unfair or immoral ways. As long as this provision is observed, an initial just distribution of goods can only lead to other just distributions, never to an unjust distribution. Those who at any point argue for a redistribution must demonstrate that some goods have been improperly acquired; otherwise they are themselves in a position of infringing moral rules by depriving certain individuals of the freedom to use their resources as they choose. For Nozick, then, a theory of justice has three main components: an account of how goods came to be held in the first place, rules governing the transfer of holdings, and principles for rectifying unjust transfers.

The strength of this approach is its rootedness in history rather than any vision of the future. It may employ various theories to account for the origin of private property, but stresses the natural liberty of men to acquire it, use it and transfer it. If men have different talents, abilities and inclinations in these respects, then some will have the means to secure more benefits than others. To prevent individuals from achieving this sort of superiority is to interfere with their natural liberty. As with men, so with states. If individuals can claim exclusive rights to certain goods, so must a group of individuals be able to enjoy possession of common goods to the exclusion of other groups. The shift from individual to group is not automatic but it is reasonable and corresponds to the practice of groups in their relations with one another. It is, significantly, a major embarrassment to Marxist theory in that a communist state in a less than communist world must find

itself asserting exclusive property rights over its territory and resources.
. . .

To maintain that justice is essentially national in origin is not necessarily to deny that justice has no place in international relations. One school of thought, epitomised in various ways by Hegel, Machiavelli and Hobbes, does see justice stopping at the water's edge. For them states are morally separate and cannot subordinate themselves to any common principles of justice. Hegel, while recognising universal principles, argued that they could only be made real through the individual state. Similarly, Machiavelli accepted the existence of principles of right and wrong but maintained that they had to be overridden by the demands of the state. Only Hobbes represents a purely positivist view: such moral obligations as exist derive from the command of the sovereign and extend only to the limit of his authority.

But the other school of thought, in which the liberal realist tradition is firmly planted, does see a certain limited scope for justice. States pursue their own interests but, by virtue of a measure of overlapping interests among some or all of their number and of their longstanding interrelationship in a single system, they are able to find room for certain rules of behaviour, including principles of justice, in their relations with one another. What distinguishes the realist from the idealist is simply the extent to which each sees national interests as overlapping. The idealist can discern, actually or potentially, a perfect harmony of interests.

The national approach to justice also finds much support in the practice of states, including many who are vocal in condemning the injustice of contemporary international relations. The principle of sovereign equality has become an axiom, asserting the right of each state to manage its own affairs and hence to create its own principles of justice. Third World states in particular are anxious to confirm their ownership of resources within their national boundaries regardless of their ability or inability to exploit them. Similarly with the world's oceans, states are looking more to expand national control than to an international regime. Demands for justice, it must also be noted, are couched in terms of aid to governments rather than to individuals. For each state wishes to retain control over the manner in which goods are distributed within its boundaries. And while it may be true that this is a demand of governments made for the sectional purposes of a ruling elite, it does not follow that the citizens of such governments would lightly abandon the idea of national autonomy for the sake of an improvement in their food consumption.

Justice, on this view, is founded in the state so that the mere fact of contact between states does not mean that new concepts of justice must replace the old. On the contrary, global economic interdependence has led to a reassertion of the demand for national autonomy. It is leading not to a world society with its own principles of justice but must rather be taken as a warning against the erosion of independence. . . .

It is possible to take issue with the idea of national justice in two ways: by tackling the theories of justice as such or by arguing their applicability to some society other than the state. In recent years the main exponents of this latter line of attack have looked to a broader basis for justice than the state. This will be our focus here, although the tradition of thought that sees salvation in smaller groups is far from extinct.

The arguments against taking the state as the matrix of justice need only be summarised here. They relate, on the one hand, to doubts about the capacity of the state to perform the functions expected of it, e.g. the provision of security against attack and the maintenance of minimum economic standards. Without trying to resolve these issues, it may be noted that they reflect Western anxieties more than global concerns; they are the worries of states which have known security and prosperity but have lost them rather than of states which have never known these blessings. On the other hand, a powerful volley of arguments has been launched by those who stress the changing nature of world economic activity. Modern production, it is claimed, can no longer be walled up within the state; traditional political barriers have been scaled or have been pushed down for the benefit of economic man. Two trends are emphasised: the interdependence of national economies and the dependence of some economies on others.

This is not the place to debate the facts of global economic developments. The conclusions to be deduced from them are another matter. For some the emergence of global economic relations (whether of co-operation or exploitation) necessitates a new basis for principles of justice. No longer can states be regarded as autonomous; they are bound by economic ties and in many cases this means by political ties as well. Others, however, do not reach the same conclusions. Economic interdependence, among states as among men, is seen to breed 'not accommodation and harmony but suspicion and incompatibility'. It is no answer to say that this simply demonstrates the need for a wider conception of justice. The creation of justice, moreover, has typically been possible only when men have submitted themselves to a common political authority. In the absence of world government, global justice appears to be beyond man's grasp. . . .

For the foreseeable future the most effective principles of justice will be those found within the nation-state. There is no simple way in which they can be extended to mankind at large. But while national justice is not a direct contribution to global justice and in fact makes the latter more difficult to attain, its merits ought not to be overlooked. There is a common assumption that settling for justice on a national rather than a global basis is something to be deplored, that it is to settle for second-best. Yet it does seem that part of man's nature is a sense of belonging to an exclusive group, a sense which cosmopolitanism seeks to stifle. On the other hand, the very notion of morality—moral rules which individuals as individuals ought to follow—suggests that man also has a sense of the universal. It may posit unrealisable goals but it, too, ought not to be suppressed.

The role of international justice appears to be that of mediating principles of both national and global justice. To be sure, the former will predominate, but global justice has not been ignored altogether. There is some notion of an obligation on the part of states to aid those individuals who are in the direst circumstances; but states naturally remain reluctant to accept principles which involve international redistribution of resources for this would open the door to all manner of claims against them. This emphasis on retaining autonomy is one that is shared both by the wealthy states and by those states which at present condemn the dominance of the rich.

As for economic inequalities in the world, these are indeed enormous. But the market-place perhaps offers more hope of reducing these differences than any principles of international or global justice. In the past political power that could be extended overseas gave certain states the capacity to create and maintain economic advantages for themselves. If it is the case that power is becoming more dispersed throughout the globe and more difficult to deploy abroad, then some economic imbalances may be reduced. Again, recent developments have shown that the sources of supply of many raw materials and primary products are widely spread. This will also serve to redress economic inequalities in some degree. And the more interdependent the world economy, the greater the bargaining power of those with goods in short supply.

The most intriguing question of all is how long the total stock of the earth's resources will hold out. If global shortages begin to bite they could lead to a much greater sense of a common predicament for man. Principles of justice to govern the distribution of resources in limited supply might become more appealing. But global shortages could also produce competition between states and present some countries with the opportunity to exploit a monopoly position. If what I have said about the persistence of national outlooks is correct, this more gloomy prospect also looks the more probable.

READING #27   Global Egalitarianism: Can We Make Out a Case?
Charles Beitz

Although standards of distributive justice represent a concern of many engaged in the study of world political economy, not all hold to the principles associated with equality or egalitarianism. Egalitarianism stresses the moral primacy of equality among persons or agents in society. Such an orientation is condemned by those who, as Nozick mentioned in the last reading, view such values as a threat to the right of persons to enjoy the pursuit of liberty. From this viewpoint, all claims to benefits and privileges in society stem from individual merits or deserts—never from needs. Charles Beitz, in his reading, explores several counterarguments and presents a cosmopolitan case for egalitarian principles of international distributive justice.

To accomplish his intellectual mission, Beitz raises a number of questions, including the following: What are cosmopolitan egalitarian standards, and how do they apply in the modern world economy? And can a normative middle-ground be defined such that the autonomy of states and cosmopolitan egalitarian standards are both accommodated? Beitz reviews the arguments both for and against cosmopolitan egalitarian standards of justice, including, for example, charity, reparations, and dependency; and he refers to the dependency notion of "double injustice" confronted earlier in Reading #22 by V. Kubálková and A. A. Cruickshank.

Beitz focuses his most ardent attention upon those who reject cosmopolitan egalitarian principles. Such authors include Robert W. Tucker, who, in a manner similar to that of Stephen Krasner in Reading #30, asserts that the "new egalitarianism" overlooks the realities of international politics and state power. Beitz counters such arguments by demonstrating that the basis for cosmopolitan egalitarian claims must refer to equality among persons, not necessarily to that among states or national economies.

Beitz concludes with a resounding affirmation of the validity of cosmopolitan egalitarian standards on the grounds that all persons should be treated fairly regardless of citizenship. An international economic order incorporating cosmopolitan egalitarian standards might establish procedures for closing the gap between poverty amidst plenty *within* each civil society irrespective of the boundaries established by state sovereignty. But socioeconomic disparities would remain *between* national economies in terms of their overall level of development. Thus cosmopolitan egalitarian standards, if ever imposed or realized, would not necessarily work to reduce the gaps between rich and poor countries as such. Instead, they would operate on a relative basis to reduce the distance separating the very rich and the very poor within each national economy—whether the society in question was itself rich or poor.

—E. W.

Why should global poverty concern the affluent? Why do the global poor have a claim on the sympathy, the political energy, and the economic resources of the rich?

These questions take on a new urgency as the dimensions of global poverty come to be widely recognized. Slowly, a consensus seems to be emerging that the affluent nations must undertake concerted action to help the "forgotten 40 percent" of the human population. This consensus finds an echo in the widespread sympathy with which the Third World's program for a "New International Economic Order" (NIEO) has been received. At the same time skeptical and pseudorealistic voices are declaring that the claims of the Third World on the rest of us are in fact overstated or nonexistent.

Charles Beitz, "Global Egalitarianism: Can We Make Out a Case?" *Dissent*, vol. 26, no. 1, Winter 1979. Copyright © 1979 by *Dissent*. Excerpt, pp. 59–68, reprinted by permission of *Dissent*; endnotes deleted.

As a result, the questions posed above are now being widely discussed—not merely the problem of how to help the poor nations but whether and in what ways we are obligated to do so. I propose here to examine the main arguments customarily offered for supporting such programs as the NIEO, as well as some of the problems that might follow its implementation.

The reasons for asking these questions are not entirely Socratic. Our assessment of the NIEO proposals depends largely on why we think any such proposals deserve sympathetic attention. As I hope to show, a deeper understanding of the moral basis of Third World claims will in turn make clear in what respects the NIEO is incomplete, and illuminate some potential dilemmas involved in completing them.

Charity

Why do the global poor deserve a better deal? One's immediate response is that those seriously deprived of the means of life have an automatic claim on our sympathy and, when appropriate, our political energy and economic resources. The argument rests on considerations of charity: whenever we can help alleviate human suffering, we should. The character of our relationship to those who suffer does not matter; indeed, we need have no special relationship at all. All that matters is that suffering exists; when it does, we should act to alleviate it.

This argument has undeniable force, but not so much as one might think. Arguments of charity have notorious limits. They allow us to beg off when the costs of action are significant. Other concerns, closer to home, will compete for our resources, and in any event, there always lurks in the background the question, "Why me?" That is, "Why should I sacrifice when not everybody else will?" Moreover, since arguments of charity concentrate on immediate distress rather than underlying social structures, they define the problem in superficial terms. Such arguments may seem to be satisfied when distress is relieved even though underlying causes remain untouched.

On neither point does the charity argument capture widely held views about the moral seriousness of the poor countries' claims. These claims demand concerted and potentially costly action by the rich—action aimed at the sources of poverty rather than merely its immediate manifestation. In both respects, the poor countries have attracted many sympathizers among progressives in the affluent North. Sympathy for the poor South, therefore, must be based on more fundamental moral concerns than charity.

More far-reaching arguments for the claims of the poor result from taking seriously the relative as well as absolute dimensions of world poverty. To take note of global distributive inequality is to suggest that the poverty of the many and the affluence of the few are somehow connected. If so, then the character of the connection may explain why the claims of the poor seem to carry more weight than the argument of charity allows.

Reparations

How are global affluence and global poverty connected? And what does the connection imply about Third World claims? It is sometimes said that the affluence-poverty connection is historical. The affluent countries are said to be responsible for the plight of the poor countries because, to put it crudely, in the past the rich used their political power to extract large surpluses from colonial dependencies. Indigenous social formations were broken down, economic structures distorted, and new needs created that could only be satisfied by the extractive, dependent relationship with the metropole. The colonial tie worked like a siphon: once the outward flow of resources was set in motion, it perpetuated itself, moving well beyond the temporal limits of the colonial period. Political imperialism was supplanted by economic imperialism, colonial armies by comprador military governments, and state-based trading companies by multinational corporations.

Since poverty is seen as having been exacerbated by imperialism, the demand to reverse the flow of resources can be interpreted as a demand to rectify past wrongs. And since affluence is seen as having been partly attained by taking advantage of unequal power relations, the same demand can be interpreted as a demand to restore to their rightful owners advantages unjustly gained. Either way, the poor countries' claims are claims for reparations.

No doubt, the picture sketched in the last paragraphs is overly simple. For example, the position as presented combines two logically independent empirical claims, namely, that imperialism imposed net costs on colonial countries and that it resulted in net gains for metropolitan ones. But the essential weakness of the argument does not really involve these empirical issues. Its main weakness is the unstated premise that the heirs of those who gained benefits unjustly have obligations to make restitution to the successors of the deprived. Without questioning the injustice of imperialism, present-day citizens of the rich countries might ask why they should bear the costs of rectifying injustices in which they took no part. One might be tempted to reply that their favored position is partly a *result* of these past injustices, and so the rich do not *deserve* their present, favored status. But it is a real question whether *anyone* deserves the social position that is inherited, regardless of the justice or injustice of the means by which the predecessors attained them. Suppose that Rockefeller's grandfather acquired all of his wealth in morally benign ways. Would that fact make any difference at all to our view that the present Rockefellers don't deserve all the wealth they inherited? Injustice done by previous generations seems irrelevant to whether members of *present* generations deserve what they have. If this is right, then it is no longer clear that the reparations argument for the poor countries' claim is compelling, even if its empirical premises are granted.

This is a surprising conclusion, since at first glance the reparations argument seems plausible. Why? It is not the demonstration of past injustices that is compelling but the implicit contention that these injustices continue to exist. The focus on historical considerations obscures this while it opens the argument to the sort of attack I have outlined. But if it is *present* injustice that needs to be redressed, then the complicated moral arguments and even more complicated historical arguments about the nature of imperialism are beside the point. It would be better to ask what is at present unjust about rich-poor relations.

Dependency

A natural response would be that the residue of imperialism is itself unjust. This is the moral critique implicit in various theories of economic dependency. These theories involve several claims about the effects on poor and ex-colonial countries of their economic relations with the rich, although none of these theories makes any essential reference to explicitly historical considerations.

First, it is argued that participation in the capitalist world economy produces distortions in the economic structures of poor countries, for example, by encouraging the development of capital-intensive manufacturing where there are vast numbers of unemployed persons, or by discouraging local entrepreneurs from activities aimed at satisfying the needs of the bulk of the population. Second, it is claimed that participation in the world economy produces political distortions, by generating an outward-looking elite with disproportionate political affluence that prevents the local government from governing in the interests of all its citizens. Third, it is alleged that the unequal power relations in the world economy force the poor countries to engage in trade and to accept foreign investment on exploitative terms. For example, multinational corporations with technological monopolies extract monopoly rents as the price of locating manufacturing facilities in poor countries, or they employ local labor at wages far below those paid in more developed countries. As if each claim were not bad enough, the three taken together are mutually reinforcing. Economic distortions perpetuate political ones, and both kinds reduce the ability of the dependent state to seek improvements in the terms of trade and investment.

The moral critique implicit in these charges holds that poor people in poor countries are victims of a double injustice brought on by participation in the capitalist world economy. They suffer the consequences of *domestic* social injustice because they live in societies characterized by acute inequality. Domestic income inequalities exacerbate existing poverty, while inequalities of political power make it almost impossible for disadvantaged classes to improve their position. These domestic injustices are compounded by *international* political and economic inequalities. Even if it were possible for disadvantaged classes in poor countries to redress domestic injustices, they would still find themselves up against the overwhelming political power of rich countries and the economic resources of multinational corporations based there. On the other hand, even if poor countries succeeded in reordering the world economy in a way that secured better terms of trade and investment, the disadvantaged classes in poor countries would still find themselves up against domestic social injustices. Clearly, the double injustice identified by dependency theory means that adequate strategies of change must simultaneously address domestic and international injustices, and the structures that perpetuate them.

Considered as the basis of an argument for the poor countries' claims, dependency theory has two advantages over the other arguments here considered. It does not rest the demand for present remedial action only on assertions about wrongs done by previous generations; and it does assert that a connection exists between present affluence and present poverty. Thus it can be argued that the income of the global rich is being unjustly won, and that the world economy should be reordered to reallocate income to those being unjustly deprived.

But the dependency argument also has weaknesses, although not fatal ones. In particular, the argument seems to depend on the accuracy of saying that the relations between rich and poor countries are exploitative. The rich are said to prosper *because of* their relations with the poor, and the poor to suffer *because of* their relations with the rich. What is pictured is the contemporary equivalent of the "siphoning off" that was supposed to result from imperialism.

This picture is controversial in at least three ways. First, the gains to the rich from their relations with the dependent poor may not be very significant. It is often pointed out, for example, that income from trade with the poor countries contributes only a small percentage of the combined national incomes of the industrial countries. If so, it is implausible to suggest that the rich stay rich because they exploit the poor. Second, it is sometimes said that the dependent poor are only *relatively* (but not absolutely) disadvantaged by participation in the capitalist world economy. Nonparticipants would be far worse off than those in the most dependent of poor countries. Third, it is not generally true that the degree of a country's dependence varies with the depth of its poverty. For example, if a country's degree of dependence can be roughly measured by the percentage of foreign ownership of its capital stock or by the percentage of its national income attributable to trade, then it can be shown that the poorest of the poor countries are not the most dependent. If so, it is not clear that dependency is an essential cause even of relative disadvantage.

Egalitarianism

To each of these possible objections to the dependency argument, there are replies of varying plausibility. I shall not pursue them, however, since there is another argument for the poor countries' claims, involving a straightforward appeal to distributive justice that builds on some elements of dependency theory while avoiding the problematic conclusion that dependency relations are the main *causes* of the extreme global disparities of wealth and poverty.

The problem of distributive justice is customarily considered in domestic society, so we might begin to think about it at that level. As philosophers such as Aristotle and Hume have recognized, the problem arises because a society is not merely a collection of self-sufficient individuals; it is a group in which a division of labor exists such that no one (or almost no one) produces all that he or she needs. The problem of distributive justice is to determine the morally best way in which the social product can be shared among the members of society. It can be argued (although I won't do so here) that the just society is one whose institutions distribute the social product relatively equally—"relatively" because some inequalities might be justified by considerations of desert, or need, or (as John Rawls has argued) the requirements of raising the absolute position of society's worst-off group. The point is that relative equality is at least a rough approximation of what distributive justice requires. It goes without saying that the main concern of distributive justice is not with setting terms for each particular transaction, but rather with identifying political-economic institutions most likely to yield just distributions over time.

Though familiar enough, all this is necessary to set the background for a more immediate question: why should distributive justice stop, as it were, at a country's borders? Distributive justice gets its grip on us as people who occupy positions in a social division of labor. But if the division of labor is global, then the logic that supports domestic egalitarianism appears to support global egalitarianism as well.

The egalitarian argument does not involve controversial premises concerning the particular costs and benefits of dependency. In fact, it makes clear that what is truly significant—and not in dispute—about dependency is that it characterizes a global division of labor. The world's aggregate product is a *social* product, raising the question of how that product should be shared. If one believes that distributive claims rest on a person's participation in social production, it appears that one should assess international distributive claims just as one assesses domestic ones. In a world in which state boundaries do not set off discrete systems of social production, egalitarianism in one country does not make sense. A consistent egalitarianism must take the world as its subject.

The egalitarian argument does not dispute another key thesis of dependency theory, namely, that one of the main mechanisms of inequality is the dependent state itself. Thus, a commitment to global egalitarianism need not limit itself to the reform of inegalitarian structures at the international level. To the extent that social structures in dependent states contribute to internal inequalities, global egalitarianism yields a moral case for internal reform as well.

Two objections to this position recently have been voiced by Robert W. Tucker.

First, while recognizing the growth of a world economy involving an international division of labor, Tucker claims that state boundaries continue to delimit communities within which egalitarianism is a plausible distributive principle: "It is the state that, more often than not, has created the degree of interdependence identified with community."

This is a true, historical observation. But it is not clear why Tucker's historical observation is relevant to the egalitarian argument. If the mark of a community is the existence of a social division of labor and the economic interdependence it entails, and if the existence of community, so defined, is a precondition of distributive justice, then the facts of international economic life leave no alternative to accepting the egalitarian argument, globally applied. Tucker's reading of the history of states does not undermine this reasoning.

But perhaps Tucker means to press a different argument. Correctly noticing that some forms of socioeconomic cooperation are more intense than others, he might want to claim that only cooperation within states is sufficiently intense to trigger the familiar requirements of distributive egalitarianism. This reformulation does not salvage his argument, however, because even domestic cooperation varies in intensity, and it is plausible that many to whom we readily acknowledge egalitarian distributive obligations make only marginal contributions to economic life and are only marginally affected by it. If so, the point about the intensity of cooperation does not distinguish global from domestic justice.

Neither does it help to point out the subjective differences between domestic and global societies. No one would seriously dispute that people generally feel stronger ties to other members of their own societies than to those elsewhere. But the temptation should be resisted to draw inferences about the limits of distributive obligations, since it is not clear how feelings of community affiliation are relevant to the argument of egalitarianism. Indeed, such feelings are notoriously unreliable guides to the limits of moral ties, more often functioning as rationalizations for inaction than as true indicators of the reach of our responsibilities.

Tucker's second objection is more frequently heard and more easily disposed of. It is that the poor countries' claims are claims for equality among *states*, whereas the egalitarian argument given above urges equality among *persons*. To some, like Tucker, it seems mistaken to advance the egalitarian argument in support of the poor countries' claims. It is a confusion, he suggests, to apply an interpersonal standard internationally.

There is a confusion, but it is Tucker's. Since countries contain people, international redistribution *is* interpersonal redistribution. Moreover, it is not implausible to suggest that the goal of interpersonal egalitarianism might be served by promoting transfers from rich to poor countries. Of course, this goal will not be achieved by transfers alone; as dependency theory makes clear, a country's domestic structure might keep large infusions from the outside from ever reaching the bottom. Tucker's confusion is to take this possibility as an objection in principle to international egalitarianism, whereas the possibility, in fact, counsels caution about what can be expected from interstate transfers unaccompanied by reforms inside poor societies. The egalitarian argument not only does not ignore such reforms, but might require them.

CHAPTER SEVEN

The Liberal International Economic Order and Distributive Justice

READING #28 The Liberal International Economic Order
Miriam Camps, with Catherine Gwin

Liberalism, an influential philosophy of economic growth based on the precepts of competitive markets and free international trade, has guided the character of the international economic order since modern states began to mature. The flourishing of states and the prospering of Western society are often attributed to the values of liberalism and to the economic theories developed by its great classical proponents, Adam Smith, David Ricardo, and, later, John Stuart Mill.

In the following reading, Miriam Camps, assisted by Catherine Gwin, examines the manner in which the modern Liberal International Economic Order incorporates the values of classical and neoclassical liberal economic analysis, including efficiency, equity, and autonomy. She reveals how these basic values are in turn reflected in the policies of the major intergovernmental organizations that help to regulate the Liberal International Economic Order. As this reading assumes an understanding of the logic and values of liberalism, we should briefly explore the nature and import of liberal perspectives on markets and socioeconomic values.

The basic logic of classical liberalism is straightforward:

1. Personal self-interest and private egoism leads to collective efficiency.
2. Collective efficiency leads to economic productivity and prosperity.
3. Greater prosperity leads to equity.

What lends liberalism its historic theoretical influence is its emphasis on efficiency and its rejection of leveling philosophies that would appear to threaten all personal initiative by imposing upon it the social straightjackets of equity. Indeed, one of the great assumptions in liberal economic thought is that *public good* derives from *private egoism*. Classical and neoclassical liberals thus envision the prescriptive norms of distributive justice as artificial contrivances that, once introduced into national or international economic policies, work to stifle private enterprise. Thus liberals favor normative principles grounded in prudential notions of self-interest, autonomy, and efficiency.

As implied by Camps and Gwin, these classical presumptions have guided the operations of the main institutions of the Liberal International Economic Order. For many liberals, the fault of those who stress distributive justice as a social standard is that they stress socioeconomic outcomes rather than processes of interaction. An emphasis upon process, however, leads in the liberal view to a recognition of the central role of markets in producing wealth or plenty in the most efficient manner.

Liberals assert that markets work to protect economic freedom by creating an infinite number of entry points for individuals and corporate organizations to pursue profits and economic gain. Markets consequently facilitate distribution of social and economic benefits—from personal consumption to wide-scale social values and welfare. The reason is simple: As markets tend to be the sites of individual judgment and pursuit of self-interest, they constitute the springboards of aggregate economic prosperity.

A liberal economic perspective thus regards market exchange devoted to fostering private egoism as the prime source of distributive justice. This faith in the capacities of consumer self-interest to generate collective good is linked to the fundamental conviction that open markets promote efficiency. If markets are permitted to release the energies of self-interest, the *invisible hand* of collective efficiency will be strengthened. The special appeal of markets is not that they are a victory for private egoism alone, therefore, but that they are the main instrumentalities for harnessing the energies of individual self-interest in a socially productive manner.

This firm belief that markets foster collective efficiency through private egoism represents the conceptual key to liberalism and suggests why this perspective so closely identifies competitive economic freedom with efficiency and, ultimately, with distributive justice. Herein lies the logic of values embedded within the Liberal International Economic Order: Markets are the means to national economic efficiency; national economic efficiency is the means to world economic productivity and international prosperity; and international prosperity is the optimal means for achieving international distributive justice. As Camps and Gwin observe, the Liberal International Economic Order has introduced regulatory policy mechanisms specifically geared to the expansion of international distributive justice, but only in limited and highly abbreviated ways.

Regulatory policies within the Liberal International Economic Order have, as a result, aimed at the following objectives:

1. coordination among states of trade and monetary policy by means of the General Agreement on Tariffs and Trade and the International Monetary Fund, the two main intergovernmental organizations of the Liberal International Economic Order;
2. promotion of nondiscriminatory trade practices;
3. free circulation and convertibility of currencies in foreign exchange markets and balance-of-payments stability; and
4. encouragement of private enterprise and development of market-oriented economies.

Behind these policies stand the classical and neoclassical doctrines of free trade liberalism, which will also be discussed in Reading #29.

—E. W.

Today, four main normative principles (or perhaps, more precisely, simply desiderata) attract strong support when considering the procedures, rules, and other institutional arrangements that should govern economic interaction at the international level. For short, these desiderata can be called efficiency, equity, autonomy, and order (not in the sense of "system" but in the sense of predictability, stability, and reliability). Tension and incompatibility among the four instantly appear if any one of them is given an overriding importance, and much of the argument in international forums today arises because countries differ on their relative importance. It seems clear enough that rules and procedures needed at the global level will not command sufficient support to be widely honored unless they go some way toward satisfying each of these rather different desiderata. It is therefore worth looking more closely at some of the arguments.* . . .

Efficiency

The rules and other institutional arrangements that governed the trade and payments of the central system for most of the period since World War II were designed to reduce friction among states by providing certain "rules of the road." Beyond that, they were intended to facilitate the expansion of trade and thus to promote a better international division of labor and a more efficient use of resources. To achieve these positive goals, they relied

---

Miriam Camps, with Catherine Gwin, *Collective Management.* Copyright © 1981 by the Council on Foreign Affairs. Excerpt, pp. 82–88, reprinted with permission of the Council on Foreign Affairs.

*Obviously, states desire other things as well, such as increasing their power and influence over others.

explicitly on market forces. Both the goal of "efficiency" and the reliance on the market are today being challenged.

If one puts aside for the moment the question of how much reliance can or should be placed on market forces and focuses first on the goal of the most efficient use of the world's resources, acceptance of this goal clearly assumes a world that is far closer to being a global community than in fact it is. We do not have today, nor are we likely to have soon, the political infrastructure and the social attitudes that would make strict allegiance to the principle of comparative advantage a realizable goal in the foreseeable future. How is it, then, that it could have been the implicit if not the explicit goal of the postwar trade and payments system?

There are at least three reasons why, until recently, the most efficient use of global resources has seemed, like peace, a blameless goal. In the first place, like peace, it was regarded as a remote goal, not an achievable target. The Bretton Woods system dealt in relatives, not absolutes: *freer* trade and payments, not *free* trade and payments. And in the context of the highly protected system of the late 1940s and 1950s, reducing barriers tended to expand trade without posing serious problems of adjustment. Second, although the international trade and payments system was conceived of as a global system, the system was fully operative for the most part only for the industrialized, market-economy countries. Thus, although "efficiency on a global basis" was the norm implicit in the rules, the "universe" to which the rules really applied was far more restricted. For the most part, it was a "universe" of reasonably homogeneous states in terms of living standards and social and economic outlook. In the third place, the General Agreement on Tariffs and Trade (GATT) and the International Monetary Fund (IMF) provided ways of slowing down the process of removing barriers if a country suffered from the process—that is, if structural changes were, in fact, probable—but there were few provisions to encourage adjustments to new situations and nothing beyond reliance on market forces to bring about change.

Today, the situation is very different. The efficient use of resources on a global basis, which was endorsed by the developed market-economy countries when it was simply a remote goal without much operational significance, has become unacceptable to them when application of the principle means domestic hardship. Even holding to present levels of liberalization is difficult precisely because larger shifts in production patterns than can be easily accommodated now seem likely to follow. The goal of a better international division of labor has—at the rhetorical level—changed hands and become a slogan of the Group of 77.* But the LDCs interpret the goal in a highly selective way, invoking other principles when their own very high tariffs and other restrictive measures come under scrutiny. They want a new international division of labor, but they would be even

---

*It has also become a slogan in some of the smaller countries of Eastern Europe but, again, with a selective application.

more unwilling than the advanced countries to see comparative advantage be the only test.

Today, there are two main objections to basing global rules *simply* on the norm of the efficient use of global resources. The first is the unwillingness of any country really to accept the heterogeneous world of today as the unit for which welfare is to be optimized. The second is the equally pervasive unwillingness to accept the most efficient use of global resources as an overriding goal. Many LDCs would put a different distribution of the world's wealth and production capacity well ahead of "efficiency," and most developed countries would insist that shifts to patterns of international production which would reflect a more efficient use of resources on a global basis should be slow enough so that the problems of adjustment could be handled without provoking substantial social unrest or economic hardship.

Yet, if one is to have any *global* trade and payments rules, the universe for which they are designed must, by definition, be the globe. And few, if any, governments would deny that encouragement of a more efficient use of resources should be *one* objective, indeed a central objective, of the rules system.

In addition to the objections to giving an overriding priority to the norm of efficiency, today we hear much criticism of the further assumption underlying the postwar trade and payments system that the way to achieve efficiency in the use of resources is by removing barriers and putting one's faith in the market. Perfect markets exist in textbooks but seldom in real life. Sometimes markets are distorted or deliberately rigged by monopolies or oligopolies; sometimes they are interfered with by governments to serve other ends, such as defense, social welfare, environmental protection; and sometimes they are simply inadequate and do not accurately reflect social and other costs.

Most of the authors of the postwar trade rules had rather less faith in the perfection of markets than some of the present criticism would suggest: the International Trade Organization (ITO) Charter reflected great awareness of the distortions caused by concentrations of economic power. But increased social demands and the acceptance by most governments of a greater responsibility for general welfare have inevitably led to more use of subsidies, taxes, and similar measures, sometimes designed simply to ensure that markets take into account social, environmental, and other costs, but frequently to produce results different from those that would result from a "perfect" market. Similarly, although multinational enterprises are not new phenomena, their ability to distort markets or to strengthen their own competitive position in ways not open to others has been greatly increased by the revolution in communications. Nevertheless for most tradable goods, market competition is a stimulus to efficiency—as the increase in the use of markets by the planned economies of Eastern Europe testifies—and it is usually the best guide we have to comparative advantage. The prevalence of distortions, intentional and unintentional, and of governmental intervention to further desired social, economic, and political purposes does not mean that markets are no longer useful, but, rather, that the maintenance of truly competitive markets frequently requires not a policy of laissez faire but one of positive intervention to eliminate or offset distortions. This is true at both the national and the international levels. Like the norm of efficiency, so the instrument of market guidance needs to be supplemented, not abandoned. . . .

Equity

Equity is a poor shorthand term, because, as recourse to a dictionary shows, it can mean either "fair" or "equal," two different concepts. It has become a portmanteau term covering several things, all of which, as different groups argue with varying degrees of intensity, the international economic system should provide. In addition to the term's dual meaning, the demands that international economic arrangements should be more "equitable" use the concepts of equality and of fairness to apply sometimes to relationships between states, sometimes to relationships between people. It may be useful, therefore, to begin by unpacking the many different things that are frequently bundled together under this heading.

The easiest objective to agree upon need not detain us long: the international economic system should be fair in the sense that the rules, procedures, and so forth that govern international economic intercourse should not be biased—intentionally or unintentionally—against poor or weak countries, or indeed against or in favor of any country or group of countries. This principle would seem to need no elaborate justification.

Difficulties soon arise, however, because views differ about what constitutes bias and about the criteria that should govern the weights accorded to countries in the management of the institutions. For example, views differ about how far the same rules applied to countries that are very differently endowed are biased in their result if not in their intent. Some argue that only a system built upon the principle of one state, one vote is equitable; others, that only a system in which voting strength corresponds to some measure that more accurately reflects the true weight of the country in the system, or is more representative of the numbers of people involved, is truly equitable. . . .

Another kind of "equity" that, during the last decade or so, has become of central concern has to do with the issue of how the world's goods are distributed, both as among states and as among people. Here, much of the recent argument has focused on the emotive issue of growing gaps. Not surprisingly, the gap in the levels of per capita GNP between the rich countries and the poor, and the "unfairness" of a situation in which countries with about 25 percent of the world's population consume about 75 percent of its resources, have figured most prominently in statements by representatives from the LDCs. In contrast, it is the gap between the incomes of the rich and the poor within countries—particularly within the developing ones—and the "unfairness" of transfers which sometimes seem to result in the poor in the rich countries helping the rich in the poor countries that receive most of the emphasis in the rich nations.

It may well be that a pattern of income distribution which narrows the differentials between rich and poor within countries is a necessary ingredient of programs designed to eliminate abject poverty and to promote national development. But as a definition of the "equity" that should characterize or be a norm of the international economic system, the narrowing of gaps in personal incomes within states or across national boundaries goes well beyond what most people have in mind or would be prepared to advocate. The concept of equity as applied to welfare, rather than to fairness in decision-making, is used very loosely and broadly. Normally, it embraces the need for an improvement in the living standards of the poorest people and the raising of the GNPs of the poor countries to a level that would enable them to provide, without further outside help, an adequate standard of living for their peoples. But because some would define adequate as being not grossly dissimilar from what is enjoyed by the rich countries, we are back once again on the treacherous and emotive ground of gaps.

The necessity of providing for the poorest and most disadvantaged section of domestic society is one that all the advanced, industrialized, democratic states, and a good many others, today accept. In part out of conscience, in part as a result of the pressures that the disadvantaged can apply, in part because growth and affluence have made it relatively painless to do so, there has been a marked expansion in the roles governments are expected to play, not only in putting floors under poverty but in seeing to it that the floors are rising ones and that the means are found, through education, housing, medical care, etc., to increase the opportunities for a satisfying life for all their citizens. Nevertheless, distributional arguments remain at the center of the political process in all countries. Normally, political bargaining keeps the tensions within more mature societies within acceptable limits, but occasionally they flare into open confrontation. One of the defining characteristics of a viable modern society is its ability to find a rate of social change and of redistribution that is acceptable to most of its citizens most of the time.

Clearly, many of the same forces that have produced domestic change are present today on the international scene: conscience, powerfully assisted by television, and pressure, powerfully assisted by the new experience of the vulnerability of the rich "advanced" societies. But although the forces making for change are there, the crucial element, the sense of belonging to a common society, is, as yet, woefully weak, and no global political compact exists from which to derive rights and obligations.

The difficulties of agreeing on how equity goals should be defined, on what instruments should be used to promote them, and on how divergent and conflicting views should be mediated are daunting. Perhaps . . . it will be possible to agree that international arrangements should exist so that the worst forms of abject poverty can be eradicated during the next decade, that is, that the resources needed to do so should be made available by the international community if the governments concerned are prepared to try.

The quest for equity with all its ambiguities will undoubtedly continue. Pushed to an extreme, the demands for fair shares can, at times, produce the perverse result of smaller amounts. But if it is ignored, the result is not only hardship but usually a poorer society. Although equity will be a more ambiguous and controversial norm than efficiency, in many parts of the world it is likely to be a more powerful one. Equity must be pursued, but, like efficiency, it will never be fully attained. And, like efficiency, although it must be one test of the adequacy of any regime or system, it cannot be the sole test. . . .

READING #29   Protectionism and the Myths of Liberal Doctrine
Susan Strange

The basic principles of the Liberal International Economic Order are under attack by virtue of the spread of protectionism and the growing influence of the doctrines of neomercantilism. These occurrences reflect the growing prominence of transnational modes of production and the new transnationalism discussed in Part Two. Susan Strange examines the impact of the new protectionism upon the dynamics of the world economy. Her aim is to evaluate liberal assumptions regarding free international trade now that it is falling under severe protectionist restraint.

Mercantilism advocates policies of economic nationalism in the name of state sovereignty and power. **Neomercantilism**, shaped by the modern world economy, regards the economic imperatives of states to be critical. It also recommends the forging of alliances among government, business, and finance; indeed, it is this embrace, in an era of keen economic competition between national economies, that renders neomercantilism such a powerful influence. Indeed, neomercantilism has attained a stature virtually comparable to that of free trade liberalism as a guide to the economic policies and practices of states. This is the starting point of the analysis provided by Susan Strange in the reading that follows. Her analysis assumes an understanding of the basic precepts of mercantilism, neomercantilism, and the new protectionism.

Neomercantilist policies employ a variety of methods, from export promotion to nontariff restrictions on imports; their means, however, include not only economic measures but the political mechanisms available to any government as well. No longer does economic nationalism represent the *means* of state policy and state sovereignty its *end*, as in the case of mercantilism. The fundamental design of neomercantilism is economic superiority. The objectives of neomercantilist policies, therefore, involve the pursuit of national predominance over world markets, especially with respect to important revenue-producing industries or sectors of critical importance to other economies—as in the case of control over the world's semiconductor market, for example.

The fears generated by neomercantilism create a kind of mirror image. The policy objectives of mercantilism, involving as they do a drive toward economic superiority, lead to the concern that one's national economy will become subordinated by advances in production and finance on the part of competing national economies. Such nightmares have become so influential in recent years that the doctrines of neomercantilism and its policy counterparts, **strategic competition** and the **new protectionism**, have begun to challenge the basic norms and principles of the Liberal International Economic Order.

Neomercantilist policies typically assume one of the two forms just noted: strategic competition or the new protectionism. Strategic competition involves

1. active participation by governments
2. in economic and business decisions
3. within specified economic sectors
4. to obtain control of set proportions of world markets
5. by means of export subsidies, tax incentives, and loan or credit guarantees.

The new protectionism involves

1. protectionist restrictions
2. designed to limit international competition
3. among suppliers of commodities and services
4. by means of a battery of new protectionist devices largely consisting of nontariff barriers, which require that imported goods contain a percentage of domestically produced components.

The very terms, *strategic competition* and the *new protectionism,* suggest the character of the new kinds of competitive programs in world markets based upon neomercantilist partnerships between governments and transnational business enterprises. Strategic competition and the new protectionism are thus demonstrably connected to the **new transnationalism**—that is, to the emergence of transnational business enterprises and transnational modes of production.

—E. W.

Much public debate and speculation in many Western countries today—in political parties and government circles, in the business community and among academics—is about international trade. It concerns both the prospects for the future and the policies that governments should, or should not, adopt in their own interest or for the general welfare of world society.

In this debate it is high time students of international relations and international political economy finally threw off the intellectual bondage of liberal economics and began to think for themselves about international trade and its part in the international system. This cultural dependence has led them to accept too easily the liberal assumption that the connection between international trade and international relations works both ways, that not only do better trade relations result from better political relations but that better political relations result from better trade relations. Historical experience does indeed sustain the contention that more and freer trade improves political relations. However, the second, Cobdenite assertion, that restricted trade damages political relations, is much more doubtful.

Yet its wide acceptance has led to a further assumption. Positive corrective measures have to be consciously taken, its proponents hold, to secure international trade against the shortsighted tendency of states to interfere with it—to the detriment not only of efficiency and wealth in the economic system but of peace in the political system. These measures, it has been widely supposed, must be either imposed by the power of a hegemonial strong trader with a self-interest in freer trade or else engineered on the basis of negotiated rules strong enough to restrain the perverse and misguided nationalist impulses of states to obstruct commerce.

The gloom and despondency of liberal economics notwithstanding, trade experience in the early 1980s tells us that protectionism in fact poses no great threat to the world's trade system. On the contrary, the only really serious disorders in the system result from ten years' mismanagement of money and credit and to some extent from an interrelated instability in the world oil market.

The explanation for this gulf between theory and experience, I shall argue, is to be found in a changing world production structure and its effects both on the decisions of governments and on the decisions of corporations. Because national wealth, and eventually power, depend on success in a world market, the argument goes, governments have a natural resistance, widespread and growing, to protectionist pressures from special interests. And because a corporation's survival also depends on success in a world market, trade between countries in goods and services will be, and is being, sustained by a complex network or web of transnational, bilateral bargains—bargains between corporations and other corporations, between

Susan Strange, "Protectionism and World Politics," *International Organization*, vol. 39, no. 2, Spring 1985. Copyright © 1985 by *International Organization*. Excerpt, pp. 233–246, 248–249, excluding tables, and 251–255, reprinted by permission of the author and The MIT Press; endnotes deleted.

corporations and governments, and between governments. The interest of both parties to these bilateral exchanges is (and will continue to be) a far more powerful influence on the level, the direction, and the content of international trade than the puny efforts of states to interfere with market forces.

It follows that the collapse of the system of rules which people (still, alas) refer to as a regime is of little moment—except to those with a vested professional or ideological interest in it. The alleged decline of the hegemonial power is also irrelevant to this particular issue, except insofar as it may lead to war or civil disorder.

The argument has both policy implications and intellectual implications. Politicians and officials need to know what the real choices are in trade matters; yet they are still apt, as Keynes remarked, to be the mental prisoners of defunct economists. And some academics, at least, seek a better understanding regardless of ideology of what is going on. The analytic implications of the argument are clear: trade in the international system has to be seen as a *secondary* structure. It is subsidiary to four primary structures of the international political economy: the security structure; the production structure; the money and credit structure; and the knowledge structure. The security structure includes both external security and internal security; it determines whether there is war or peace in the international political system of states and whether and how governments within states are able to maintain domestic order. Trade is obviously highly vulnerable to both. It is also responsive to the production structure, which together with the knowledge structure decides what is to be produced, how (i.e., with what technology), where, by whom, and for whom; and it is vulnerable to the money and credit structure, which decides who can pay for traded goods or services and how.

It follows that if war and civil disorder can be avoided in the security structure and if (a big if) the money and credit structure can be even moderately well managed, the production and knowledge structures, between them, will take care of the future of world trade. If we abandon both the hegemonial and the multilateral regime model as inadequate approximations to reality in trade matters, and if we adopt instead a web-of-contracts model, we may begin to hope that trade will satisfy more basic values of political economy than either of the other two models leads us to expect. Trade, we might realize, is more stable and durable than we had thought because it is better able to sustain growth in the face of technical and economic change. It may be more equitable because it may redress some of the asymmetry between North and South. And it may ease the coexistence of a unified world economy with a political system of divided authority, allowing states more leeway to choose freer trade or protection—or both at the same time for different sectors—without risking damage either to world peace or to world prosperity.

A first step in the argument must be to rehearse, for the benefit of those still in bondage to them, the myths of liberal economics and the reasons, derived from a study of international history, why they need no longer be taken too seriously.

The Myths of Liberal Doctrine

The main tenet of liberal economics regarding international trade is that the less governments intervene to obstruct the flow of trade, the better. The more generally liberal policies are adopted toward foreign competition, the better the national welfare and global welfare will be served. Free trade, it is held, allows the most effective allocation of resources to the production of goods and services and thus maximizes the production of wealth for the community. Protection, conversely, encourages inefficiency and impoverishes both individual consumers and the society as a whole.

Much conventional liberal opinion goes on to argue that protectionism adopted by one country provokes retaliatory protectionism in others, setting off a vicious spiral. To avoid this vicious spiral, it is held essential to maintain the momentum of multilateral diplomacy aimed at the reduction of trade barriers. The more protectionist policies multiply, the more imperative for world order it becomes that the states that have signed the General Agreement on Tariffs and Trade (GATT) should make a "new joint initiative," in the words of the 1983 GATT report, to stop the rot. Moreover, it is sometimes argued, the economic effects are apt to spill over into politics, poisoning international relations and contributing if not actually leading to conflict between allies and to war between states that might otherwise have been content to coexist.

Like most other simple doctrines, liberal economics is held with enormous passion but with rather less than unassailable logic or strict regard for historical facts. The chief fallacies, false premises, and historical misrepresentations that sustain the liberal doctrine can be fairly briefly stated, since most of them have already been perceived and identified.

The basic premise that state policy should, or even can, be based on the single criterion of maximizing efficiency in the production of goods and services for the market is demonstrably false. Efficiency never has been, *and never can be*, the sole consideration in the choice of state policies. Given an international political system in which the world is divided territorially among states over whom there is no reliable higher authority to prevent conflict among them, security from external attack and the maintenance of internal order are and always have been the first concern of government in each state. Efficiency can be given priority only if the provision of security, internally and externally, is taken for granted—as indeed it is by many if not most liberal economists.

Some, it is true, have acknowledged that guns must sometimes take priority over butter. Adam Smith himself saw that the defense of the realm and security from invasion had to be an objective of political economy for the state. Some modern liberal economists will admit that military production can count as part of the national product, even though it is not exactly consumable or productive in the usual sense. They may even concede, if reluctantly, that it is rational for the state in the interests of national security to adopt a "second-best" strategy, maintaining a less than fully efficient agriculture or coal-mining or textile industry to make the country less vulnerable in wartime to the cutting off of imports of food, fuel, or clothes.

Where liberal economists are reluctant to follow the logic of the admission that security is a basic value is where internal order and the security of government are concerned, for it is no more irrational to sacrifice efficiency in the allocation of resources to the need for social cohesion than it is to do so to the need for national security. An inefficient group of producers might constitute a potential group of revolutionary dissidents. It would be cheaper and quicker to pay the price of keeping them in business than to pay the police to quell their rioting. To maintain the loyalty of its citizens— a necessary condition of political security—the state in wealthier societies is also called on to provide economic security. Economic security may mean setting up a welfare or social security system for all. It may also mean making special provision for groups considered to be disadvantaged, whether the physically handicapped or those like steelworkers most acutely afflicted by the rapid rate of change in the international division of labor. From a politician's point of view there is no essential difference between the two. Both are claiming a measure of justice as the price of their continued support of and loyalty to the politician at the polls or even to the state itself. A political order within the state cannot be stable without the consent and support of major groups in society.

Efficiency, in short, is only one of four basic values that any politically organized society seeks to achieve for its members. Wealth, order, justice, and freedom; these are the basic elements of political compounds just as hydrogen, oxygen, and carbon are the essential elements of some chemical compounds. And just as chemical elements can be combined differently to produce oil, wood, or potatoes, so basic values will be combined differently in all politically organized societies to produce, for example, fast-growing authoritarian states or slow-growing democracies, or conversely, fast-growing democracies or slow-growing police states. Wealth and efficiency in the production of wealth will seem the most important objective of government only if the safety of the state and civil order within it can be taken for granted, either because consent is freely given because the existing order is thought to be just or because potential dissidents are coerced and frightened into silent compliance. It is no coincidence that the two strongest champions of free trade—19th-century Britain and mid-20th-century America—were both states secure and confident in the basic justice of the social order. They did not normally need to fear revolution from within or invasion from without. Both were so strong that they could afford to have relatively limited government. Others whose societies were actually less secure, both internally and externally, paradoxically required strong central government in order to protect their society from internal division, external attack, or both.

Freedom, too, is a basic value, and one that market economies enshrine and liberal economists extol. But it is precisely the freedom to choose to be governed differently from others, to be governed by those with whom people identify as "us" rather than "them," that is the sustaining reason for the continued existence of a society of states as prone as is the present international political system to destructive and debilitating internecine conflict and war. If history has not shown that men and women do from time to time choose freedom and justice rather than the most efficient allocation of resources, it has shown nothing. Individuals the world over, for all the superficial concessions they may make to internationalism, do tend to identify themselves with a particular national group and do give their loyalty to one particular nation-state.

Government, consequently, is a matter of finding an appropriate trade-off between these four basic values—security (or order), wealth, justice, and freedom—when it comes to making state policy. On occasion it may be necessary to sacrifice some freedom and accept binding rules (as under the GATT), if it is thought the rules are just and that greater wealth through faster economic growth will thus be attained. At other times it may be necessary to assert independence over efficiency in order to preserve the order of national unity. The French did so in the 1880s, as Alan Milward has argued, when the National Assembly voted to protect peasant farmers against cheap imported grain. That decision he characterizes as a de facto extension of democracy, "a set of stages in the widening participation of different groups in that body politic." In this sense, "the transition from mid-nineteenth century liberalisation of trade to late nineteenth century protectionism was not a regressive atavistic response by conservative agrarian pressure but a progression in political participation." After the peasants have come the steelworkers, the textile workers, and the shipbuilders, and to the needs of each important social group the policy-making process has—in order to maintain national unity in a democratic society—become more attentive.

So much for the first myth, the pursuit of economic efficiency. It raises all sorts of enticing questions of political philosophy, but exploring them is not my present purpose.

The second myth is almost a rider to the first. Liberal economists believe that the individual pursuit of private gain is consistent with the general welfare of the society, since the hidden hand of the market ensures that the producer will make what the consumer wants and at the lowest price, or else he will go out of business. Transposing the coincidence of individual and collective interest from the national to the international level produces a corollary myth. It holds that the pursuit of national interests by individual states is consistent with the general welfare of international society—or, in short, that the world economy will be well served if each individual government or state observes the law of comparative costs and sells on the world market what it produces best.

The fallacy here is that the political or economic security of the state may *not* in fact be best served by observing the law of comparative costs. The supposed coincidence of national and global welfare objectives, moreover, assumes the absence or unimportance of adjustment costs and risks. In theory, states can freely adapt either to the changing prices of factors of production or to the changing demands and conditions of the world market. In reality, the political as well as material costs of having to chop and change from one production sector to another are by no means inconsiderable, especially for poor countries or ones that do not share the high degree of conformism, respect for authority, and adaptability of, for instance, Japanese society. These costs, moreover, are probably higher now than they used to be as the pace of technical change accelerates and the cost of capital investment in the latest technology appreciates. Prompt adjustment may be in the collective interest, but it will not always be in the interest of the individual state. The law of comparative costs is an essentially static concept, ever more open to question as the world economy becomes more dynamic.

All this is not to say that political choices are always rational and always made in the best general interest. The point is simply that the choices involve a difficult trade-off among different values and value-laden objectives; and the discounting of time—that is, the weighing of certain present discomforts against uncertain future benefits—is not an easy and certainly not a scientific business. Economists are apt to complain that politicians are irrational because they make "political" choices, but what is politically rational, how one takes political values into account, is not that simple to define and cannot be assessed by quantitative methods.

The next three myths of liberal economics all concern the interpretation of 20th-century economic history. Everyone knows that two different by-standers may give totally conflicting accounts of a road accident. Similarly, two quite unbiased witnesses of a world depression may give entirely different versions of the sequence of cause and effect. But when, as I believe is the case with protectionism in the last great world depression in the 1930s, almost all those who have spent most time studying the evidence have come up with one conclusion while those liberals who have a political axe to grind have come up with a quite different one, the latter conclusion must be doubted even though it may be widely accepted as the "true" version of what happened.

Regarding the world depression of the interwar years, the conventional wisdom of liberal economics is that though it may have started with financial crisis, a main cause of shrinking markets was the raising of trade barriers. The major problem was protectionism; the system was trapped in a vicious spiral of beggar-thy-neighbor policies, in which each country retaliated against the others for barriers raised against its own products. The result was that all suffered and no one benefited.

But this is not what the economic historians say—or rather, what they said when, a few years later, they finally got around to sifting the evidence and looking at the figures. Unfortunately, that was just the time when all over the world people's attention was already turning to the impending outbreak of another world war, or when that war had actually started, threatening the very survival of states and political systems. The result was that the economic historians' verdict on the Depression was little heeded and soon forgotten. What they said was that tariffs, though substantially raised, had made surprisingly little difference either to the volume of world trade or to its direction. (Even Frank Taussig concurred with this view.) Nor had retaliation been the significant motive. There was not much tit for tat. It was just that as markets shrank, politicians were everywhere under pressure to handicap foreign producers against domestic ones, to keep jobs open at home if it could be done. Yet the handicaps actually did little to alter the pattern of trade flows. Instead, as Arthur Lewis concluded, "The decline of trade in manufactures was due neither to tariffs nor to the industrialisation of new countries. The trade in manufactures was low and only because the industrialised countries were buying too little of primary products and paying so low a price for what they bought." They were buying too little not only because commodity prices had tumbled long before tariffs had been raised but also because credit had dried up in London and New York, especially credit for foreign borrowers. By comparison, the effects of tariffs (and that other bogey of the historical imagination, competitive devaluation of currencies) were minimal.

Why, then, did the myth gain such popularity that it persists to this day? The answer is simple. Americans correctly perceived themselves as the strong traders of the postwar world, both because they were technologically more advanced and because American corporations were better organized to produce for and to sell to a mass market of consumers. They also regarded British and other Europeans' sheltered colonial markets as obstructing their conquest of the world market after the war, and the destruction of preferential barriers against American exports was the first target of U.S. commercial policy. The myth that protectionism had been the main cause of the prewar Depression, propagated by economists led by Clair Wilcox, was echoed by U.S. policy makers. The Europeans, including the British, accepted the argument, recognizing that whether or not trade barriers had done much harm, they certainly had done little good, and that a fresh start at the end of the war would probably be in everyone's interest.

Another historical myth holds that the postwar recovery of Europe and the unprecedented growth of all industrialized countries' economies in the 1960s was primarily the result of multilateral tariff reduction conducted under the aegis of the GATT—and perhaps of the earlier cuts in quotas and quantitative restrictions which the Americans demanded of the Europeans as a condition of Marshall Plan aid. That these tariff-bargaining rounds were an important innovation in economic diplomacy and that they helped make business more confident about expanding markets for most capital and consumer goods is not in doubt. But were tariff reductions the *main* cause of postwar prosperity? No one can ever prove conclusively which of two factors was the more decisive. Correlation can be demonstrated, but causation in either direction can only be implied, never proven.

In this case it seems to me far more probable that prosperity permitted liberalization. Trade revived after the war, and continued to grow, because the United States injected large doses of purchasing power into the system at a rate that pretty well matched the physical ability of enterprises to increase production. Impelled by a perceived national interest in holding the line against Soviet expansion, in Europe and elsewhere, the United States came up first with UNRRA aid and the British Loan, then with the European Recovery Program, and finally with military aid to NATO and other allies (which even financed British wheat imports) and with dollars to pay for the stationing of U.S. troops abroad. By that time the U.S. private sector was able to take over from the government a share of the task of maintaining an outflow of dollars to the rest of the world. Americans bought up foreign companies or invested in new plants for foreign affiliates, allowing their allies and associates to rebuild their monetary reserves (composed largely of dollar IOUs) to the point where most of them—Britain excepted—no longer needed to fear the political consequence of a temporary deficit on their balance of trade. Eventually, of course, and especially after the mid-1960s, the injection of dollar purchasing power became increasingly inflationary as the U.S. government also took on the financing of social welfare. But that it was instrumental for a generation in spreading purchasing power more widely throughout the whole economy is hardly in doubt.

When it comes to more recent history and the present state of the world economy, one must be careful not to overstate what the liberals say. There are, of course, substantial differences of emphasis both in their analyses of past events and in their prescriptions for future policy. But three general observations crop up again and again, observations that do not always accord well with the analysis that precedes them. One is that the main problem afflicting the world economy is the deterioration in the trade system. Sometimes this is explicitly stated, sometimes it is implicit in recommendations for governments.

Another is that if the drift toward protectionism is not arrested, things will get a lot worse. We might call it the "bicycle theory," since it says that if you do not keep up the momentum of trade liberalization, disaster will follow. For instance, Miriam Camps and William Diebold wrote recently for the Council on Foreign Relations in New York that "Doing nothing will lead to trouble." "Hanging on"—by which they meant protesting devotion in principle to the GATT and its rules while in practice giving in to protectionist pressures—is a "prescription for deterioration." Similarly, a recent experts' report written for the Commonwealth Secretariat in London stated flatly, and apparently without any supporting evidence, that recent expansionary trends in the exports of developing countries "cannot continue even if world expansion is soon resumed unless the drift toward protectionism is arrested and reversed."

The final historical myth is the unwarranted but very widespread assumption that the only hope lies in multilateral agreement, negotiated through international organization. This assumption rests, of course, on that biased interpretation of postwar history which ascribes so much importance to multilaterally negotiated reductions in trade barriers and so little to other factors. It greatly underrates the importance of some key bilateral relationships within the American alliance, specifically those of the United States with Britain, with Canada, with Germany, and with Japan. Each of the four had its own reasons for complying with American policy objectives. It also underrates the steady creation of credit first by the U.S. government, then through the investment of dollars abroad by U.S. corporations, and finally, after the first oil price rise of 1973, by international bank lending through the Eurodollar and other Eurocurrency markets.

By contrast with these rather dogmatic assertions, the analysis that leads up to them often gives far more importance to the disorder of the monetary and financial system than it does to the state of trade. (World trade fell only in 1982, after nearly a decade of mounting protectionism, and by 1%, a trivial amount compared with the 28% fall in world trade in 1926–35. The inflation-adjusted increase in world trade in 1973–83 has been of the order of 6 or 7%.) . . .

Except for a few academic economists particularly interested in international finance, and for people engaged with financial markets whether as central or commercial bankers, there is a curious distaste for acknowledging the tremendous structural changes that have taken place in financial markets and thus the reason why tighter monetary policies in the United States should have had such enormous worldwide consequences. The relation between monetary disorder and either the commodity boom of the early 1970s or the commodity slump of the early 1980s (the worst in 15 years according to the World Bank) is thus glossed over. And so is the coincidence of the slackened demand that accompanied recession with the major structural changes in the international division of labor, which have in fact buoyed up the exports of manufacturers from developing countries even in the face of mounting protection.

Why should there be this widespread reluctance to face up to the financial and monetary factors contributing to present difficulties or to the structural changes in production resulting from the internationalization of business? There are several possible explanations. At the lowest possible level there is the institutional interest of international bureaucracies in preserving their role and their importance. Ever since the fiasco of the trade ministers' meeting at Geneva in November 1982, the GATT secretariat, for instance, has had to face the uncomfortable fact that the road to further progress in trade liberalization was firmly closed by yawning gulfs of disagreement between the Americans and the Europeans, between the Europeans and the Japanese, and between all the industrialized countries and the Group of 77 developing countries. No wonder the GATT reports sound so full of doom and gloom. The truth is that if the whole organization were wound up, and its tax-exempt officials made redundant with a golden handshake, the world's trade would be remarkably little affected. At a somewhat higher level, there is a natural preference among many academic economists for an interpretation of economic change that allows them both to ignore politics and to be rather self-righteous about it. They can thus condemn politicians for their lack of moral fiber while telling their students that all would have been well if only their priestly advice had been heeded. That is much easier and a lot more fun than trying to come to grips with the complexities of a monetary and financial conundrum to which no one has a sure or simple answer. . . .

Recent Trends in Trade

Even the most cursory examination of recent trends in world trade shows that while world trade, as pointed out earlier, declined only a trivial 1 percent, growth rates, output, and employment suffered a much more severe setback. In the early 1980s the world passed through quite a severe recession, and indeed it may not yet have fully emerged from it. Yet recession did not have nearly so violent an effect on the volume of international trade as the Depression of the 1930s. The reasons for this paradox are not at all well understood, but one plausible explanation implicates the growth of what Judd Polk first described as *international production*—that is to say, production for a world market by large corporations that operate with a global strategy and not only sell abroad but actually produce in more than one country. Charles-Albert Michalet has made a further useful distinction between two kinds of international production. One takes place in a "relay affiliate," which merely reproduces abroad the production process developed at home—a practice that fits with product-cycle theory. The other takes place in "workshop affiliates," where one stage of a production process is farmed out, as it were, to another country where labor is cheaper or more docile or taxes are lower.

Whatever the reason, trade in manufactures has grown very much faster than trade in primary products. Moreover, there is far more trade between industrialized countries than trade between them and the developing countries. The conventional notion holds that trade is determined by differences in resource endowment. But, as Fred Meyer has argued, technology and the accelerating rate of technical change has a lot more to do with the drive to produce for the world market. For, as technology becomes more complex, and expensive, each new plant or process a company installs is dearer and is destined to more rapid obsolescence than the one it replaces. In most industries it becomes impossible to recoup the investment fast enough by selling on only a local or national market. One result is that trade in semimanufactures—half-finished goods—has also grown faster than the average rate of growth. Thus a totally Swedish Volvo car or a totally American Boeing aircraft, even a totally South Korean ship, no longer exists. Components are put together from all over, and the figures on trade collected by international organizations tell only half-truths inasmuch as they allow us to continue to think in these obsolete terms of trade as an international exchange of national products.

A second point is that developing countries' penetration of industrialized countries' markets has been faster in manufactured goods in the 1970s than

ever before and faster than the general rise in trade in manufactures.
. . . Though textiles, shoes, and electrical goods are the sectors where Third
World exports are best known, they are by no means the only ones. Exports
of paper, paper products, and printed matter, for instance, increased by 26
percent in the 1970s, those of chemicals, petroleum, coal, rubber, and plastic
products by 25 percent, and those of all fabricated metal products, machinery,
and equipment by nearly 33 percent.

It is clear from these figures that protectionism does not work as a
check on the industrial development of developing countries. Very precise
arrangements, bilaterally negotiated between industrialized countries such
as Japan and the United States, for well-defined products, do apparently
check market penetration. Quota restrictions and tariffs, and even voluntary
export agreements reached with developing countries, apparently do not.
. . . The only export markets where LDC manufactures did take a knock
in 1982 (and probably in 1983 too) were the OPEC countries, then suffering
from the falling oil price and the other LDCs, then suffering from falling
commodity prices (and therefore earnings of foreign exchange) and the
shrinkage of credit associated with debt problems. But no one has suggested
that the drift toward protectionism has been most marked in either of these
groups of countries. They may perhaps have been protectionist, but it is
the developed countries that have become markedly more protectionist in
the last decade.

Throughout the period of the so-called new protectionism the developed
countries have continued to lose their share of total markets and of other
countries' markets. In an analysis conducted for the World Bank, H. Hughes
and A. Krueger concluded that "the rate of increase of LDC market shares
was sufficiently great that it is difficult to imagine that rates would have
been significantly higher in the absence of any protectionist measures."
Welfare losses, presumably therefore, fell not on the developing but on the
developed countries.

The new international division of labor appears to be unstoppable. The
move of manufacturing industry to the Third World is structural, not cyclical.
Though more visible in the export-oriented economies of South Korea and
Taiwan, it is also happening in India and Brazil where an expanding mass
market—for clothes, radios, even computers—is increasingly satisfied by
domestic production rather than by imports from the old industrialized
countries. (No one would deny that this is so, though statistics on consumption
in such countries are sometimes so scanty that it is hard to find statistical
evidence.)

The progress of the newly industrialized countries that are the main
targets of protectionism is indicated by the figures . . . on South Korean
exports and in . . . the exports of Taiwan—a country arbitrarily excluded
from most UN statistics because of its anomalous legal status. Though the
value of Korean exports to the United States of primary products (fruit,
vegetables, and tobacco) took something of a knock between 1981 and 1983,
Korean exports of most manufactures continued to grow rather substantially.

In the space of two supposedly bad recession years Korean exports of textiles to America grew by 60 percent, of machinery and transport equipment by 140 percent, of steel by 20 percent, of rubber by 24 percent, and of clothing and shoes by 27 percent. Overall, the growth in U.S. imports from Korea was 43 percent.

The figures for Korean exports to Japan, . . . though on a smaller scale, show equally striking growth rates. Over four years clothing textile exports more than quadrupled, iron and steel exports increased seven times, and machinery and transport equipment increased by more than five times. Exports of textile fiber and manufactures were up in some years and down in others, but they were in any case not as important as any of the other categories of manufactures. . . .

A similarly strong upward trend can be seen in Taiwan's exports of manufactures until 1982, the last year for which figures are available. Here, the only hiccup is from 1981 to 1982 (and from 1974 to 1975, when slack demand interrupted the upward trend), except in transportation equipment— mainly container ships, of which Taiwan is now the second most important producer in the world.

The conclusion is surely clear: protectionism is far less important to LDCs than the rate of growth in the world economy as a whole. Although it may well be, as Corden has suggested, that these exports would have been greater still had it not been for the barriers they encountered, the rate of growth remains astonishing. It is far beyond anything anticipated by economic forecasts made in the 1960s. The record of the four leading East Asian NICs (South Korea, Taiwan, Hong Kong, and Singapore) is of course streets ahead of the ASEAN group and still further ahead of the Latin American countries. Nevertheless, the point is still valid that if protectionism has not effectively held back the leaders (those whose products pose the greatest threat to the domestic industries of the developed countries), then protectionism cannot be the main problem. . . . All the evidence, in fact, points to volatility in the availability of credit as the dominant factor. . . .

As Lewis observed about the 1930s, trade declined primarily because of a lack of purchasing power. Significantly, this lack has affected LDC trade with the industrialized countries more than it has their trade with each other. More than one-third of their exports of manufactures now go to other LDCs, and in some cases even more than that. Over half of South Korea's growing exports of cars and trucks—now nudging the half-million mark— go to other LDCs, even though ten years ago the industry did not exist. The explanation for this expanding trade in manufactures within the Third World may lie in the growing number of regional and bilateral trade arrangements between the countries concerned.

Finally, there is no doubt that other, domestic factors have heavily affected the divergent experience of trade which marks the Third World scene in the 1970s and early 1980s. World Bank studies have shown, for example, that though wages in Colombia were no higher than in East Asia, labor productivity was much lower. Because of government policies, moreover, imported raw materials were often dearer and management less prompt in executing orders and making deliveries. It was neither quotas nor tariffs that was holding Colombia back. Mexico, which in its border zones long enjoyed preferential treatment from the United States over other developing countries, was yet unable to compete with less favored LDCs, mainly because its own import-substituting, protectionist policies kept its prices high and the quality of its products low.

By about the mid-1980s, however, in Mexico and in several other previously protectionist countries, a change was beginning. It was due less to the exhortations of liberal economists or the urging of international organizations than to the urgent need to earn foreign exchange. Governments of all political kinds began to perceive the handicap that protection imposed on national competitiveness in world markets and to extol the advantages of opening the home market to more competition. The South Koreans, for example, declared that they would learn by Japan's mistakes and allow in many more foreign firms to compete with local enterprise in the home market. Bob Hawke, a Labour prime minister of Australia who might have been expected to be under pressure from unions to protect jobs, not only liberalized restrictions on foreign banks but declared his government's intention of dismantling the defensive barriers surrounding (and, he argued, choking) the Australian car industry. In these and other instances governments were responding to the imperative need to be competitive in at least some sectors in a world market.

Their need is one very strong reason why protectionism is not such a great threat, why the bicycle theory is unconvincing, and why the fear of retaliatory trade wars has even less foundation today than in the past. It is even possible that governments in some industrialized countries—the United States, for instance—are shadowboxing with their protectionist lobbies. Ostentatiously appearing to respond with quotas or other barriers to foreign competition, they succeed in quelling the clamor of protest. But at the same time they are well aware that the barriers (e.g., against LDC clothing or shoes) will soon be breached. They may even think that the broad national interest will be better served if they are.

Another reason is that the developing countries are getting much better at finding ways to wriggle around the barriers raised against them. In the well-known case of Hong Kong, quotas on low-cost textiles and clothes forced exporters to go up-market, where barriers were fewer, thus actually increasing the total value of exports. Provenance and final destination in trade are always tricky matters, as those running blockades or strategic embargoes soon find out. There are always third-party go-betweens ready and willing to pass on consignments above the producers' quota as their own exports.

Most important of all in explaining why protectionism is not working to keep out LDC manufactures is the connivance of the transnational corporations. Between them and the governments of developing countries there is a strong symbiotic relationship that accelerates the shift of manufacturing industry from North to South. It is this symbiosis that leads TNCs to negotiate complex bargains with other corporations and with state enterprises and governments around the world. Some estimates of the proportion of world trade which is actually trade between different sections of transnational corporations suggest that intrafirm transfers account for as much as half of some countries' total imports.

Many developing countries, in consequence, recognize that the bargaining which the government conducts with the private sector—foreign banks and foreign corporations—is a good deal more important than ordinary diplomacy with other states. Ecuador's negotiations with Gulf Oil in recent years, for example, have probably been more important to the country than its diplomatic relations with its neighbors. In this new form of diplomacy the state's control of territory gives it control over access to its markets as well as to its natural resources, its work force, and its financial resources and borrowing capacity. The corporation, on its side, can be taxed for revenue and often has new technology based on its R&D capacity; it has managerial experience and the capacity to market products in other countries, all of which it can exchange for the access that the state alone can give or withhold. A mutuality of interest exists which both parties acknowledge when they bargain with each other but which both often deny in public.

Yet the extent of these trade-creating agreements between states and corporations is unknown. No one has a vested interest in collecting the figures comparable to the interest that governments have always had (originally for tax and revenue reasons) in collecting statistics about the volume of goods entering or leaving their territory. . . .

Such spotty and uncoordinated evidence as we have, chiefly from the financial press, strongly suggests that this bilateral network of contracts is not only sustaining—despite the financial disorder—the continued expansion of world trade but is actually doing a great deal more than debates in the United Nations to achieve the much-discussed New International Economic Order. This quiet commercial diplomacy produces more tangible results in the shape of new investments, new jobs, and new production in the South than all the resolutions, codes of conduct, guidelines, and declarations on which so much official time has been spent. . . .

What has happened between the 1930s and the 1980s is that international corporations have taken over in large part from governments in arranging trade deals across frontiers. This bilateralism is regarded with disdain in international organization circles and by liberal economists, but their attitudes are more than a little biased, by self-interest in the first case and by ideology in the second. It seems at the least arguable that the model of a web of bilateral contracts is capable of producing a more durable and generally satisfactory trade-off among the basic values of political economy than any other. It would appear capable—always given the necessary monetary management—of sustaining growth and efficiency in the production of wealth. By aiding the changing international division of labor to benefit the NICs, it is also bringing about some more just and equitable distribution of the benefits of economic integration. And it is certainly giving greater freedom to states to be openly inconsistent (instead of covertly, as before) in their trade policies. For political security reasons they may choose to be protectionist in one sector (German shipbuilding) while open and competitive in others (German automobiles). The choice is theirs, and there is no reason why governments should not change their mind in either direction.

In any case, the next few years will show whether world trade can continue to survive despite the deadlock in the GATT and despite a certain amount of increased protectionism. My contention is that a combination of political and economic interests, reinforced by structural change in the international division of labor brought about by the mobility of capital and technology, is preventing a world depression from seriously arresting or reversing the steady growth in world trade.

READING #30   What the Third World Really Wants
Stephen D. Krasner

During the 1970s, a clamor arose within the international community regarding distributive justice. Rarely, if ever, has the Third World acted—as it did then—in as unified a fashion or as determinedly to deplore the prevalence of poverty amidst plenty within the world economy. The complex network of intergovernmental organizations and agencies within which lesser developing countries actively debate international economic policy, particularly the so-called Group of 77 and the United Nations Conference on Trade and Development (UNCTAD), galvanized what seemed to be their collective resources to the delivery of a call for a new international economic bargain designed to transfer resources from the wealthy North to the impoverished South. In time, these appeals were consolidated into the program known as the New International Economic Order (NIEO). The NIEO was formally accepted by the Sixth Special Session of the UN General Assembly in 1974 and was also officially incorporated in the UN Charter of Economic Rights and Duties of States adopted by the General Assembly on December 12, 1974.

The NIEO represents an interesting experiment in world political economy. First, it was dedicated to the norms of international distributive justice. Second, its approach was multinational in character. The NIEO was not to be achieved piecemeal or by means of direct bilateral negotiations, its proponents declared; rather, it was a program that required multilateral action since it was aimed at nothing less than a "global deal." Thus the single distinguishing feature of the NIEO was its maximalist approach to diplomacy and economic change. It demanded nothing less than a radical revision of the rules of the game around which the Liberal International Economic Order operates.

The demands of the NIEO included

1. alterations in the terms of trade between advanced and lesser developing countries;
2. measures to promote industrial production in the Third World;
3. expansion of the General System of Preferences, thereby providing open access to rich country markets for the exports of lesser developing economies;
4. acceptance of an international code of conduct governing operations of transnational business enterprises with respect to circulations of technology, finance, and other operations;
5. substantial increases in foreign economic assistance;
6. extensive cancellation of Third World indebtedness and/or reductions in interest payments; and
7. increased voting authority for Third World states in the World Bank and IMF.

Not surprisingly, given these somewhat grandiose aims, the NIEO failed. It came to naught because it threatened the sovereign prerogatives of some of the most powerful and wealthy societies within the international community, including the United States, and promised to erode the viability of the international society of states as a "practical association." In Stephen Krasner's view, it would have corroded the very political foundations of the Liberal International Economic Order as a regime regulating the international economic policies of states.

In the following reading, Krasner seeks to demonstrate the reasons for which the NIEO represented, first, a political movement and, only secondarily, an economic program advancing the cause of distributive justice. His discussion provides succinct definitions of such terms as **norms**, **principles**, and **decisionmaking rules** or **procedures**, all of which are relevant to the concept of **regime** and central to an understanding of the operations of intergovernmental organizations. Krasner's analysis of the NIEO parallels that of Robert W. Tucker, who is criticized by Charles Beitz in Reading #27. Like Tucker, Krasner holds to the traditions of **realism** and the doctrines of the **morality of states** in denying the relevance of cosmopolitan and egalitarian standards to the economic policies of states.

—E. W.

What do Third World countries want? More wealth. How can they get it? By adopting more economically rational policies. What should the North do? Facilitate these policies. How should the North approach global ne-

Stephen D. Krasner, *Structural Conflict*. Copyright © 1985 by The Regents of the University of California. Excerpt, pp. 1–4, reprinted with permission of the University of California Press; endnotes deleted.

gotiations? With cautious optimism. What is the long-term prognosis for North-South relations? Hopeful, at least if economic development occurs. This is the common wisdom about relations between industrialized and developing areas in the United States and in much of the rest of the North. Within this fold there are intense debates among adherents of conventional liberal, basic human needs, and interdependence viewpoints. But the emphasis on economics at the expense of politics, on material well-being as opposed to power and control, pervades all of these orientations. . . .

In this [reading], I set forth an alternative perspective. I assume that Third World states, like all states in the international system, are concerned about vulnerability and threat; and I note that national political regimes in almost all Third World countries are profoundly weak both internationally and domestically. This [reading] offers a very different set of answers to the questions posed in the preceding paragraph. Third World states want power and control as much as wealth. One strategy for achieving this objective is to change the rules of the game in various international issue areas. In general, these efforts will be incompatible with long-term Northern interests. Relations between industrialized and developing areas are bound to be conflictual because most Southern countries cannot hope to cope with their international vulnerability except by challenging principles, norms, and rules preferred by industrialized countries.

Political weakness and vulnerability are fundamental sources of Third World behavior. This weakness is a product of both external and internal factors. Externally, the national power capabilities of most Third World states are extremely limited. The national economic and military resources at the disposal of their leaders are unlikely to alter the behavior of Northern actors or the nature of international regimes. Southern states are subject to external pressures that they cannot influence through unilateral action. The international weakness of almost all less developed countries (LDCs) is compounded by the internal underdevelopment of their political and social systems. The social structures of most LDCs are rigid, and their central political institutions lack the power to make societal adjustments that could cushion external shocks. They are exposed to vacillations of an international system from which they cannot extricate themselves but over which they have only limited control.* The gap between Northern and Southern capabilities is already so great that even if the countries of the South grew very quickly and those of the North stagnated (an unlikely pair of assumptions in any event), only a handful of developing countries would significantly close the power gap within the next one hundred years. The physical conditions of individuals in developing areas may improve dramatically

---

*The two major exceptions to this generalization are the small number of developing countries that are so large that they can limit external interactions, notably China and India, and a few smaller developing states that have flexible and effective sociopolitical and economic structures that allow them to adjust to international conditions, such as the newly industrializing countries (NICs) in Southeast Asia—South Korea, Taiwan, Singapore, and Hong Kong.

without altering the political vulnerabilities that confront their political leaders.

Third World states have adopted a range of strategies to cope with their poverty and vulnerability. Strategies directed primarily toward alleviating vulnerability are most frequently played out in international forums concerned with the establishment or maintenance of international regimes. Regimes are principles, norms, rules, and decision-making procedures around which actor expectations converge. Principles are a coherent set of theoretical statements about how the world works. Norms specify general standards of behavior. Rules and decision-making procedures refer to specific pre-scriptions for behavior in clearly defined areas. For instance, a liberal international regime for trade is based on a set of neoclassical economic principles that demonstrate that global utility is maximized by the free flow of goods. The basic norm of a liberal trading regime is that tariff and nontariff barriers should be reduced and ultimately eliminated. Specific rules and decision-making procedures are spelled out in the General Agreement on Tariffs and Trade. Principles and norms define the basic character of any regime. Although rules and decision-making procedures can be changed without altering the fundamental nature of a regime, principles and norms cannot. Regimes define basic property rights. They establish acceptable patterns of behavior. They coordinate decision making. They can enhance global well-being by allowing actors to escape from situations in which individual decision making leads to Pareto-suboptimal outcomes. Changes in regimes can alter the control and allocation of resources among actors in the international system. Every state wants more control over international regimes in order to make its own basic values and interests more secure.

The Third World has supported international regimes that would ame-liorate its weakness. As a group, the developing countries have consistently endorsed principles and norms that would legitimate more authoritative as opposed to more market-oriented modes of allocation. Authoritative allocation involves either the direct allocation of resources by political authorities, or indirect allocation by limiting the property rights of nonstate actors, including private corporations. A market-oriented regime is one in which the allocation of resources is determined by the endowments and preferences of individual actors who have the right to alienate their property according to their own estimations of their own best interests.

For developing countries, authoritative international regimes are attractive because they can provide more stable and predictable transaction flows. External shocks and pressures are threatening to developing countries because their slack resources and adjustment capabilities are so limited. Shocks are particularly troubling for political leaders because they are the likely targets of unrest generated by sudden declines in material well-being. Authoritative regimes may also provide a level of resource transfer that developing countries could not secure through market-oriented exchange. Given equal levels of resource transfer, developing states prefer authoritative to market-oriented regimes. Even when market-oriented regimes are accompanied by substantial increases in wealth, as has been the case in the post–World War II period, developing states have still sought authoritative regimes that would provide more security. I do not claim in this study that developing countries prefer control to wealth; rather I argue that authoritative regimes can provide them with both, whereas market-oriented ones cannot. I do not claim that LDCs are uninterested in wealth for its own sake. Purely wealth-oriented activities can be pursued within existing international regimes at the same time that developing states seek basic changes in principles and norms. But I do claim that the South has fundamentally challenged the extant liberal order, most visibly in the call for a New International Economic Order.

READING #31   The International Monetary Fund, Conditionality, and Basic Needs
Richard E. Feinberg

During recent years, a crisis in international finance has developed within the world economy characterized by massive capital flights from lesser developing economies and by historically unprecedented levels of national indebtedness. In 1987, for example, lesser developing countries owed approximately $1.2 trillion to commercial banks. Interest charges necessary to service this ocean of debt came to some $153 billion during the previous year alone. This problem of Third World indebtedness underscores the need for international monetary management in a world economy that operates without a single world currency. It also illustrates the predicaments of the International Monetary Fund as it seeks to maintain a monetary regime in a political universe defined by state sovereignty.

The mounds of indebtedness confronting the international financial community propelled the IMF into the role of a modified central bank for the world economy. Its economic prescriptions increasingly prompted it, however, to become engaged in the domestic affairs of member-states. The impacts of its lending policies thus became controversial—indeed, politicized in several instances. In mid-September 1987, for example, the democratic president of Argentina, Raul Alfonsín, blamed his party's defeat in midterm elections upon IMF conditions, or what he called "ridiculous prescriptions which have nothing to do with the needs of the people."

Richard E. Feinberg, in the following reading, undertakes the difficult task of investigating the extent to which the lending policies, or **conditionality**, of the IMF have diminished the capacities of lesser developing countries to provide for the basic needs of the poorest of the poor. His analysis presumes a rudimentary understanding of the operations of IMF conditionality. One must thus briefly examine the operations of the IMF and its conditions for adjustment assistance.

The lending operations of the IMF consist of a series of ingenious mechanisms that function, in effect, like revolving-doors that allow countries to borrow from themselves and from other member-states by purchasing the equivalents of what they have contributed to IMF financial resources. Currency transactions between a member-government and the IMF assume one of two forms: **straight drawings** or **standby agreements**. In straight drawings, a government "buys," on a one-shot basis, a given amount of foreign exchange in return for the "sale" of an equivalent amount of its own currency. Standby assistance, on the other hand, creates a line of foreign exchange credit available to a government against its own currency for specified periods. Controversy regarding IMF conditionality has centered, in recent years, on the rules governing extension of standby assistance.

The maximum amount of currency a member-government may purchase depends upon its quota, which, as just noted, is based on its contributions to the IMF. Access to the credit reserves of the IMF occurs in **tranches**, the French word for "slices."

Conditions governing adjustment assistance become more stringent as a government moves past the initial set of tranches. The first tranche, for example, is granted automatically to member-governments. It is called the "gold tranche" because it merely returns to member-governments a proportion of the gold and currency reserves they had originally given to the IMF. Typically, the gold tranche consists of the equivalent of one-fourth of a country's quota. The subsequent slice, or "first credit tranche," permits member-governments to tap resources equivalent to the next 25 percent of its quota—also on relatively easy terms. But after this, the rules become more severe and the issue of IMF conditionality begins to loom larger and larger.

The rules governing adjustment assistance beyond the first credit tranche are politically charged because they require member-governments to enact national policy changes that have not only international but also demonstrable domestic impacts. These internal impacts usually affect the general population adversely, even though they may also represent the first stages of national, aggregate, or macroeconomic health.

In recent experience, the basic thrust of IMF conditionality is that a government must commit itself to deflationary economic policies at home. These policies usually involve one or a combination of the following measures, none of which in the *short term* appear to help the poor or the middle classes, but all of which impose certain costs that are borne directly by them:

1. suppression of domestic demand through decreases in spending on the part of both government and general population;
2. elimination of government supports and subsidies on such staples as bread, often rendering domestic products more expensive;
3. reduction of the numbers of workers employed by the state, and a general lowering of salary or wages;

4. currency devaluations, making exports more expensive and imports less so; and
5. increases in taxation.

However necessary such measures might be to protect the viability of a national economy, they often tend to distribute the costs of economic revitalization disproportionately to the lower and middle classes, which endure the worst of their effects.

As Richard E. Feinberg now proceeds to demonstrate, IMF conditionality has correctly come to be associated with economic austerity—even hardship. Indeed, several countries—including Brazil, Argentina, the Dominican Republic, and Egypt—have witnessed serious rioting in protest against its impacts. Yet many economists deem the use of deflationary policies, however painful they may seem in the immediate or short term, to be the only path to longer-range economic health. Thus the dilemmas posed by IMF conditionality illuminate the difficulties of pursuing distributive justice in a world economy characterized by plenty. Feinberg's analysis of the role and impacts of IMF adjustment assistance and of related domestic economic policies pursued by the governments of lesser developing countries points ahead to the conclusion to our study as well as back to the subjects of political economy of development with which we started.

—E. W.

Introduction

Because the International Monetary Fund has so frequently become involved in countries at crucial moments in their histories, it has attracted considerable attention and criticism. In Brazil in the mid-1960s, in Bolivia in the early 1970s, and in Chile, Argentina, and Uruguay in the mid-1970s, the Fund signed stand-by arrangements at critical junctures. In Peru and Mexico, IMF stand-bys were signed as populist periods (the presidencies of Velasco Alvarado and Echevarría) were giving way to the governments of Bermúdez and López Portillo. Most recently, the IMF has found itself enmeshed in politically convulsed Nicaragua and Jamaica. In Latin America, one could say that the International Monetary Fund has been the midwife of change.

Observers who have identified with those social forces that did poorly during these historic conjunctures have tended to place considerable blame on the IMF. Most notably, the IMF has been accused of imposing severe austerity programs on weak developing countries. In fact, an IMF agreement cannot proceed without the approval of the government in question, which,

Richard E. Feinberg, "The International Monetary Fund and Basic Needs: The Impact of Stand-by Arrangements," in Margaret E. Crahan, ed., *Human Rights and Basic Needs in the Americas.* Copyright © 1982 by Georgetown University Press. Excerpt, pp. 190–197, reprinted with permission of Georgetown University Press; endnotes deleted.

however unpopular, usually reflects the predisposition of important societal interests. Moreover, in many cases, overheated economies living beyond their means had no remaining options but to depress living standards to seek to adjust their external and internal financial accounts to sustainable levels. The issue cannot be framed in terms of whether or not to adjust. Rather, what requires examination is which societal groups bore the heavier burdens of adjustment, and whether the adjustment was carried out efficiently, i.e., at minimum loss of output and employment.

Another way to analyze the division of the burden of adjustment is to examine the impact of stabilization programs on the basic needs of the poor. Both absolute and relative measures of poverty are relevant. A decline in absolute standards of living at the depth of the adjustment period is insufficient evidence to prove that the poor suffered disproportionately. When severe adjustment is required, an equal sharing of the burden of adjustment can still leave the poor absolutely worse off. This [reading] first describes the short-term and longer term "structural" components of IMF stand-bys, and then relates them to a basic needs approach to stabilization and development. The various economic instruments that typically are employed in an IMF stabilization program are scrutinized for their potential impacts on income distribution, when viewed in isolation and when implemented as a package. The implications for basic needs of the Fund's preference for market mechanisms over official intervention are also discussed. An attempt is made to offer some explanations as to why IMF programs have so frequently failed to meet their own stated goals, and in the process proved more costly than necessary. Finally, corrective policy recommendations are offered.

The likelihood that the IMF will become even more important in the near future makes an examination of these issues especially pressing. The looming recession in the industrial countries, skyrocketing oil prices, and burgeoning debt burdens inflated by high interest rates will increase the developing countries' demand for external financing at the very moment when the commercial banks are expressing growing concern about their extensive overseas exposure, and New International Economic Order (NIEO) proposals for a rapid and massive expansion of development assistance appear to be floundering. In these circumstances the International Monetary Fund will be standing by as a major source of balance-of-payments financing. Once the currently programmed increase in quotas is completed, the Fund will have 58 billion ($75 billion) in Special Drawing Rights (SDR) of normal quota resources to lend, plus another $10 billion in the special Supplementary Financing Facility (Witteveen Facility). The oil importing developing countries will potentially have access to approximately one-fourth of these resources.

Basic needs are generally discussed in the framework of development strategy. Some might contend that, since the division of labor of the Bretton Woods institutions has traditionally placed the IMF in charge of short-term financial stabilization and given the World Bank jurisdiction over longer term development matters, the World Bank, and not the IMF, should be concerned with basic needs. (Indeed, this essay ought never to have been written!) In reality, this sharp dichotomy between the short term and the long term, between stabilization and development, is obscured in concrete cases.

An IMF stabilization program involves a comprehensive package of measures which go well beyond merely seeking to control the money supply, and seeks to alter fundamentally the structure of the economy. If successful, these changes set the parameters within which development planners will have to operate. The blending between stabilization and development has been implicitly recognized by the IMF in its establishment in the mid-1970s of the Extended Fund Facility (EFF). Under an EFF, a country has three years rather than the normal one year to undertake the necessary adjustments, to allow time for "structural" changes. Among the structural issues that the EFF addresses are food and energy supplies, typically considered priority development problems. At the same time, seeing some of its own projects threatened by immediate financial squeezes, the World Bank has begun to offer quick-disbursing "program loans" for balance-of-payments assistance.

Fortunately, the IMF itself has begun to recognize the inevitable repercussions of stabilization programs on income distribution, and at least two staff studies have been written. The Fund has not yet, however, begun to integrate systematically this incipient concern for basic needs into its routine procedures for drawing up stand-by arrangements.

I. IMF Structuralism

In recent years, the IMF has attempted to negotiate stand-by arrangements with numerous Latin American and Caribbean countries, including Argentina, Bolivia, Chile, Costa Rica, the Dominican Republic, El Salvador, Guyana, Haiti, Jamaica, Mexico, Nicaragua, Panama, Peru, and Uruguay. In some cases no agreement was reached, or the program was abandoned before complete disbursement. While the particular conditions of each case were, of course, different, the Fund's analysis and prescription generally bore important similarities, and might be paraphrased as follows. Persistent balance-of-payments deficits resulted from internal inflation and overvalued exchange rates. Inflation was caused by excessive domestic demand, the product of government budget deficits financed by borrowing from the banking system, i.e., printing money. Excess demand both raised domestic prices and increased the demand for imports, and the overvalued exchange rate further reduced the relative profitability of exports. Confronted with a deteriorating balance of payments and vanishing international reserves, desperate governments resorted to import controls and the rationing of scarce foreign exchange through multiple exchange rates or direct administrative allocation.

In many cases, while widening fiscal deficits and rising aggregate demand were viewed as the immediate causes of the balance-of-payments crisis, the Fund saw deeper causes, the products of years of mistaken economic management in pursuit of policies associated with import-substitution industrialization. Beginning in the late 1930s, and intensifying after the Second World War, many Third World governments attempted to speed national industrialization by overvaluing the exchange rate, subsidizing capital investment, and stimulating aggregate demand through public sector spending and, sometimes, increasing the earnings of the urban work force. Official controls over foreign exchange allocation, administration of the prices of many commodities, and public sector ownership of key industries often accompanied the drive to establish a domestic industrial base.

The Fund's prescription involves a two-pronged approach, one to deal with the immediate external and internal financial imbalances, and a second structural one to halt the imposition of exchange and trade controls and, preferably, to move toward dismantling these and other elements of the skeleton of import-substitution industrialization strategies. The immediate disequilibria are normally dealt with by increasing the profitability of the export, and import-competing sectors through currency devaluation and the wringing out of "excessive" demand, by closing the budget deficit, controlling wages, and restricting credit. The Fund's emphasis on controlling the money supply, as a principal instrument to squeeze out excessive demand, has earned it the lable monetarist, but it would be a major mistake to believe that the Fund is only or even primarily concerned with tracking the monetary aggregates. The Fund's vision of an efficiently functioning economy encompasses a much broader range of variables.

The Fund will frequently take advantage of a country's immediate financial difficulties to press for deeper structural reforms. A stand-by arrangement is the product of often prolonged negotiations between the Fund and the government of the member country. When the Fund feels that an important segment of local opinion shares its views, or that the country's desperate need for foreign exchange leaves it with few options, it will press hard for structural reforms. These are often already being advocated by some within the government, and the entrance of the Fund strengthens their hand.

Without demanding perfection, the Fund will propose at least a partial removal of such restraints on the free movement of goods and capital, as, for example, important licensing systems, import quotas, multiple exchange rates or other more direct means of allocation of foreign exchange. The Fund does not limit itself to policy instruments that directly affect its official purpose of restoring equilibrium to a member's balance of payments. While a stand-by may contain only four or five explicitly quantified "performance criteria" (usually targets deal with the size of the government deficit, the rate of growth of domestic credit and the money supply, and the amount of new external borrowings and/or other balance-of-payments tests), the accompanying documents will detail a much wider plan that will be taken into account when the Fund determines, at quarterly intervals, whether performance has been satisfactory enough to warrant further disbursements.

This detailed plan generally concentrates on stimulating private capital formation by offering adequate incentives to savers and producers, and by creating a general atmosphere of business confidence. The efficient allocation of this capital will best be guaranteed by allowing price signals to be set by the free market. This logic, in turn, reinforces the view that government controls over relative prices (other than wages) should be removed. In many cases, the Fund also advocates that the relative size of the state sector itself be reduced, to reserve a larger proportion of economic activity and of available credit to the private sector.

Beginning with the mandate, enunciated in its *Articles of Agreement*, to help restore a balance-of-payments equilibrium, the Fund moves from a concern to reduce imports to controlling aggregate demand, from the need to expand exports to the wisdom of reducing the size of the state sector in order to stimulate private investment in exportables. The involvement goes deeper and deeper, as controlling aggregate demand leads to establishing ceilings on wages, to curtailing fiscal expenditure, and to eliminating subsidies on particular items such as bread or bus fares.

The profound implications of this two-pronged approach of financial stabilization and structural reform explain the heatedness of the controversy in Latin America over Fund policies. The inevitable discontent generated by austerity measures is amplified by policies which attack a development model erected over two generations.

II. The IMF and Basic Needs

In the pursuit of external balance and financial stability, the IMF becomes involved with a wide range of problems. The basic needs of the poor, however, are not a direct concern. Some measures may indirectly benefit the poor, such as the creation of employment in export-oriented industries that are also labor intensive, and steadier prices, if applied to essential consumer items, which halt the erosion of workers' purchasing power. In essence, however, the Fund adheres to the trickle-down approach whereby aggregate growth in GNP is thought to lead to full employment and rising real incomes.

The Fund's emphasis on the free market and a circumscribed public sector biases it against official provision, whether through subsidies or directly, of five basic needs—food, health care, education, shelter, and water and sanitation. Moreover, the Fund tends to view such budgetary allocations for "consumption expenditures" as expendible, as it concentrates on laying the foundations for savings and investment in physical capital. This focus contrasts sharply with the World Bank's increasing emphasis on human resource development, for investment in human capital, as central to improving labor productivity and generally fostering development. While the IMF tends to see expenditures on basic needs as postponable, the World Bank now views them as foundation-laying investments.

While not generally made explicit, the Fund's belief in the market carries with it all the assumptions that lie behind the neoclassical paradigm, including an acceptance of given or market-determined factor endowments (assets and income), consumer sovereignty and the noncomparability of consumption between individuals. If a basic needs approach implies that the consumption levels of the better off ought to be restrained until the basic needs of all or nearly all of society are being met, then the Fund's basic philosophy would place it in opposition.

The Fund is not alone among economic institutions in viewing both production and consumption as aggregates, while a basic needs approach is, by definition, taking a disaggregated view that confers priority on particular goods and services. The Fund seeks to create an economic environment that fosters aggregate growth, with the market determining the mix of production. In such a paradigm, the issue of basic needs does not arise.

III. Stabilization Measures and Income Distribution

Although the Fund does not routinely worry about basic needs, its stabilization programs can significantly alter both the relative and absolute income levels of the poor. Analyzing these effects involves several hazards. Unfortunately, comprehensive income data to compare distribution before and after the program is rarely available. Resort must often be made to less disaggregated statistics on functional or urban-rural distribution, or to data across productive sectors. The results may be contradictory. For example, as one study found in the case of Peru, while functional data on urban wages and profits suggested an increasingly skewed distribution of income, rising food prices may have benefited the rural population where many of the poor are concentrated. More generally, the impact of changing relative prices may be marginal on subsistence farmers less integrated into the monetary economy. An additional hazard involves the choice of timeframe: the differential impact on incomes of a stabilization program during its first year or two may be misleading. Finally, whereas some variables (e.g., wage controls, selective credit allocation) have a direct effect, many others have indirect distributional results that are harder to trace.

Notwithstanding these caveats, considerable evidence suggests that under many IMF-supported stabilization programs the wealthy elites have fared better than the rest of the population, and significant sectors of the poor have suffered disproportionately. To date there is no in-depth study which argues that IMF programs have actually improved income distribution. These findings are generally based on the cumulative effect of the stabilization package. It would not be inconsistent to discover that particular policies may have had a more ambiguous or even positive impact on income distribution. The disaggregated analysis which follows is intended to elucidate the potential distributional effects of policies commonly employed in IMF stabilization programs. *Ceteris paribus* conditions are invoked for simplicity and space allows for only a suggestive treatment of each variable. The cumulative impact of packages of measures will then be considered.

Devaluation. Devaluation can affect income distribution in numerous ways. Consumers find imported goods to be more costly, but the composition of a nation's imports will determine the relative effect on different social groups. If luxury goods are a major component, the wealthier classes may suffer more, but if food is a major component the impact may fall most heavily on the poor. Devaluation renders exports more profitable and, if effective, will move more resources into the export sector. In the Argentine case, where agriculture remains the major export and where land tenure is concentrated, devaluation has historically benefited the landed elite and hurt the urban workers who had to pay more for foodstuffs. However, where export agriculture is potentially labor intensive, the introduction of new labor-using technology allows both for the possibility of higher real wages and for increased rural employment. Mexican agriculture might fit this mold. Devaluation also affects holders of cash balances; holders of foreign currency gain relative to holders of local currency, thereby altering the value of assets within the monied classes. Also, foreign investors suddenly find assets priced in local currency relatively cheaper to purchase.

The Relaxation of Exchange Controls. The relaxation of exchange controls will adversely affect those groups that benefited from the existing exchange regime. If controls were administered with a high degree of corruption and official favoritism of the wealthy, unification of exchange rates and reduced administrative allocation of scarce foreign exchange might actually improve income distribution. Thus, in the case of the ill-fated stand-by with Nicaragua in the spring of 1979, the Fund's insistence on the elimination of advance import deposits and deposits for obtaining foreign exchange, and injunctions against any further official restrictions on international transactions, might have reduced at least one avenue whereby the Somoza regime funnelled privileges to its adherents. On the other hand, Jamaica maintained a dual exchange rate system as a means of holding down the prices of imports consumed by low-income groups. The Fund prevailed on Jamaica to unify the exchange rate in 1978.

Credit Restrictions. Squeezing credit to the private sector, in the absence of selective controls, would most likely harm those smaller firms that lack privileged access to banking institutions. In the absence of controls over private foreign borrowing, larger firms may also use their access to international credit in order to offset domestic restrictions.

Easing of Price Controls. Releasing price controls, while generally increasing the return to capital unless wages keep pace, may redound to the benefit of the rural poor if internal terms of trade are administered to benefit urban food consumers, and if the revenues from higher prices reach the small farmers and landless laborers. However, in the presence of structural tendencies for internal terms of trade to move against agriculture, the removal of price controls may ultimately harm the rural sector.

Elimination of Interest Rate Ceilings. Removing interest rate ceilings, and the creation of domestic capital markets with positive real rates of return, if resulting in efficient capital markets, can benefit small savers (but not the very poor, who do not have financial assets) by offering higher rates of return on deposits. However, very high rates of return on financial instruments, and excessive spreads between rates paid to lenders and borrowers, can divert resources into speculation and away from more productive, employment-creating investment. This adverse effect of a liberation of capital markets in the absence of a healthy climate for productive investment seems to have occurred during the stabilization processes in both Chile and Argentina in the mid-1970s. The holders of the speculative assets, and owners of the financial intermediaries, benefit, while the other sectors, including workers left without jobs for lack of investment in real capital, lose.

Wage Controls. Notwithstanding occasional disclaimers to the contrary, IMF stand-bys frequently establish ceilings on wage increases significantly under the projected rate of inflation. If certain assumptions regarding quickly adjusting labor markets hold, new hirings could offset some of the adverse effect of decreased real wages on income distribution. This is unlikely to occur, however, in the context of falling aggregate demand and sluggish investment. The partial incomes policy of the IMF, whereby wages but not other prices are controlled, is designed to increase the return on capital to stimulate savings and investment. The immediate effect on the functional distribution of income is to reduce labor's share of national income.

Budget Restraint. The impact of budget restraint naturally depends upon whether fiscal balance is sought by increased taxes or reduced expenditures, and the incidence of such measures. While the Fund will sometimes recommend selective tax increases, the emphasis is generally on expenditure reduction. In that case, the burden may fall on public-sector workers whose wages or numbers decrease, on consumers who lose their subsidies, and on workers who had planned to work on investment projects that were postponed.

Limits on Public-Sector Enterprises. In its drive to reduce state subsidies, the IMF sometimes advocates the transference of state-owned enterprises to the private sector. This transfer could allow for reduced taxation and more efficient production, and thereby benefit the entire society. However, if this transfer occurs at bargain prices, as appears to have occurred in the Chilean case, then the new owners can look forward to very high rates of return on their investments. The Fund tends to look askance at the forced redistribution of assets within the private sector or from the private sector to collective ownership. Land reform would generally be seen as prejudicial to investor confidence. President Luis Echevarría's dramatic gestures favoring land redistribution toward the end of his term were viewed as contributing to the drop in private investment in Mexico preceding the 1976 stand-by arrangement. In the Peruvian case, the Fund regarded the watering down of the industrial community law, whereby labor was to be given increasing equity and a commensurate voice in management, as conducive to business confidence.

Redistribution of land is obviously an explosive political subject with ramifications well beyond the scope of this paper. A recent World Bank staff study, however, concluded that, among eight middle-income, semi-industrialized countries examined, a key factor in determining income distribution was the distribution of land. The poor showings of Brazil and Mexico were partly attributed to this variable. Of special relevance was the conclusion that, in the cases of more even income distribution, agrarian reform had occurred before the period of accelerated growth. This finding would appear relevant to stabilization programs which are attempting to lay the foundations for future growth with equity.

Stabilization and Inflation. The main stated objective of a number of these stabilization measures—restricting credit, fiscal restraint, controlling wages—is to reduce inflation. It is frequently assumed that inflation harms the weaker, generally poorer, sectors most. The prices of basic needs may rise especially fast and the poor are less able to defend their wage levels. Inflation also allows a government considerable leeway to alter relative prices. The Brazilian government consciously adjusted certain wage scales by less than the actual inflation rates. This partial indexation was intended both to decelerate inflation and to hold down real labor costs. As Barbara Stallings has shown in the case of successive regimes in Chile, different governments adjusted wage levels with respect to inflation depending upon their respective sources of political support. Governments representative of business interests (e.g., the administration of President Jorge Alessandri, 1958–1964) turned the functional distribution of income against labor, whereas the prolabor government of Salvador Allende (1970–1973) favored its constituents.

Social Costs of Stabilization Policies. This discussion suggests that the distributional impact of particular stabilization measures is not at all obvious. Within a generally declining national income, certain sectors may actually benefit while others will suffer disproportionately. An important factor is the nature of the governments that preceded and are implementing the stabilization program. In the presence of a new government concerned with income distribution that had recently displaced a corrupt or elite-oriented regime, selective and carefully targeted implementation of some of the above measures could actually advance income distribution. The removal or modification of administrative controls and other fiscal policies that primarily benefited the ruling elite could assist the poor in the short and long run. More generally, a government concerned with income distribution, but forced by circumstances to undertake a stabilization program, can consciously select measures to reduce the burden on the poor. For example, in determining the depth of a devaluation, the capital-labor ratios in the most affected productive sectors could be considered. Tax increases and expenditure cuts could be made with income distribution effects in mind. Public-sector enterprises should be sold off only at prices that reflect their future productive worth. As certain restraints on capital markets are removed, nonproductive speculation should be discouraged. Where otherwise desirable measures unavoidably cut more deeply against the poor, offsetting subsidies would be in order.

Less effort, however, is required in implementing orthodox stabilization measures that avoid considerations of income distribution. Under such circumstances, it is easy to envision the poor suffering both in absolute and relative terms. At the disaggregated level of individual stabilization measures, the above analysis indicated numerous possibilities for measures impinging most severely on the poor. Devaluation or the removal of multiple exchange rates can raise the price of imported foodstuffs. The removal of price controls may work to the detriment of real wages and to the benefit of producers. The reduction of fiscal expenditures will harm those more who depend upon official subsidies to obtain the basic services. High interest rates will, in absolute terms, benefit large owners of financial assets the most.

Perhaps most devastating on the poor is the cumulative and reinforcing nature of these stabilization measures. Although it is true that in perfectly functioning markets adjustment would occur through relative price changes under continuing full employment, in reality adjustment occurs through price increases and rising unemployment. The real wages of the workers fall, while the unemployed may find their unemployment benefits reduced if they exist at all. The IMF will typically restrain the hand of a government considering using administrative controls over prices or resource allocation to ameliorate these adverse consequences.

From a basic needs perspective, even a strictly proportionate distribution of the economic burden is not sufficient. The wealthier have a thicker cushion on which to lean before their access to basic needs is affected, while the poor may have no cushion at all. A basic needs approach to stabilization would argue for shifting the burden disproportionately onto the wealthier groups (although the longer run economic impact of such measures would have to be taken into account). A government especially sensitive to the needs of the poor might attempt such basic needs strategy, but the political obstacles—namely, the ability of the wealthier groups to resist—are likely to be effective constraints in most cases. It would be a major step forward for the IMF to strive consciously for a proportional distribution of the burden of adjustment.

Conclusion:
The Morality of States
and Cosmopolitan Justice

The Impacts of International Regimes:
Realism Revisited

The morality of states is a morality grounded in the requirements of survival. Thus it assumes that distributive justice is less essential to the interests of the state than is the pursuit of power and security. From this viewpoint, normative standards within the international society of states reflect the priority of state sovereignty over any body of transnational rules or any kind of international authority exercised by agents seeking to act for the society as a whole; the paramountcy of power and force as the essential mechanisms for survival; and the primacy of states over persons as the subjects or agents of international morality.

The morality of states, established by the seminal writings of Niccolo Machiavelli and John Hobbes, denigrates the moral standing of international economic relations and of distributive justice as a normative guide to interstate behavior. Political power and its pursuits impose their own set of obligations upon states—obligations that may or may not include such secondary economic aims as distributive justice.

Attempts to revise this realist rendering of the morality of states, such as the one developed earlier by Beitz, have tended to concentrate upon the role of international economic relations, including the dynamics of international exchange in commodities, finance, and commercial services as well as upon transnational modes of production. The speed and intensity of international economic relations, these arguments suggest, are now such that few states can be regarded as islands of economic isolation. On the contrary, states have become swept up in a sea of economic interrelatedness, with major and demonstrable domestic consequences. Such impacts are certainly subject to evaluation according to the terms of cosmopolitan morality and egalitarian standards of distributive justice.

Debates thus arise over what *analytical* weight economic relations among states should receive in assessing the *moral* weight to be bestowed upon distributive justice. In cases where the domestic impacts of international economic relations are demonstrable, the claims of distributive justice may apply at home, between or across states. Once such claims are recognized,

263

they can then become politically incorporated into the economic policies of international economic regimes. Analysis of the extent to which this has occurred is the precise focus of the reading that follows.

Freedom and Justice:
Theoretical Questions and Political Answers

International economic policies that are true to the international society of states, but also suffused with the principles of distributive justice, must work within the tensions created by the values of freedom and justice: They must foster reductions in poverty, but not at the expense of the foundations' plenty, and they must promote greater prosperity, but not at the cost of impoverishing the many.

For in the end, we must remember, as we did in the beginning, that poverty amidst plenty is the only crime against humanity in which the victims not only suffer from its brutal punishments but also are blamed for it. Thus, the Liberal International Economic Order will continue to face the challenge of having to become a realm in which both the morality of states and the cosmopolitan morality of distributive justice serve as fulfillments of each other.

We are left, finally, with the question: What is a just economic order? This, of course, is the very question with which we started. As we learned, theories do not always provide the correct answers, but they do allow us to raise the most telling questions. Our immediate question thus leads to others:

1. On what national, international, or transnational grounds can cosmopolitan appeals of distributive justice be made?
2. How does one justify claims to moral obligation (if any can be said to exist at all) between rich and poor and across as well as within national boundaries?
3. What is a "just" international order, given that justice includes economic or distributive rather than legal or political criteria?
4. Does the applicability of distributive justice become altered according to whether one conceives of the universe of human relations as a world economy or as an international society of states, and why?
5. How can the values of cosmopolitan egalitarian morality supportive of distributive justice be strengthened within the Liberal International Economic Order, given the morality of states?
6. How can cosmopolitan and egalitarian standards become better enforced by the international regimes of the Liberal International Economic Order?

The quest for analytical clarity and normative relevance in political economy does not stop with theoretical answers, for theoretical answers are by definition merely the means to future questions. In addition, we must remain ardent in our attempts to bring about distributive justice within a world economy in which the gaps between poverty and plenty are widening. That we remain so is the test of our quality as political participants in the history of our times and the measure of our mettle as moral agents worthy of any age.

READING #32   The Future of Distributive Justice
Robert O. Keohane

Robert O. Keohane concludes our series of readings with a lament for the failures to achieve international distributive justice within the world economy; but his lament is combined with a note of cautious optimism in light of the cooperative regimes that have arisen within the Liberal International Economic Order. Like Camps and Gwin in Reading #28, he suggests that intergovernmental organizations and the international regimes of the Liberal International Economic Order veer between the polar tensions created by the values of political autonomy and distributive justice. Keohane, however, refers to autonomy in specific terms as the **morality of states.** He also associates distributive justice with **cosmopolitan morality** in a manner resembling that of Charles Beitz in Reading #27.

The major obstacle to the achievement of a cosmopolitan egalitarian morality supportive of distributive justice within the international regimes of the Liberal International Economic Order remains, in Keohane's view, the morality of states. Yet, as he implies, the morality of states preserves the autonomy of states essential for the pursuit of national self-interest. Cosmopolitan programs that reject the legitimacy of such self-interest, Keohane concludes, are built on foundations of "sand."

Thus, Keohane sees some virtue in sin and some sin in virtue. States within the Liberal International Economic Order, he suggests, are often insensitive to the plight of the poor, but an absence of intergovernmental organizations, such as the GATT or IMF, would aggravate the dire circumstances endured by the poor. His conclusion is sober but hopeful: "On consequentialist grounds, therefore, contemporary international economic regimes may be superior to politically feasible alternatives, although the principles on which they are based are morally deficient." These are the issues with which we began. On the basis of Keohane's examination, they are also the ones with which we are left at the end.

—E. W.

What is the moral value of the patterns of cooperation discussed here? Can they be justified on the grounds of a defensible moral theory? Attempting

---

Robert O. Keohane, *After Hegemony: Cooperation and Discord in the World Political Economy.* Copyright © 1984 by Princeton University Press. Excerpt, pp. 247–257, reprinted with permission of Princeton University Press; endnotes deleted.

to answer this question requires careful evaluation of criteria for ethical judgment.

Either of two competing doctrines could form the basis for our evaluation. We could rely on the "morality of states" or on a "cosmopolitan" view. The doctrine of the morality of states holds that "states, not persons, are the subjects of international morality." Major features of this view are its emphasis on state autonomy and the absence of any principle of distributive justice: "there are no moral rules regarding the structure and conduct of economic relations between states." A cosmopolitan perspective, by contrast, denies that state boundaries have deep moral significance, holding that "there are no reasons of basic principle for exempting the internal affairs of states from external moral scrutiny, and it is possible that members of some states might have obligations of justice with respect to persons elsewhere." . . .

On the basis of the morality of states, genuinely voluntary cooperation among states is easy to justify. The primary value from the standpoint of this doctrine is state autonomy. Since international regimes help states to pursue their interests through cooperation, but without centralized enforcement of rules, an adherent of the doctrine of the morality of states would hold a strong presumption in their favor. The only serious issue would be to establish that a given regime was indeed formed on the basis of voluntary agreement and maintained through voluntary compliance. Yet . . . it is difficult to distinguish clearly voluntary from involuntary political action. Is my decision to give a robber my money, or a government my allegiance, "voluntary" if I make this choice at the point of a gun? To apply the morality of states doctrine, we would have to establish a threshold of constraint above which we would not consider actions to be voluntary, or autonomous. Once having found that the level of constraint in a given cooperative relationship fell below that threshold, we would be able to justify cooperation as promoting state purposes without violating state autonomy.

I believe that the international regimes discussed in this [reading] would be regarded by an adherent of the doctrine of the morality of states as, on the whole, morally justifiable. It is true that different states face different constraints, or opportunity costs, in deciding whether to join or remain in regimes, so effective equality is not achieved. But equality is not a requirement of the morality of states doctine, which is based on a keen awareness of the prevalence of inequality in world politics. In any case, most international regimes seem to be less constraining of the autonomy of weak states than politically feasible alternatives, which would presumably involve bilateral bargaining on the basis of power rather than of general rules. The International Monetary Fund may be an exception to this judgment, since IMF practices for dealing with debtor countries involve considerable constraint on the autonomy of these countries' governments. But a hard-nosed proponent of the morality of states doctrine would reject even this criticism, since she would deny that rich lenders have any obligation to provide resources to poor borrowers in the first place. Such an observer could regard loans as properly conditional on the voluntary acceptance by borrowers of obligations to repay them, implying that the constraints imposed by the IMF on a borrower's autonomy would not constitute moral wrongs but simply consequences of the latter's earlier voluntary acts.

Critics of the morality of states doctrine, such as Charles Beitz, have pointed out that since ethical theory normally takes the individual person as the moral subject, special justification must be offered for abandoning this principle where international relations is involved. Beitz argues for a cosmopolitan conception, which "is concerned with the moral relations of members of a universal community in which state boundaries have a merely derivative significance." . . . As Beitz suggests, the burden of argument should be on those who would ascribe rights to what E. H. Carr, in attempting to provide such a justification, referred to as "the fiction of the group-person." . . . Even those who argue that there is justification for the morality of states doctrine must admit that "there is a relation between the rights of individuals and the rights of states. The latter are not unlimited and unconditional. States are artificial constructs." . . . That is, states cannot be considered independent subjects of moral theory; a justification of the morality of states doctrine must ultimately be made in terms of the rights or interests of individual human beings.

No effort will be made here to resolve the argument between advocates of the morality of states and cosmopolitanism, although I have a great deal of sympathy for the cosmopolitan view. It is important to note, however, that the closer we come to this view the more demanding must our criteria be for the evaluation of cooperation. If individuals in different societies have moral obligations toward one another, even a voluntary agreement that was beneficial for all citizens of the states entering into it could be considered immoral if it damaged people elsewhere in the world. To the extent that we accept a cosmopolitan morality, we have to examine the system-wide consequences of action, rather than narrowly focusing on the autonomy of the states involved in cooperative activity.

Such a cosmopolitan morality could rest either on utilitarianism or on a conception of rights. Cosmopolitan utilitarianism is attractive in many ways, since the criterion of attaining the greatest happiness of the greatest number worldwide seems consistent with the individualist orientation of cosmopolitanism. But utilitarianism encounters serious philosophical problems. In one respect, it seems *too demanding*, since it appears to imply an almost unlimited moral obligation to help anyone, anywhere, who is less well-off than oneself. . . . This requires a high level of altruism. It also encounters difficulty in dealing with cross-cultural disparities in standards of living and social customs. A citizen of the United States who retained only enough income to live at the subsistence level of an Indian peasant would actually be more deprived than that peasant, since the American would be virtually cut off from her own culture and society, whereas the peasant would not. Yet if cultural standards were introduced into the utilitarian comparison, huge economic inequalities would again be sanctioned. In other respects, however, utilitarianism seems *insufficiently strict*, since it can be used to justify the view that innocent people can legitimately be sacrificed in the interests of the "greatest happiness of the greatest number." This may well seem intuitively unjust, and is so subject to abuse or manipulation that many reflective people find it repugnant. . . .

The principal alternative to utilitarianism is a theory of rights. According to John Rawls's influential formulation of this view, one begins such an analysis by asking how certain features of society would be evaluated "behind the veil of ignorance." That is, how would we regard particular institutions or rules if we had to evaluate them without knowing our place in society and therefore how they would affect us? Rawls's principles of justice emphasize liberty and equity. Of particular importance for a moral evaluation of international economic regimes is his "difference principle," which requires that "social and economic inequalities are to be arranged so that they are . . . to the greatest benefit of the least advantaged." . . .

Although Rawls has resisted doing so, Charles Beitz . . . has extended this reasoning to international relations. A follower of Beitz's argument would ask whether she would approve of international regimes and the cooperation they entail even without knowing her nationality or her position within the structure of her society. "Behind the veil of ignorance," with only one chance in six or seven of being a citizen of an industrialized market-economy country, would she approve of these institutions and the policy coordination that they facilitate?

Notice that this rights-based argument depends in practice on estimates of the consequences of action. Like utilitarianism, it focuses on the act rather than the intention—whether pure or not—of the actor. This emphasis makes sense for both practical and conceptual reasons. It is often impossible to know the motivation of political leaders; and even if they could be reliably discovered, it would be odd to use our judgments about the moral worth of individuals as a basis for evaluating their actions as statesmen. Cooperation that has benign effects should be praised even if we do not extend our blessings to its architects; and cooperation that leads to bad outcomes is subject to criticism even if the intentions of those who engage in it are pure. Students of international relations do not praise the appeasement in which the British government engaged at Munich in 1938 because Neville Chamberlain genuinely desired peace; nor do they condemn Richard Nixon's rapprochement with China on the grounds that Nixon took this step largely for selfish reasons.

Since both a consequentialist rights-based evaluation relying on the difference principle and a utilitarian standard focusing on aggregate welfare depend on an analysis of consequences, the distinction between intentions and consequences does not differentiate them from one another. The major difference between these two views is found in the willingness of utilitarians, and the refusal of rights-oriented thinkers, to justify losses of small increments of welfare by disadvantaged people in exchange for larger gains for more favored individuals. In practice, however, this distinction may be blurred, since utilitarians can use the principle of diminishing marginal utility to argue that a small gain in monetary terms for a poor person is really worth much more, in utility, than a much larger gain for someone who is already rich. The distinction between rights-oriented and utilitarian theories has fewer implications, therefore, for our evaluation of international regimes than the distinction between the doctrine of the morality of states and cosmopolitanism.

How would the international regimes discussed in this [reading] fare when evaluated on cosmopolitan grounds, whether according to principles of utilitarianism or Rawls's difference principle? . . .

Evaluating Effects of Regimes on a Global Basis

Mention of less developed countries brings us to the final aspect of our evaluative task: how to judge international regimes on cosmopolitan grounds if we consider their effects on the world as a whole, not just the advanced industrialized countries. When poor countries are taken into account, it seems even more clear that the principles of contemporary international economic regimes would be found morally deficient by the standards of cosmopolitan moral theory. These principles would fail an egalitarian util-itarian test because the benefits in terms of human welfare of redistributing resources to poorer countries would be greater than the costs of doing so. . . . They would fail the test implied by the difference principle because any of them could be changed to benefit poor and weak individuals more. It is debatable whether the liberal principles of GATT and the IMF help the advanced industrialized countries more than the less developed ones; but it certainly is clear that changes in both regimes to reallocate more resources to poorer countries, and to direct those resources toward some of the world's least advantaged people, would be morally desirable either on utilitarian grounds or on the basis of Rawls's difference principle. The moral status of these regimes would be improved if the IMF were to devote more attention to helping poor people in debtor countries, if GATT were to give more generous preferences to the export of developing countries' manufactured goods insofar as doing so would have positive effects on employment and income redistribution, and if the IEA [International Energy Agency] were to enact and implement provisions for subsidizing use of oil by people at the margin of subsistence in the Third World.

Thus it is compelling to argue that the principles on which present patterns of cooperation are based show insufficient sensitivity to the interests of disadvantaged people in the Third World. This suggests, however, not that there is too much cooperation, but that its orientation towards the interests of the rich is morally questionable. Contemporary monetary, trade, and oil regimes help the advanced industrialized countries to cooperate with each other, serving their interests. They create some benefits for poor countries, but these are small compared to what would be needed to correct gross violations of basic human rights that take place when people die of hunger or are continually miserable because of lack of clean water, adequate health care, or decent shelter. Greater empathy between rich and poor people— across national borders as well as within them—would not only be desirable; sharing more generously with poor people abroad is arguably the moral duty of affluent citizens of Europe, Japan, and North America, as well as of other countries.

Like the argument made above about the advanced industrialized countries, this argument suggests the moral inadequacy of the principles on which international regimes rely. Yet it does not imply that contemporary international regimes themselves should be abandoned or overturned. The principles underlying the rules and practices of the IMF, GATT, or the IEA reflect the interests and ideologies of the most powerful states in the international system. The cooperation that the institutions themselves foster, however, probably works to mitigate some of the harsher inequities inherent in the principles. Exchange of information and personal contacts between northern and southern elites, and the creation of organizations such as the World Bank and some of the United Nations specialized agencies, which are charged with promoting development, may marginally divert resources from North to South and slightly limit the tendency of advanced industrialized countries toward selfishness and exploitation. On consequentialist grounds, therefore, contemporary international economic regimes may be superior to politically feasible alternatives, although the principles on which they are based are morally deficient. This conditional acceptability of international economic regimes, however, does not relieve citizens of the advanced industrialized countries of the obligation to seek to modify the principles on which these institutions are based.*

Improvements (as judged by cosmopolitan moral standards) are more likely to be incremental than sudden, building on the knowledge of one another created by successful cooperation. The trick is not to ignore self-interest but to redefine it, to make it less myopic and more empathetic. Empathy by the advantaged may be more likely to develop in the context of well-functioning international institutions than in an international state of nature that approximates Hobbes's "war of all against all." Closer approximation to the ideals of cosmopolitan morality is therefore more likely to be promoted by modifying current international regimes than by abandoning them and attempting to start all over. Abstract plans for morally worthy international regimes, which do not take into account the reality of self-interest, are like castles constructed in the air, or—if implemented in a fit of absent-mindedness by governments—on sand.

---

*My formulation of the conditional acceptability of international economic institutions, despite the deficiency of the principles on which they are based, has been influenced by a paper by my colleague, Susan Moller Okin . . . on the American Catholic bishops' pastoral letter on nuclear war. The bishops hold deterrence, though evil, to be conditionally acceptable because it is better than politically feasible alternatives; but they impose the condition that people relying on it must seek to find a better way to manage their relations.